Here are five representative plays from the sixties—when some thought the American theatre was in its death throes. This period, however, brought forth new experiments and diverse influences which promise to be the seeds for vital new forms of theatre.

HARLOD CLURMAN, distinguished director, critic and lecturer, is one of the most vigorous figures in the American theatre. A founder of the Group Theatre (1931-1941), he directed that company's production of *Awake and Sing*. Since then he has directed a notable succession of Broadway plays: McCullers' *The Member of the Wedding,* Inge's *Bus Stop,* Giraudoux's *Tiger at the Gates,* Anouilh's *The Waltz of the Toreadors,* O'Neill's *A Touch of the Poet.* Mr. Clurman has served as drama critic of The Nation since 1953 and has written three engrossing books on the theatre: *The Fervent Years, Lies Like Truth,* and *The Naked Image.*

*Other volumes in the Laurel*
*Famous American Plays Series include:*

**FAMOUS AMERICAN PLAYS OF THE 1920s**
*Selected and Introduced by Kenneth Macgowan*

**FAMOUS AMERICAN PLAYS OF THE 1930s**
*Selected and Introduced by Harold Clurman*

**FAMOUS AMERICAN PLAYS OF THE 1940s**
*Selected and Introduced by Henry Hewes*

**FAMOUS AMERICAN PLAYS OF THE 1950s**
*Selected and Introduced by Lee Strasberg*

*Selected and introduced by*

HAROLD CLURMAN

# FAMOUS
# AMERICAN PLAYS
# OF THE

# 1960s

THE LAUREL DRAMA SERIES

Published by
Dell Publishing Co., Inc.
1 Dag Hammarskjold Plaza
New York, New York 10017

Laurel ® TM 674623, Dell Publishing Co., Inc.

ISBN: 0-440-32609-5

Printed in the United States of America
First printing—August 1972
Second printing—July 1974
Third printing—August 1975
Fourth printing—February 1977
Fifth printing—September 1978

# Contents

INTRODUCTION   13

BENITO CERENO / *Robert Lowell*   23

HOGAN'S GOAT / *William Alfred*   79

WE BOMBED IN NEW HAVEN / *Joseph Heller*   175

THE INDIAN WANTS THE BRONX / *Israel Horovitz*   275

THE BOYS IN THE BAND / *Mark Crowley*   311

# FAMOUS AMERICAN PLAYS
## OF THE 1960's

# Introduction

This volume marks the continuation of a series of similar paperbacks that began with selections from the American theatre of the twenties. They were named *Famous American Plays*. All the plays in the series are actually typical. Apart from whatever intrinsic merits they may possess, they represent various tendencies which have manifested themselves since our theatre's coming-of-age with the emergence in 1920 of Eugene O'Neill as our foremost dramatist.

Here we are dealing with the sixties, an era which Robert Brustein, as drama critic for *The New Republic*, called the "seasons of discontent," and which I spoke of as a time that produced a "dramaturgy of the maimed." The historian Richard Hofstadter planned to write a book about the same era which he proposed to entitle "the age of rubbish"!

The plays within these covers are not rubbish: they are dramatizations of the causes and effects which led to the sorrowful or angry epithets just cited. When a playwright depicts an unhappy or an ugly condition it does not follow that his work is forbidding or disgusting. Only the bad play is a symptom of the disease undergoing examination. One must distinguish between the material a dramatist deals with and his attitude toward it. The playwright is to be judged by the quality of his talent and perception.

The rubbish Hofstadter referred to, the cause for so much of our discontent (in and out of the theatre), is due to an erosion of our sensibilities. Many fear that our civilization is at its ebbtide. The significant dramatists of the sixties were grieved at the prospect. They do not favor the explosion (the signal for our extinction) which they foresaw, although at times they seem to. On the contrary, they con-

template it with loathing. There are more curses than
prayers in their plays, more cries of "help" than propagan-
da. Their blasphemies are often avowals of holiness. Their
raucous laughter is a substitute for tears. Obscenities are
often reactions to defilement.

Some playwrights do not understand the process by
which we have arrived at our disarray. They are to some
extent its victims, and this leads to moral and intellectual
debility. That is what maims them. Their vices are unfortunate derivatives of their virtues. The cure, if it exists, cannot be contempt—which is a form of hostile hypocrisy—
but the patient courage of confrontation with what ails us.
Despair may be transcended only by realizing the paths
which led to it and by avoiding accusation aimed at others.
We are all responsible.

If our format permitted a much larger choice of plays,
and if all of them were available to us, I might have included not only more "straight" (non-musical) drama but ex-
amples like *Hair* and such dubious "events" as *Oh! Calcut-
ta.* Edward Albee's *Who's Afraid of Virginia Woolf* is
"famous" enough though in certain respects I prefer his less
conspicuous *A Delicate Balance.* There is also social meaning in his *Box-Mao-Box.* The Living Theatre's *Franken-
stein,* certainly merits mention though the orthodox might
contest its validity as a "play."

The development of a black theatre—both playwrights
and organizations—is an important event of the last decade. Lonnie Elder's *Ceremonies in Dark Old Men,* Charles
Gordone's *No Place to be Somebody,* and the work of Ed
Bullins, Adrienne Kennedy, Ronald Miller and Le Roi
Jones—particularly *Dutchman*—would surely occupy a
prominent place in a complete roster. The Black Theatre,
apart from the assets and debits of particular cases, is on
the whole a sign of health amid the less fortunate aspects of
the contemporary scene, though it too suffers from the dis-
abilities which beset us all.

New playwrights, several of them associated with small
institutional groups off-Broadway and off-off-Broadway
(The Open Theatre, Café La Mama, The American Place

Theatre, The Public Theatre) demand recognition. I have in mind Kenneth Brown's *The Brig,* Jean Claude Van Itallie's *America, Hurrah!,* John Guare's *Muzeeka,* Sam Shepard's *Red Cross* (and other plays of his), Arthur Kopit's *Oh Dad! Poor Dad! Mama's Hung You in the Closet and I'm Feelin' So Sad* and the same author's *Indians.*

*Dionysus in '69,* Richard Schechner's Performance Group adaptation of Euripides' *The Bacchae,* is typical of a recent trend in our theatre. This is also true of Joseph Chaikin's Open Theatre's more ritualistic *The Serpent,* which uses passages from the Book of Genesis as its starting point. For a total picture of the theatre of the sixties such performances (as distinct from traditional playtexts) as that of Megan Terry's *Viet Rock* are essential. These plays belong to what recently has come to be designated new or vanguard theatre. New theatre combines diverse media to achieve effects which are purely theatrical rather than strictly verbal. It frequently invites audience participation and depends to some degree on improvisation.

Howard Sackler's *The Great White Hope* was a great Broadway hit made especially memorable by the splendor of James Earl Jones' acting as the black heavyweight champion and the delicate pathos of Jane Alexander as his wife. To this we should be obliged to add plays by dramatists whose beginnings date from earlier periods: Lillian Hellman's *Toys in the Attic,* Tennessee Williams' *The Night of the Iguana,* Arthur Miller's *After the Fall* and *Incident at Vichy,* and Eugene O'Neill's incomplete *More Stately Mansions.*

It is to be understood that the cutting up of artistic epochs into decades may be a convenience but that it is also to some degree a falsification. Much of what we ascribe to the theatre of the sixties is the outgrowth of seeds sown in the fifties. And some of the more recent impulses may gather further impetus in the future—providing that the chaotic economics of our theatre do not drive it into the wilderness or the underground.

We cannot fail to recognize in some of the plays of the sixties a number of foreign influences: the writing of Beckett, Pinter, Ionesco, Genet; the production methods of Brecht and Grotowski; and the documentary theatre of fact, a predominantly German development (Peter Weiss' *The Investigation* is the best example, and *The Trial of the Catonsville Nine*, the Berrigan brothers case, is an American documentary play). The possibilities for American theatre include further extension from these roots or a withering away followed by a refreshed and broadened realistic tradition.

Robert Lowell's *Benito Cereno*, the most powerful piece in his *Old Glory* triptych, is especially interesting. It synthesizes various dramatic methods of which the use of verse is the most obvious but perhaps the least important. It is not so much a poetic as a "social" play. It exemplifies our ever-growing concern with the black "problem." Unexpectedly, it is not a plea, and if it is in any way a prophecy it is a rather pessimistic one.

*Benito Cereno* is based on Herman Melville's story of the same name. Melville's tale, which takes place circa 1830, communicates the American inability to comprehend evil. Melville's Captain Amasa Delano is an innocent: he cannot imagine why there should be any cause for rebellion aboard the Spanish ship which he generously attempts to aid.

Lowell's captain is a serene libertarian, proud to be helpful to those less favored than himself. But in the face of a threat to his dominance he does not hesitate to kill. When Babu, the black leader, asserts that the future belongs to those who like himself will rise up against white oppression, the captain unhesitatingly empties six barrels of his pistol into Babu's body with the words, "This is your future." What Lowell suggests with pained but dignified impassivity is that black insurrection when it seriously threatens the ruling powers will meet with murder. This assessment of the future is implied in such lines as Delano's reflection, "If you looked into our hearts, we all want slaves." The American is a puritan, in Lowell's words, "all faith and fire," a conclusion which explains the gloominess of Delano's "God save America from Americans!"

The play is lucidly classic in manner and, though written

in verse, has a realistic viewpoint. It is melodrama with an eye to colorful effect. It serves as a model for what may be achieved in dealing with one of the most crucial issues of our day by fashioning revised materials inherited from the past.

*Hogan's Goat* by William Alfred purports to be a tragedy. Though it fails in this, it possesses other merits. Like Lowell's play, the action of *Hogan's Goat* is situated in the past and its language is verse. In both cases this mode is stageworthy. There is a speech in the latter piece describing the immigrants' overseas passage in steerage from the old sod to the new (American) soil which rises to true eloquence. The passenger in this case is Irish and the place in which he set himself down is the then independent city of Brooklyn. The play savors of its locale in 1890. This aspect of the play is particularly noteworthy because Americans, both in life and in drama, tend to neglect the past. Indeed we carry on as though we had none.

The past may instruct us as to the present. So Stanton, the protagonist of *Hogan's Goat,* after the hardships attendant upon his arrival in the new land, made a ". . . vow, I'd fight my way to power if it killed me." The playwright proposes to show the tragic price Stanton and those close to him (the unseen Agnes Hogan and his wife Kathleen Stanton) must pay on account of his drive to power. But this is less convincing than another facet of the play. What arrests us is the vigorous picture presented of the place and the time and the racy types characteristic of them.

Alfred's Brooklyn is very much a corrupt frontier town. It is rank with its politicians, lackeys, intrigues, whores, drinking, its still superstitious ties with its old religion, habits, and hearth. There is a neighborhood charm in all this: warmth and gaiety in the midst of poverty, graft, internecine rivalry. The atmosphere is rife with a mixture of rage and sentimentality: booze, dirt, song, and gestures of patriotic and sacramental devotion. People here are as quick to fury as to love. Holding all together is the tenacious oldtime political boss whose ambition, achievement, and pride are summed up in the boast, "I kept my office." Many cities all over America at the time, and perhaps in our time too, were very much like that.

Joseph Heller's *We Bombed in New Haven* was first produced at the Yale School of Drama and later ran on Broadway. It should not surprise us that the Vietnam War did not occasion more plays concerning it. Broadway is understandably timid in regard to controversial matters. (Megan Terry's *Viet Rock* in the new theatre vein also appeared on the Yale Theatre program.) In his play, Heller, already well known for his novel *Catch-22,* combines some of the jocose elements of the freewheeling new theatre technique with a touch of Pirandello. He applies them to the absurdities of Army discipline and the military consequences, both farcical and pathetic.

Actors as actors play soldiers in this wry lampoon, while they never lose their identity as actors. The first part is all fun and games; the second becomes grim and finally hortatory in a way which I, for one, find moving. The justification for Heller's peculiar treatment of such material is that actors are as unreal or as real as those soldiers, unknown to us, whose names we read on the casualty lists of the papers. We contemplate Heller's "game" with a double vision: it is an alienation effect, rendering the play's situation so strange that the audience does not view it as an actual, literally realistic event, but rather stands apart from the action and makes its own critical judgments as to its validity.

The bomb in the play is a toy which the men juggle. War becomes meaningless. In the process of training for it everything, including the man-woman relationship, becomes equally meaningless. "Why are we killing Turks?" an enlisted man asks. To which the major answers, "That's none of our business. . . . This is a good mission you people are flying today. If everything goes well, there shouldn't be a single thing in Constantinople left alive." Both the company idiots and the intelligent are caught in the same vise. Nothing under the circumstances can make sense.

The young man sent off to die in stupid battle by his sorrowing father says, "It is your fault! What were you doing all this time, when you could have been doing something [to prevent war]. . . . If I were still a baby in a baby carriage, and someone wanted to take me away and kill me, you wouldn't let them, would you? Are you really going to let them take me away now to be killed?" The message is not dated in 1971. When shall it be?

Israel Horovitz's *The Indian Wants the Bronx* (at this writing it is being acclaimed in Paris) stands for a number of other short pieces written in the sixties which reflect the savage temper of the times. The subject is violence. When the moral structure of a civilization begins to crumble, violence becomes a way of life. Some people appear to exult in it (this is often rationalized as a form of protest) while others anathematize it. Horovitz is not simply horrified by it, he tries to suggest its roots.

The apparently gratuitous terror of the cities is projected with special force. In many instances it begins as "play," a cruel game practiced at the expense of the innocent. What explains such mindlessness? The ditty tunelessly hummed by the two delinquents of *The Indian Wants the Bronx* provides a clue. "I walk the lonely streets at night, A 'lookin' for your door, I look and look and look and look, But, baby, you don't care. Baby, you don't care. Baby, no one cares." Callousness envelops them like poison in the air.

Of this devastating state *The Indian Wants the Bronx* is very nearly a graph or pantomime. The setting—the lonely street corner at night, its public telephone booth with a garbage can by its side—is the image of disembodied evil.

Now we come to the most decidedly famous of the chosen plays. Mart Crowley's *The Boys in the Band* was sensationally successful not only in its first New York run but on the stages of many countries abroad. Its importance, apart from clever dialogue and skillful construction, lies in its bold handling of subject matter that not many years ago would have struck audiences as infamous—homosexuality. The forbidden words which have now become commonplace on stage and screen were first freely employed in this play; the words, the ideas, the acts associated with them. Happily there is abundant humor in the mixture.

It was necessary to break the ice for the stage in this field. Homosexuality had to be faced not as a sin or as a matter for clinical study but as it appears in our society.

The birthday party at which the "boys in the band" appear is not an orgy. There is nothing clandestine or sinister about it. There are as many different types among the characters as there might be at any gathering where ordinary young people meet for pleasant foolery and possible dalliance.

*The Boys in the Band* is a sentimental comedy. I prefer the comedy to the sentiment. Some of the laughter aroused by the dialogue is due to the unexpected shock of a first encounter. This will soon wear off. But there is still enough shrewd intelligence in the delineation of the *dramatis personae* and the interaction among them to make the play really funny, which is one reason why it "holds up," even for those who take its material for granted. After Thomas Mann, Proust, and Gide, homosexuality is an open theme. Set in a big American city, the emphasis in this play is on a purely local aspect of the matter. One sign of its Americanism is the facile Freudianism which attributes the homosexual phenomenon to maternal overindulgence of the son or the son's excessive attachment to the mother.

What the play seriously implies is that the homosexual nearly always hates himself. A "campy" arrogance or boastfulness which is sometimes characteristic of certain homosexuals is the mask of self-contempt. This, I believe, is morally unfortunate and unnecessary, as is all aggressive defensiveness among minorities. We are as wrong to pity homosexuals as they are to pity themselves. As the cliché has it: they are first of all human beings. Crowley's attitude is somewhat ambiguous: he appears to assume that the tearful self-pity of the play's central character voiced at the final curtain is a conclusive statement on the subject. That is what renders the play sentimental.

The insufficiency of Crowley's assumption points to a deeper fault. The play's characters appear in the main to be nothing more than homosexual. No person can be entirely understood or judged in terms of his or her sexual nature—whatever it may be. The homosexual may be Michelangelo, Christopher Marlowe, Tchaikovsky, Oscar Wilde, or a prostitute. The range of characterization in *The Boys in the Band* in this respect is limited.

Still the play's effect is salutary, despite the fact that its free treatment of one kind of sexuality is symptomatic of an obsession of the period. It was said in the twenties that the "enlightened" young spoke and behaved as if they had invented sex. They were in rebellion against our puritan hangovers. Today the interest in sex is due in large part to our lack of faith in virtually anything else. Since we feel ourselves everywhere encased in deception and fraud, nothing substantial seems left except the reality of the body. Hence the prevalent fascination with nudity. This is certainly no disgrace. But when the body remains the sole humanly sustaining factor, it too becomes trivial. The credibility gap epidemic among us in every walk of life cannot be filled by the body alone. Exultation in sex as an absolute ultimately leads to sadism and despair.

If the foregoing description of the spirit of the sixties strikes the reader as too downbeat, I offer two healthier specimens as counterproof of my basic contention. *Fiddler on the Roof* and *Man of La Mancha* (a New York Drama Critics prizewinner for the 1965-1966 season) were and still are enormous successes. How explain the audience attraction of these two musicals? It is not enough to speak of the excellent productions given them—settings, dance, lyrics and music. Other shows possess similar attributes.

In the angry atmosphere of the sixties, *Fiddler on the Roof* is the image and reminder of a community bound together by love. The idealistic core of Dale Wasserman's "book" for *Man of La Mancha*—the romantic assertion of belief in goodness, gallantry, and determined service on behalf of others—is at the root of the public infatuation with this entertainment. To endure, humanity ever stands in need of these virtues. In spite of the knight of La Mancha's failure to achieve the noble aims he sets for himself, we know that the hope of humanity lies in the persistence of this quest. His servant Sancho Panza can't rationally explain his loyalty to his mad master except by saying, "I like him." But the audience responds with spontaneous enthusiasm to the key refrain, "To dream the impossible dream, to fight the unbeatable foe. . . . To fight without question or pause, to be willing to march into hell without question for a heavenly cause. . . . And the world will be better for this!"

There is some irony in the fact that both these musicals are adaptations of works of another time and place—a sort of never-never land. Despite all that is indisputably morbid in the tone and texture of the day we still crave for a lost wholeness. Any glimmer of it is taken to our hearts. It is the promise of recovery.

HAROLD CLURMAN

# BENITO CERENO

*by Robert Lowell*

*First production, November 1, 1964*
*at the American Place Theatre, New York,*
*with the following cast:*

CAPTAIN AMASA DELANO, *Lester Rawlins*
JOHN PERKINS, *Jack Ryland*
DON BENITO CERENO, *Frank Langella*
BABU, *Roscoe Lee Browne*
ATUFAL, *Clayton Corbin*
FRANCESCO, *Michael Schultz*
AMERICAN SAILORS, *Conway W. Young, Robert Tinsley,*
    *Richard Kjelland, E. Emmet Walsch,*
    *Howard Martin*
SPANISH SAILORS, *Luke Andreas, William Jacobson,*
    *James Zaferes*
NEGRO SLAVES, *Woodie King, Lonnie Stevens,*
    *George A. Sharpe, Hurman Fitzgerald,*
    *Ernest Baxter, Aston Young, June Brown,*
    *Mary Foreman, Gene Foreman, Judith Byrd,*
    *M. S. Mitchell, Lane Floyd, Paul Plummer,*
    *Walter Jones, Ethan Courtney*

# The scene

*About the year 1800, an American sealing vessel, the* President Adams, *at anchor in an island harbor off the coast of
Trinidad. The stage is part of the ship's deck. Everything is
unnaturally clean, bare and ship-shape. To one side, a pol-
ished, coal-black cannon. The American captain,* AMASA
DELANO *from Duxbury, Massachusetts, sits in a cane chair.
He is a strong, comfortable-looking man in his early thirties who wears a spotless blue coat and white trousers. In-
congruously, he has on a straw hat and smokes a corncob
pipe. Beside him stands* JOHN PERKINS, *his bosun, a very
stiff, green young man, a relative of* DELANO'S. THREE
SAILORS, *one carrying an American flag, enter.* EVERYONE
*stands at attention and salutes with machinelike exactitude.
Then the* THREE SAILORS *march off-stage.* DELANO *and*
PERKINS *are alone.*

DELANO.
  There goes the most beautiful woman in South America.
PERKINS.
  We never see any women, Sir;
  just this smothering, overcast Equator,
  a seal or two,
  the flat dull sea,
  and a sky like a gray wasp's nest.
DELANO.
  I wasn't talking about women,
  I was calling your attention to the American flag.
PERKINS.
  Yes, Sir! I wish we were home in Duxbury.

DELANO.

We are home. America is wherever her flag flies.
My own deck is the only place in the world
where I feel at home.

PERKINS.

That's too much for me, Captain Delano.
I mean I wish I were at home with my wife;
these world cruises are only for bachelors.

DELANO.

Your wife will keep. You should smoke, Perkins.
Smoking turns men into philosophers
and swabs away their worries.
I can see my wife and children or not see them
in each puff of blue smoke.

PERKINS.

You are always tempting me, Sir!
I try to keep fit,
I want to return to my wife as fit as I left her.

DELANO.

You're much too nervous, Perkins.
Travel will shake you up. You should let
a little foreign dirt rub off on you.
I've taught myself to speak Spanish like a Spaniard.
At each South American port, they mistake me for a
Castilian Don.

PERKINS.

Aren't you lowering yourself a little, Captain?
Excuse me, Sir, I have been wanting to ask you a question.
Don't you think our President, Mr. Jefferson, is
    lowering himself
by being so close to the French?
I'd feel a lot safer in this unprotected place
if we'd elected Mr. Adams instead of Mr. Jefferson.

DELANO.

The better man ran second!
Come to think of it, he rather let us down
by losing the election just after we had named this ship,
the *President Adams.* Adams is a nervous dry fellow.
When you've travelled as much as I have,
you'll learn that that sort doesn't export, Perkins.

Adams didn't get a vote outside New England!

PERKINS.

He carried every New England state;
that was better than winning the election.
I'm afraid I'm a dry fellow, too, Sir.

DELANO.

Not when I've educated you!
When I am through with you, Perkins,
you'll be as worldly as the Prince Regent of England,
only you'll be a first class American officer.
I'm all for Jefferson, he has the popular touch.
Of course he's read too many books,
but I've always said an idea or two won't sink
   our Republic.
I'll tell you this, Perkins,
Mr. Jefferson is a gentleman and an American.

PERKINS.

They say he has two illegitimate Negro children.

DELANO.

The more the better! That's the quickest way
to raise the blacks to our level.
I'm surprised you swallow such Federalist bilge, Perkins!
I told you Mr. Jefferson is a gentleman and an American;
when a man's in office, Sir, we all pull behind him!

PERKINS.

Thank God our Revolution ended where the French
   one began.

DELANO.

Oh the French! They're like the rest of the Latins,
they're hardly white people,
they start with a paper republic
and end with a toy soldier, like Bonaparte.

PERKINS.

Yes, Sir. I see a strange sail making for the harbor.
They don't know how to sail her.

DELANO.

Hand me my telescope.

PERKINS.

Aye, aye, Sir!

DELANO [*With telescope*].

I see an ocean undulating in long scoops of swells;
it's set like the beheaded French Queen's high wig;
the sleek surface is like waved lead,
cooled and pressed in the smelter's mould.
I see flights of hurried gray fowl,
patches of fluffy fog.
They skim low and fitfully above the decks,
like swallows sabering flies before a storm.
This gray boat foreshadows something wrong.

PERKINS.

It does, Sir!
They don't know how to sail her!

DELANO.

I see a sulphurous haze above her cabin,
the new sun hangs like a silver dollar to her stern;
low creeping clouds blow on from them to us.

PERKINS.

What else, Sir?

DELANO.

The yards are woolly
the ship is furred with fog.
On the cracked and rotten head-boards,
the tarnished, gilded letters say, the *San Domingo*.
A rat's-nest messing up the deck,
black faces in white sheets are fussing with the ropes.
I think it's a cargo of Dominican monks.

PERKINS.

Dominican monks, Sir! God help us,
I thought they were outlawed in the new world.

DELANO.

No, it's nothing. I see they're only slaves.
The boat's transporting slaves.

PERKINS.

Do you believe in slavery, Captain Delano?

DELANO.

In a civilized country, Perkins,
everyone disbelieves in slavery,
everyone disbelieves in slavery and wants slaves.
We have the perfect uneasy answer;

in the North, we don't have them and want them;
Mr. Jefferson has them and fears them.

PERKINS.

Is that how you answer, Sir,
when a little foreign dirt has rubbed off on you?

DELANO.

Don't ask me such intense questions.
You should take up smoking, Perkins.
There was a beautiful, dumb English actress—
I saw her myself once in London.
They wanted her to look profound,
so she read Plato and the Bible and Benjamin Franklin,
and thought about them every minute.
She still looked like a moron.
Then they told her to think about nothing.
She thought about nothing, and looked like Socrates.
That's smoking, Perkins, you think about nothing and
   look deep.

PERKINS.

I don't believe in slavery, Sir.

DELANO.

You don't believe in slavery or Spaniards
or smoking or long cruises or monks or Mr. Jefferson!
You are a Puritan, all faith and fire.

PERKINS.

Yes, Sir.

DELANO.

God save America from Americans!
   [*Takes up the telescope*]
I see octagonal network bagging out
from her heavy top like decayed beehives.
The battered forecastle looks like a raped Versailles.
On the stern-piece, I see the fading arms of Spain.
There's a masked satyr, or something
with its foot on a big white goddess.
She has quite a figure.

PERKINS.

They oughtn't to be allowed on the ocean!

DELANO.

Who oughtn't? Goddesses?

PERKINS.
   I mean Spaniards, who cannot handle a ship,
   and mess up its hull with immoral statues.

DELANO.
   You're out of step. You're much too dry.
   Bring me my three-cornered hat.
   Order some men to clear a whaleboat.
   I am going to bring water and fresh fish to the
      *San Domingo*.
   These people have had some misfortune, Perkins!

PERKINS.
   Aye, aye, Sir.

DELANO.
   Spaniards? The name gets you down,
   you think their sultry faces and language
   make them Zulus.
   You take the name *Delano*—
   I've always thought it had some saving
   Italian or Spanish virtue in it.

PERKINS.
   Yes, Sir.

DELANO.
   A Spaniard isn't a Negro under the skin,
   particularly a Spaniard from Spain—
   these South American ones mix too much with the
      Indians.
   Once you get inside a Spaniard,
   he talks about as well as your wife in Duxbury.

PERKINS [*Shouting*].
   A boat for the captain! A whaleboat for Captain Delano!
   [*A bosun's whistle is heard, the lights dim. When they
   come up, we are on the deck of the* San Domingo, *the
   same set, identical except for litter and disorder.*
   THREE AMERICAN SAILORS *climb on board. They are
   followed by* PERKINS *and* DELANO, *now wearing a
   three-cornered hat. Once on board, the* AMERICAN
   SAILORS *salute* DELANO *and stand stiffly at attention
   like toys.* NEGROES *from the* San Domingo *drift silently and furtively forward*]

DELANO.

I see a wen of barnacles hanging to the waterline of
this ship.

It sticks out like the belly of a pregnant woman.

Have a look at our dory, Bosun.

PERKINS.

Aye, aye, Sir!

[*By now, about twenty blacks and* TWO SPANISH SAIL-
ORS *have drifted in. They look like some gaudy, shabby,
unnautical charade, and pay no attention to the Americans, until an unseen figure in the rigging calls out a
single sharp warning in an unknown tongue. Then
they all rush forward, shouting, waving their arms and
making inarticulate cries like birds. Three shrill warnings come from the rigging. Dead silence. The men
from the* San Domingo *press back in a dense semicir-
cle. One by one, individuals come forward, make
showy bows to* DELANO, *and speak*]

FIRST NEGRO.

Scurvy, Master Yankee!

SECOND NEGRO.

Yellow fever, Master Yankee!

THIRD NEGRO.

Two men knocked overboard rounding Cape Horn,
Master Yankee!

FOURTH NEGRO.

Nothing to eat, Master Yankee!

NEGRO WOMAN.

Nothing to drink, Master Yankee!

SECOND NEGRO WOMAN.

Our mouths are dead wood, Master Yankee!

DELANO.

You see, Perkins,

these people have had some misfortune.

[*General hubbub, muttering, shouts, gestures, ritual
and dumbshow of distress. The rigging, hitherto dark,
lightens, as the sun comes out of a cloud, and shows*
THREE OLD NEGROES, *identical down to their shabby
patches. They perch on cat's-heads; their heads are
grizzled like dying willow tops; each is picking bits of*

*unstranded rope for oakum. It is they who have been
giving the warnings that control the people below. Everyone,* DELANO *along with the rest, looks up.* DELANO
*turns aside and speaks to* PERKINS]

It is like a Turkish bazaar.

PERKINS.

They are like gypsies showing themselves for money
at a county fair, Sir.

DELANO.

This is enchanting after the blank gray roll of the ocean!
Go tell the Spanish captain I am waiting for him.

[PERKINS *goes off. Sharp warnings from the* OAKUM-
PICKERS. *A big black spread of canvas is pulled creak-
ingly and ceremoniously aside.* SIX FIGURES *stand
huddled on a platform about four feet from the deck.
They look like weak old invalids in bathrobes and
nightcaps until they strip to the waist and turn out to
be huge shining young Negroes. Saying nothing, they
set to work cleaning piles of rusted hatchets. From
time to time, they turn and clash their hatchets together with a rhythmic shout.* PERKINS *returns*]

PERKINS.

Their captain's name is Don Benito Cereno,
he sends you his compliments, Sir.
He looks more like a Mexican planter than a seaman.
He's put his fortune on his back:
he doesn't look as if he had washed since they left port.

DELANO.

Did you tell him I was waiting for him?
A captain should be welcomed by his fellow-captain.
I can't understand this discourtesy.

PERKINS.

He's coming, but there's something wrong with him.

[BENITO CERENO, *led by his Negro servant,* BABU,
*enters.* BENITO, *looking sick and dazed, is wearing a
sombrero and is dressed with a singular but shabby
richness. Head bent to one side, he leans in a stately
coma against the rail, and stares unseeingly at*
DELANO. BABU, *all in scarlet, and small and quick,*

*keeps whispering, pointing and pulling at* BENITO'S
*sleeve.* DELANO *walks over to them*]

DELANO.

Your hand, Sir. I am Amasa Delano,
captain of the *President Adams,*
a sealing ship from the United States.
This is your lucky day,
the sun is out of hiding for the first time in two weeks,
and here I am aboard your ship
like the Good Samaritan with fresh food and water.

BENITO.

The Good Samaritan? Yes, yes,
we mustn't use the Scriptures lightly.
Welcome, Captain. It is the end of the day.

DELANO.

The end? It's only morning.
I loaded and lowered a whaleboat
as soon as I saw how awkwardly your ship was making
    for the harbor.

BENITO.

Your whaleboat's welcome, Captain.
I am afraid I am still stunned by the storm.

DELANO.

Buck up. Each day is a new beginning.
Assign some sailors to help me dole out my provisions.

BENITO.

I have no sailors.

BABU [*In a quick sing-song*].

Scurvy, yellow fever,
ten men knocked off on the Horn,
doldrums, nothing to eat, nothing to drink!
By feeding us, you are feeding the King of Spain.

DELANO.

Sir, your slave has a pretty way of talking.
What do you need?

    [DELANO *waits for* BENITO *to speak. When nothing
    more is said, he shifts awkwardly from foot to foot,
    then turns to his* SAILORS]

Stand to, men!

    [*The* AMERICAN SAILORS, *who have been lounging and*

*gaping, stand in a row, as if a button had been pressed*]
Lay our fish and water by the cabin!

[*The* SAILORS *arrange the watercans and baskets of
fish by the cabin. A sharp whistle comes from the
OAKUM-PICKERS. Almost instantly, the provisions disappear*]

Captain Cereno, you are surely going to taste my water!

BENITO.

A captain is a servant, almost a slave, Sir.

DELANO.

No, a captain's a captain.
I am sending for more provisions.
Stand to! [*The* AMERICAN SAILORS *stand to*]
Row back to the ship. When you get there,
take on five hogsheads of fresh water,
and fifty pounds of soft bread.

[FIRST SAILOR *salutes and goes down the ladder*]

Bring all our remaining pumpkins!

[SECOND *and* THIRD SAILORS *salute and go down the
ladder*]

My bosun and I will stay on board,
until our boat returns.
I imagine you can use us.

BENITO.

Are you going to stay here alone?
Won't your ship be lost without you?
Won't you be lost without your ship?

BABU.

Listen to Master!
He is the incarnation of courtesy, Yankee Captain.
Your ship doesn't need you as much as we do.

DELANO.

Oh, I've trained my crew.
I can sail my ship in my sleep.

[*Leaning over the railing and calling*]

Men, bring me a box of lump sugar,
and six bottles of my best cider.

[*Turning to* BENITO]

Cider isn't my favorite drink, Don Benito,
but it's a New England specialty;

I'm ordering six bottles for your table.

[BABU *whispers and gestures to* DON BENITO, *who is exhausted and silent*]

BABU.

*Une bouteille du vin* [*to* NEGROES]

My master wishes to give you a bottle
of the oldest wine in Seville.

[*He whistles. A Negro woman rushes into the cabin and returns with a dusty beribboned bottle, which she holds like a baby.* BABU *ties a rope around the bottle*]

BABU.

I am sending this bottle of wine to your cabin.

When you drink it, you will remember us.

Do you see these ribbons? The crown of Spain is tied to one.

Forgive me for tying a rope around the King of
Spain's neck. [*Lowers the wine on the rope to the whaleboat*]

DELANO [*Shouting to his* SAILORS].

Pick up your oars!

SAILORS.

Aye, aye, Sir!

DELANO.

We're New England Federalists;
we can drink the King of Spain's health.

[BENITO *stumbles off-stage on* BABU'S *arm*]

PERKINS.

Captain Cereno hasn't travelled as much as you have;
I don't think he knew what you meant by the New England Federalists.

DELANO [*Leaning comfortably on the rail, half to himself and half to* PERKINS]

The wind is dead. We drift away.

We will be left alone all day,

here in this absentee empire.

Thank God, I know my Spanish!

PERKINS.

You'll have to watch them, Sir.

Brown men in charge of black men—

it doesn't add up to much!
This Babu, I don't trust him!
Why doesn't he talk with a Southern accent,
Like Mr. Jefferson? They're out of hand, Sir!

DELANO.

Nothing relaxes order more than misery.
They need severe superior officers.
They haven't one.
Now, if this Benito were a man of energy . . .
a Yankee . . .

PERKINS.

How can a Spaniard sail?

DELANO.

Some can. There was Vasco da Gama and Columbus . . .
No, I guess they were Italians. Some can,
but this captain is tubercular.

PERKINS.

Spaniards and Negroes have no business on a ship.

DELANO.

Why is this captain so indifferent to me?
If only I could stomach his foreign reserve!
This absolute dictator of his ship
only gives orders through his slaves!
He is like some Jesuit-haunted Hapsburg king
about to leave the world and hope the world will end.

PERKINS.

He said he was lost in the storm.

DELANO.

Perhaps it's only policy,
a captain's icy dignity
obliterating all democracy—

PERKINS.

He's like someone walking in his sleep.
Ah, slumbering dominion!
He is so self-conscious in his imbecility . . .
No, he's sick. He sees his men no more than me.
This ship is like a crowded immigration boat;
it needs severe superior officers,
the friendly arm of a strong mate.

Perhaps, I ought to take it over by force.
No, they're sick, they've been through the plague.
I'll go and speak and comfort my fellow captain.
I think you can help me, Captain. I'm feeling useless.
My own thoughts oppress me, there's so much to do.
I wonder if you would tell me the whole sad story of
    your voyage.
Talk to me as captain to captain.
We have sailed the same waters.
Please tell me your story.

BENITO.

A story? A story? That's out of place.
When I was a child, I used to beg for stories back in
    Lima.
Now my tongue's tied and my heart is bleeding.
    [*Stops talking, as if his breath were gone. He stares
    for a few moments, then looks up at the rigging, as if
    he were counting the ropes one by one.* DELANO *turns
    abruptly to* PERKINS]

DELANO.

Go through the ship, Perkins,
and see if you can find me a Spaniard who can talk.

BENITO.

You must be patient, Captain Delano;
if we only see with our eyes,
sometimes we cannot see at all.

DELANO.

I stand corrected, Captain;
tell me about your voyage.

BENITO.

It's now a hundred and ninety days . . .
This ship, well manned, well officered, with several
    cabin passengers,
carrying a cargo of Paraguay tea and Spanish cutlery.
That parcel of Negro slaves, less than four score now,
was once three hundred souls.
Ten sailors and three officers fell from the mainyard off
    the Horn;
part of our rigging fell overboard with them,
as they were beating down the icy sail.

We threw away all our cargo,
Broke our waterpipes,
Lashed them on deck
this was the chief cause of our suffering.

DELANO.

I must interrupt you, Captain.
How did you happen to have three officers on
    the mainyard?
I never heard of such a disposal,
it goes against all seamanship.

BABU.

Our officers never spared themselves;
if there was any danger, they rushed in
to save us without thinking.

DELANO.

I can't understand such an oversight.

BABU.

There was no oversight. My master had a hundred eyes.
He had an eye for everything.
Sometimes the world falls on a man.
The sea wouldn't let Master act like a master,
yet he saved himself and many lives.
He is still a rich man, and he saved the ship.

BENITO.

Oh my God, I wish the world had fallen on me,
and the terrible cold sea had drowned me;
that would have been better than living through what
I've lived through!

BABU.

He is a good man, but his mind is off;
he's thinking about the fever when the wind stopped—
poor, poor Master!
Be patient, Yankee Captain, these fits are short,
Master will be the master once again.

BENITO.

The scurvy was raging through us.
We were on the Pacific. We were invalids
and couldn't man our mangled spars.
A hurricane blew us northeast through the fog.
Then the wind died.

We lay in irons fourteen days in unknown waters,
our black tongues stuck through our mouths,
but we couldn't mend our broken waterpipes.

BABU.

Always those waterpipes,
he dreams about them like a pile of snakes!

BENITO.

Yellow fever followed the scurvy,
the long heat thickened in the calm,
my Spaniards turned black and died like slaves,
The blacks died too. I am my only officer left.

BABU.

Poor, poor Master! He had a hundred eyes,
he lived our lives for us.
He is still a rich man.

BENITO.

In the smart winds beating us northward,
our torn sails dropped like sinkers in the sea;
each day we dropped more bodies.
Almost without a crew, canvas, water, or a wind,
we were bounced about by the opposing waves
through cross-currents and the weedy calms,
and dropped our dead.
Often we doubled and redoubled on our track
like children lost in jungle. The thick fog
hid the Continent and our only port from us.

BABU.

We were poor kidnapped jungle creatures.
We only lived on what he could give us.
He had a hundred eyes, he was the master.

BENITO.

These Negroes saved me, Captain.
Through the long calamity,
they were as gentle as their owner, Don Aranda,
    promised.
Don Aranda took away their chains before he died.

BABU.

Don Aranda saved our lives, but we couldn't save his.
Even in Africa I was a slave.
He took away my chains.

BENITO.

I gave them the freedom of my ship.

I did not think they were crates or cargo or cannibals.

But it was Babu—under God, I swear I owe my life
to Babu!

He calmed his ignorant, wild brothers,

never left me, saved the *San Domingo*.

BABU.

Poor, poor Master. He is still a rich man.

Don't speak of Babu. Babu is the dirt under your feet.

He did his best.

DELANO.

You are a good fellow, Babu.

You are the salt of the earth. I envy you, Don Benito;

he is no slave, Sir, but your friend.

BENITO.

Yes, he is salt in my wounds.

I can never repay him, I mean.

Excuse me, Captain, my strength is gone.

I have done too much talking. I want to rest.

    [BABU *leads* BENITO *to a shabby straw chair at the
    side.* BENITO *sits.* BABU *fans him with his sombrero*]

PERKINS.

He's a fine gentleman, but no seaman.

A cabin boy would have known better

than to send his three officers on the mainyard.

DELANO [*Paying no attention*].

A terrible story. I would have been unhinged myself.

    [*Looking over toward* BABU *and* BENITO]

There's a true servant. They do things better

in the South and in South America—

trust in return for trust!

The beauty of that relationship is unknown

in New England. We're too much alone

in Massachusetts, Perkins.

How do our captains and our merchants live,

each a republic to himself.

Even Sam Adams had no friends and only loved the mob.

PERKINS.

Sir, you are forgetting that

New England seamanship brought them their slaves.

DELANO.

Oh, just our Southern slaves;
we had nothing to do with these fellows.

PERKINS.

The ocean would be a different place
if every Spaniard served an apprenticeship on an
      American ship
before he got his captain's papers.

DELANO.

This captain's a gentleman, not a sailor.
His little yellow hands
got their command before they held a rope—
in by the cabin-window, not the hawse-hole!
Do you want to know why
they drifted hog-tied in those easy calms—
inexperience, sickness, impotence and aristocracy!

PERKINS.

Here comes Robinson Crusoe and his good man Friday.

DELANO.

We don't beat a man when he's down.
      [BENITO *advances uncertainly on* BABU's *arm*]
I am glad to see you on your feet again,
That's the only place for a Captain, sir!
I have the cure for you, I have decided
to bring you medicine and a sufficient supply of water.
A first class deck officer, a man from Salem,
shall be stationed on your quarter deck,
a temporary present from my owners.
We shall refit your ship and clear this mess.

BENITO.

You will have to clear away the dead.

BABU.

This excitement is bad for him, Yankee Master.
He's lived with death. He lives on death still;
this sudden joy will kill him. You've heard
how thirsty men die from overdrinking!
His heart is with his friend, our owner, Don Aranda.

BENITO.

I am the only owner.

[*He looks confused and shaken.* BABU *scurries off and brings up the straw chair.* BENITO *sits*]

DELANO.

Your friend is dead? He died of fever?

BENITO.

He died very slowly and in torture.
He was the finest man in Lima.
We were brought up together,
I am lost here.

DELANO.

Pardon me, Sir. You are young at sea.
My experience tells me what your trouble is:
this is the first body you have buried in the ocean.
I had a friend like yours, a warm honest fellow,
who would look you in the eye—
we had to throw him to the sharks.
Since then I've brought embalming gear on board.
Each man of mine shall have a Christian grave on land.
You wouldn't shake so, if Don Aranda were on board,
I mean, if you'd preserved the body.

BENITO.

If he were on board this ship?
If I had preserved his body?

BABU.

Be patient, Master!
We still have the figurehead.

DELANO.

You have the figurehead?

BABU.

You see that thing wrapped up in black cloth?
It's a figurehead Don Aranda bought us in Spain.
It was hurt in the storm. It's very precious.
Master takes comfort in it,
he is going to give it to Don Aranda's widow.
It's time for the pardon ceremony, Master.
    [*Sound of clashing hatchets*]

DELANO.

I am all for these hatchet-cleaners.
They are saving cargo. They make

an awful lot of pomp and racket though
about a few old, rusty knives.

BENITO.

They think steel is worth its weight in gold.

[*A slow solemn march is sounded on the gongs and
other instruments. A gigantic coal-black* NEGRO *comes
up the steps. He wears a spiked iron collar to which a
chain is attached that goes twice around his arms and
ends padlocked to a broad band of iron. The* NEGRO
*comes clanking forward and stands dumbly and like a
dignitary in front of* BENITO. TWO SMALL BLACK BOYS
*bring* BENITO *a frail rattan cane and a silver ball,
which they support on a velvet cushion.* BENITO
*springs up, holds the ball, and raises the cane rigidly
above the head of the* NEGRO *in chains. For a moment,
he shows no trace of sickness. The assembled blacks
sing, "Evviva, Benito!" three times*]

BABU [*At one side with the* AMERICANS *but keeping an eye
on* BENITO]

You are watching the humiliation of King Atufal,
once a ruler in Africa. He ruled as much land there
    as your President.
Poor Babu was a slave even in Africa,
a black man's slave, and now a white man's.

BENITO [*In a loud, firm voice*].

Former King Atufal, I call on you to kneel!
Say, "My sins are black as night,
I ask the King of Spain's pardon
through his servant, Don Benito."

[*Pause.* ATUFAL *doesn't move*]

NEGROES.

Your sins are black as night, King Atufal!
Your sins are black as night, King Atufal!

DELANO.

What has King Atufal done?

BABU.

I will tell you later, Yankee Captain.

BENITO.

Ask pardon, former King Atufal.

If you will kneel,
I will strike away your chains.

[ATUFAL *slowly raises his chained arms and lets them drop*]

Ask pardon!

WOMAN SLAVE.

Ask pardon King Atufal.

BENITO.

Go!

[*Sound of instruments. The* BLACK BOYS *take* BENITO's *ball and cane. The straw chair is brought up.* BENITO *sits.* FRANCESCO *then leads him off-stage*]

BABU.

Francesco!
I will be with you in a moment, Master.
You mustn't be afraid,
Francesco will serve you like a second Babu.

BENITO.

Everyone serves me alike here,
but no one can serve me as you have.

BABU.

I will be with you in a moment.
The Yankee master is at sea on our ship.
He wants me to explain our customs.

[BENITO *is carried off-stage*]

You would think Master's afraid of dying,
if Babu leaves him!

DELANO.

I can imagine your tenderness during his sickness.
You were part of him,
you were almost a wife.

BABU.

You say such beautiful things,
the United States must be a paradise for people like Babu.

DELANO.

I don't know.
We have our faults. We have many states,
some of them could stand improvement.

BABU.

The United States must be heaven.

DELANO.

    I suppose we have fewer faults than other countries.

    What did King Atufal do?

BABU.

    He used the Spanish flag for toilet paper.

DELANO.

    That's treason.

    Did Atufal know what he was doing?

    Perhaps the flag was left somewhere it shouldn't have
      been.

    Things aren't very strict here.

BABU.

    I never thought of that.

    I will go and tell Master.

DELANO.

    Oh, no, you mustn't do that!

    I never interfere with another man's ship.

    Don Benito is your lord and dictator.

    How long has this business with King Atufal been
      going on?

BABU.

    Ever since the yellow fever,

    and twice a day.

DELANO.

    He did a terrible thing, but he looks like a royal fellow.

    You shouldn't call him a king, though,

    it puts ideas into his head.

BABU.

    Atufal had gold wedges in his ears in Africa;

    now he wears a padlock and Master bears the key.

DELANO.

    I see you have a feeling for symbols of power.

    You had better be going now,

    Don Benito will be nervous about you.

      [BABU *goes off*]

    That was a terrible thing to do with a flag;

    everything is untidy and unravelled here—

    this sort of thing would never happen on the
      *President Adams.*

PERKINS.

  Your ship is as shipshape as our country, Sir.

DELANO.

  I wish people wouldn't take me as representative of
      our country:

  America's one thing, I am another;

  we shouldn't have to bear one another's burdens.

PERKINS.

  You are a true American for all your talk, Sir;

  I can't believe you were mistaken for a Castilian Don.

DELANO.

  No one would take me for Don Benito.

PERKINS.

  I wonder if he isn't an impostor, some traveling actor
      from a circus?

DELANO.

  No, Cereno is a great name in Peru, like Winthrop or
      Adams with us.

  I recognize the family features in our captain.

      [*An* OLD SPANISH SAILOR, *grizzled and dirty, is seen
      crawling on all fours with an armful of knots toward
      the Americans. He points to where* BENITO *and* BABU
      *have disappeared and whistles. He holds up the knots
      as though he were in chains, then throws them out
      loosely on the deck in front of him. A* GROUP OF
      NEGROES *forms a circle around him, holding hands
      and singing childishly. Then, laughing, they carry the*
      SPANIARD *off-stage on their shoulders*]

  These blacks are too familiar!

  We are never alone!

      [*Sound of gongs. Full minute's pause, as if time were
      passing.* DELANO *leans on the railing. The sun grows
      brighter*]

  This ship is strange.

  These people are too spontaneous—all noise and show,
  no character!

  Real life is a simple monotonous thing.

  I wonder about that story about the calms;
  it doesn't stick.

'Don Benito hesitated himself in telling it.
No one could run a ship so stupidly,
and place three officers on one yard. [BENITO *and* BABU
    *return*]
A captain has unpleasant duties;
I am sorry for you, Don Benito.
BENITO.
You find my ship unenviable, Sir?
DELANO.
I was talking about punishing Atufal;
he acted like an animal!
BENITO.
Oh, yes, I was forgetting . . .
He was a King,
How long have you lain in at this island, Sir?
DELANO.
Oh, a week today.
BENITO.
What was your last port, Sir?
DELANO.
Canton.
BENITO.
You traded seal-skins and American muskets
for Chinese tea and silks, perhaps?
DELANO.
We took in some silks.
BENITO.
A little gold and silver too?
DELANO.
Just a little silver. We are only merchants.
We take in a dollar here and there. We have no Peru,
or a Pizarro who can sweat gold out of the natives.
BENITO.
You'll find things have changed
a little in Peru since Pizarro, Captain.
    [*Starts to move away.* BABU *whispers to him, and he
    comes back abruptly, as if he had forgotten something
    important*]
How many men have you on board, Sir?

DELANO.

Some twenty-five, Sir. Each man is at his post.

BENITO.

They're all on board, Sir, now?

DELANO.

They're all on board. Each man is working.

BENITO.

They'll be on board tonight, Sir?

DELANO.

Tonight? Why do you ask, Don Benito?

BENITO.

Will they all be on board tonight, Captain?

DELANO.

They'll be on board for all I know. [PERKINS *makes a*
    *sign to* DELANO]
Well, no, to tell the truth, today's our Independence Day.
A gang is going ashore to see the village.
A little diversion improves their efficiency,
a little regulated corruption.

BENITO.

You North Americans take no chances. Generally,
    I suppose,
even your merchant ships go more or less armed?

DELANO.

A rack of muskets, sealing spears and cutlasses.
Oh, and a six-pounder or two; we are a sealing ship,
but with us each merchant is a privateer—
only in case of oppression, of course.
You've heard about how we shoot pirates.

BABU.

Boom, boom, come Master.

    [BENITO *walks away on* BABU's *arm and sits down, al-*
    *most offstage in his straw chair. They whisper. Mean-*
    *while, a* SPANISH SAILOR *climbs the rigging furtively,*
    *spread-eagles his arms and shows a lace shirt under*
    *his shabby jacket. He points to* BENITO *and* BABU *and*
    *winks. At a cry from* ONE OF THE OAKUM-PICKERS,
    THREE NEGROES *help the* SPANIARD *down with servile,*
    *ceremonious attentions*]

PERKINS.

> Did you see that sailor's lace shirt, Sir?
> He must have robbed one of the cabin passengers.
> I hear that people strip the dead
> in these religious countries.

DELANO.

> No, you don't understand the Spaniards.
> In these old Latin countries,
> each man's a beggar or a noble, often both;
> they have no middle class. With them it's customary
> to sew a mess of gold and pearls on rags—
> that's how an aristocracy that's going to the dogs
> keeps up its nerve.
> It's odd though,
> that Spanish sailor seemed to want to tell me something.
> He ought to dress himself properly and speak his mind.
> That's what we do. That's why we're strong:
> everybody trusts us. Nothing gets done
> when every man's a noble. I wonder why
> the captain asked me all those questions?

PERKINS.

> He was passing the time of day, Sir;
> It's a Latin idleness.

DELANO.

> It's strange. Did you notice how Benito stopped rambling?
> He was conventional . . . consecutive for the first time
> since we met him.
> Something's wrong. Perhaps, they've men below the
> decks,
> a sleeping volcano of Spanish infantry. The Malays do it,
> play sick and cut your throat.
> A drifting boat, a dozen doped beggars on deck,
> two hundred sweating murderers packed below
> like sardines—
> that's rot! Anyone can see these people are really sick,
> sicker than usual. Our countries are at peace.
> I wonder why he asked me all those questions?

PERKINS.

> Just idle curiosity. I hear

the gentlemen of Lima sit at coffee-tables from sun to sun
and gossip. They don't even have women to look at;
they're all locked up with their aunts.

DELANO.

Their sun is going down. These old empires go.
They are much too familiar with their blacks.
I envy them though, they have no character,
they feel no need to stand alone.
We stand alone too much,
that's why no one can touch us for sailing a ship;
When a country loses heart, it's easier to live.
Ah, Babu! I suppose Don Benito's indisposed again!
Tell him I want to talk to his people;
there's nothing like a well man to help the sick.

BABU.

Master is taking his siesta, Yankee Master.
His siesta is sacred, I am afraid to disturb it.
Instead, let me show you our little entertainment.

DELANO.

Let's have your entertainment;
if you know a man's pleasure
you know his measure.

BABU.

We are a childish people. Our pleasures are childish.
No one helped us, we know nothing
about your important amusements,
such as killing seals and pirates.

DELANO.

I'm game. Let's have your entertainment.

[BABU *signals. The gong sounds ten times and the canvas is pulled from the circular structure. Enclosed in a
triangular compartment, an* OLD SPANISH SAILOR *is
dipping naked white dolls in a tar-pot*]

BABU.

This little amusement keeps him alive, Yankee Master.
He is especially fond of cleaning the dolls
after he has dirtied them.

[*The* OLD SPANISH SAILOR *laughs hysterically, and
then smears his whole face with tar*]

OLD SPANISH SAILOR.

My soul is white!

BABU.

The yellow fever destroyed his mind.

DELANO.

Let's move on. This man's brain,
as well as his face, is defiled with pitch!

BABU.

He says his soul is white.

[*The structure is pushed around and another triangular compartment appears. A* NEGRO BOY *is playing chess against a splendid Spanish doll with a crown on its head. He stops and holds two empty wine bottles to his ears*]

This boy is deaf.

The yellow fever destroyed his mind.

DELANO.

Why is he holding those bottles to his ears?

BABU.

He is trying to be a rabbit,
or listening to the ocean, his mother—
who knows?

DELANO.

If he's deaf, how can he hear the ocean?

Anyway, he can't hear me.

I pass, let's move on.

[*The structure is pushed around to a third compartment. A* SPANISH SAILOR *is holding a big armful of rope*]

What are you knotting there, my man?

SPANISH SAILOR.

The knot.

DELANO.

So I see, but what's it for?

SPANISH SAILOR.

For someone to untie. Catch! [*Throws the knot to* DELANO]

BABU [*Snatching the knot from* DELANO].

It's dirty, it will dirty your uniform.

DELANO.

Let's move on. Your entertainment
is rather lacking in invention, Babu.

BABU.

We have to do what we can
We are just beginners at acting.
This next one will be better.

[*The structure is pushed around and shows a beautiful*
NEGRO WOMAN. *She is dressed and posed as the Virgin Mary. A Christmas crèche is arranged around her.
A* VERY WHITE SPANIARD *dressed as Saint Joseph
stands behind her. She holds a Christ-child, the same
crowned doll, only black, the* NEGRO BOY *was playing
chess against*]

She is the Virgin Mary. That man is not the father.

DELANO.

I see. I suppose her son is the King of Spain.

BABU.

The Spaniards taught us everything,
there's nothing we can learn from you, Yankee Master.
When they took away our country, they gave us a
    better world.
Things do not happen in that world as they do here.

DELANO.

That's a very beautiful,
though unusual, Virgin Mary.

BABU.

Yes, the Bible says, "I am black not white."
When Don Aranda was dying,
we wanted to give him the Queen of Heaven
because he took away our chains.

PERKINS.

The Spaniards must have taught them everything;
they're all mixed up, they don't even know their religion.

DELANO.

No, no! The Catholic Church doesn't just teach,
it knows how to take from its converts.

BABU.

Do you want to shake hands with the Queen of Heaven,
    Yankee Master?

DELANO.

No, I'm not used to royalty.
Tell her I believe in freedom of religion,
if people don't take liberties.
Let's move on.

BABU [*Kneeling to the Virgin Mary*].

I present something Your Majesty has never seen,
a white man who doesn't believe in taking liberties,
Your Majesty.

[*The structure is pushed around and shows* ATUFAL *in
chains but with a crown on his head*]

BABU.

This is the life we believe in.
Ask pardon, King Atufal!
Kiss the Spanish flag!

DELANO.

Please don't ask me to shake hands with King Atufal!

[*The canvas is put back on the structure*]

BABU.

You look tired and serious, Yankee Master.
We have to have what fun we can.
We never would have lived through the deadly calms
without a little amusement. [*Bows and goes off*]

[*The* NEGROES *gradually drift away.* DELANO *sighs
with relief*]

DELANO.

Well, that wasn't much!
I suppose Shakespeare started that way.

PERKINS.

Who cares?
I see a speck on the blue sea, Sir,
our whaleboat is coming.

DELANO.

A speck? My eyes are speckled.
I seem to have been dreaming. What's solid?

[*Touches the ornate railing; a piece falls onto the deck*]

This ship is nothing, Perkins!
I dreamed someone was trying to kill me!
How could he? Jack-of-the-beach,
they used to call me on the Duxbury shore.

Carrying a duck-satchel in my hand, I used to paddle
along the waterfront from a hulk to school.
I didn't learn much there. I was always shooting duck
or gathering huckleberries along the marsh with
     Cousin Nat!
I like nothing better than breaking myself on the surf.
I used to track the seagulls down the five-mile stretch
     of beach for eggs.
How can I be killed now at the ends of the earth
by this insane Spaniard?
Who could want to murder Amasa Delano?
My conscience is clean. God is good.
What am I doing on board this nigger pirate ship?

PERKINS.
You're not talking like a skipper, Sir.
Our boat's a larger spot now.

DELANO.
I am childish.
I am doddering and drooling into my second childhood.
God help me, nothing's solid!

PERKINS.
Don Benito, Sir. Touch him,
he's as solid as his ship.

DELANO.
Don Benito? He's a walking ghost!

     [BENITO *comes up to* DELANO. BABU *is a few steps be-
     hind him*]

BENITO.
I am the ghost of myself, Captain.
Excuse me, I heard you talking about dreams
     and childhood.
I was a child, too, once, I have dreams about it.

DELANO [*Starting*].
I'm sorry.
This jumping's just a nervous habit.
I thought you were part of my dreams.

BENITO.
I was taking my siesta,
I dreamed I was a boy back in Lima.
I was with my brothers and sisters,

and we were dressed for the festival of Corpus Christi
like people at our Bourbon court.
We were simple children, but something went wrong;
little black men came on us with beetle backs.
They had caterpillar heads and munched away on our
    fine clothes.
They made us lick their horned and varnished insect legs.
Our faces turned brown from their spit,
we looked like bugs, but nothing could save our lives!

DELANO.

Ha, ha, Captain. We are like two dreams meeting head-on.
My whaleboat's coming,
we'll both feel better over a bottle of cider.

    [BABU *blows a bosun's whistle. The gongs are sounded*
    *with descending notes. The* NEGROES *assemble in*
    *ranks*]

BABU.

It's twelve noon, Master Yankee.
Master wants his midday shave.

ALL THE NEGROES.

Master wants his shave! Master wants his shave!

BENITO.

Ah, yes, the razor! I have been talking too much.
You can see how badly I need a razor.
I must leave you, Captain.

BABU.

No, Don Amasa wants to talk.
Come to the cabin, Don Amasa.
Don Amasa will talk, Master will listen.
Babu will lather and strop.

DELANO.

I want to talk to you about navigation.
I am new to these waters.

BENITO.

Doubtless, doubtless, Captain Delano.

PERKINS.

I think I'll take my siesta, Sir. [*He walks off*]

    [BENITO, BABU, *and* DELANO *walk toward the back of*
    *the stage. A scrim curtain lifts, showing a light deck*
    *cabin that forms a sort of attic. The floor is matted,*

> *partitions that still leave splintered traces have been knocked out. To one side, a small table screwed to the floor; on it, a dirty missal; above it, a small crucifix, rusty crossed muskets on one side, rusty crossed cutlasses on the other.* BENITO *sits down in a broken thronelike and gilded chair.* BABU *begins to lather. A magnificent array of razors, bottles and other shaving equipment lies on a table beside him. Behind him, a hammock with a pole in it and a dirty pillow*]

DELANO.
   So this is where you took your siesta.
BENITO.
   Yes, Captain, I rest here when my fate will let me.
DELANO.
   This seems like a sort of dormitory, sitting-room,
   sail-loft, chapel, armory, and private bedroom all
      together.
BENITO.
   Yes, Captain: events have not been favorable
   to much order in my personal arrangements.
      [BABU *moves back and opens a locker. A lot of flags, torn shirts and socks tumble out. He takes one of the flags, shakes it with a flourish, and ties it around* BENITO's *neck*]
BABU.
   Master needs more protection.
   I do everything I can to save his clothes.
DELANO.
   The Castle and the Lion of Spain.
   Why, Don Benito, this is the flag of Spain you're using!
   It's well it's only I and not the King of Spain who sees
      this!
   All's one, though, I guess, in this carnival world.
   I see you like gay colors as much as Babu.
BABU [*Giggling*].
   The bright colors draw the yellow fever
   from Master's mind. [*Raises the razor.* BENITO *begins to
      shake*]
   Now, Master, now, Master!

BENITO.

You are talking while you hold the razor.

BABU.

You mustn't shake so, Master.

Look, Don Amasa, Master always shakes when I shave
him,

though he is braver than a lion and stronger than a castle.

Master knows Babu has never yet drawn blood.

I may, though, sometime, if he shakes so much.

Now, Master!

Come, Don Amasa, talk to Master about the gales and
calms,

he'll answer and forget to shake.

DELANO.

Those calms, the more I think of them the more I
wonder.

You say you were two months sailing here;

I made that stretch in less than a week.

We never met with any calms.

If I'd not heard your story from your lips,

and seen your ruined ship,

I would have said something was missing,

I would have said this was a mystery ship.

BENITO.

For some men the whole world is a mystery;

they cannot believe their senses.

   [BENITO *shakes, the razor gets out of hand and cuts
   his cheek*]

Santa Maria!

BABU.

Poor, poor Master, see, you shook so;

this is Babu's first blood.

Please answer Don Amasa, while I wipe

this ugly blood from the razor and strop it again.

BENITO.

The sea was like the final calm of the world

On, on it went. It sat on us and drank our strength,

crosscurrents eased us out to sea,

the yellow fever changed our blood to poison.

BABU.

You stood by us. Some of us stood by you!

BENITO.

Yes, my Spanish crew was weak and surly, but the blacks,
the blacks were angels. Babu has kept me in this world.
I wonder what he is keeping me for?
You belong to me. I belong to you forever.

BABU.

Ah, Master, spare yourself.
Forever is a very long time;
nothing's forever.

> [*With great expertness, delicacy and gentleness,* BABU
> *massages* BENITO's *cheeks, shakes out the flag, pours
> lotion from five bottles on* BENITO's *hair, cleans the
> shaving materials, and stands off admiring his work*]

Master looks just like a statue.
He's like a figurehead, Don Amasa!

> [DELANO *looks, then starts to walk out, leaving*
> BENITO *and* BABU. *The curtain drops upon them.*
> DELANO *rejoins* PERKINS, *lounging at the rail*]

PERKINS.

Our boat is coming.

DELANO [*Gaily*].

I know!
I don't know how I'll explain this pomp
and squalor to my own comfortable family of a crew.
Even shaving here is like a High Mass.
There's something in a Negro, something
that makes him fit to have around your person.
His comb and brush are castanets.
What tact Babu had!
What noiseless, gliding briskness!

PERKINS.

Our boat's about along side, Sir.

DELANO.

What's more, the Negro has a sense of humor.
I don't mean their boorish giggling and teeth-showing,
I mean his easy cheerfulness in every glance and gesture.
You should have seen Babu toss that Spanish flag like
a juggler,

and change it to a shaving napkin!

PERKINS.

The boat's here, Sir.

DELANO.

We need inferiors, Perkins,
more manners, more docility, no one has an inferior mind
in America.

PERKINS.

Here is your crew, Sir.

[BABU *runs out from the cabin. His cheek is bleeding*]

DELANO.

Why, Babu, what has happened?

BABU.

Master will never get better from his sickness.
His bad nerves and evil fever made him use me so.
I gave him one small scratch by accident,
the only time I've nicked him, Don Amasa.
He cut me with his razor. Do you think I will die?
I'd rather die than bleed to death!

DELANO.

It's just a pinprick, Babu. You'll live.

BABU.

I must attend my master. [*Runs back into cabin*]

DELANO.

Just a pinprick, but I wouldn't have thought
Don Benito had the stuff to swing a razor.
Up north we use our fists instead of knives.
I hope Benito's not dodging around some old grindstone
in the hold, and sharpening a knife for me.
Here, Perkins, help our men up the ladder.

[*Two immaculate* AMERICAN SAILORS *appear carrying great casks of water. Two more follow carrying net baskets of wilted pumpkins. The* NEGROES *begin to crowd forward, shouting, "We want Yankee food, we want Yankee drink!"* DELANO *grandiosely holds up a pumpkin; an* OLD NEGRO *rushes forward, snatches at the pumpkin, and knocks* DELANO *off-balance into* PERKINS's *arms.* DELANO *gets up and knocks the* NEGRO *down with his fist. All is tense and quiet. The*

SIX HATCHET-CLEANERS *lift their hatchets above their
heads*]

DELANO [*Furious*].

Americans, stand by me! Stand by your captain!

[*Like lightning, the* AMERICANS *unsling their muskets,
fix bayonets, and kneel with their guns pointing at the*
NEGROES]

Don Benito, Sir, call your men to order!

BABU.

We're starving, Yankee Master. We mean no harm;
we've never been so scared.

DELANO.

You try my patience, Babu.
I am talking to Captain Cereno:
call your men to order, Sir.

BENITO.

Make them laugh, Babu. The Americans aren't going
to shoot.

[BABU *airily waves a hand. The* NEGROES *smile.* DELANO
*turns to* BENITO]

You mustn't blame them too much; they're sick
and hungry.
We have kept them cooped up for ages.

DELANO [*As the* NEGROES *relax*].

Form them in lines, Perkins!
Each man shall have his share.
That's how we run things in the States—
to each man equally, no matter what his claims.

NEGROES [*Standing back, bleating like sheep*].

Feed me, Master Yankee! Feed me, Master Yankee!

DELANO.

You are much too close.
Here, Perkins, take the provisions aft.
You'll save lives by giving each as little as you can,
Be sure to keep a tally.

[FRANCESCO, *a majestic, yellow-colored mulatto, comes
up to* DELANO]

FRANCESCO.

My master requests your presence at dinner, Don Amasa.

DELANO.

Tell him I have indigestion.

Tell him to keep better order on his ship.

It's always the man of good will that gets hurt;
my fist still aches from hitting that old darky.

FRANCESCO.

My master has his own methods of discipline
that are suitable for our unfortunate circumstances.

Will you come to dinner, Don Amasa?

DELANO.

I'll come. When in Rome, do as the Romans.

Excuse my quick temper, Sir.

It's better to blow up than to smoulder.

[*The scrim curtain is raised. In the cabin, a long
table loaded with silver has been laid out. The locker
has been closed and the Spanish flag hangs on the
wall.* DON BENITO *is seated,* BABU *stands behind him.
As soon as* DELANO *sits down,* FRANCESCO *begins serv-
ing with great dignity and agility*]

FRANCESCO.

A finger bowl, Don Amasa.

[*After each statement, he moves about the table*]

A napkin, Don Amasa.

A glass of American water, Don Amasa.

A slice of American pumpkin, Don Amasa.

A goblet of American cider, Don Amasa.

[DELANO *drinks a great deal of cider,* BENITO *hardly
touches his*]

DELANO.

This is very courtly for a sick ship, Don Benito.

The Spanish Empire will never go down, if she keeps
her chin up.

BENITO.

I'm afraid I shan't live long enough to enjoy
your prophecy.

DELANO.

I propose a toast to the Spanish Empire
on which the sun never sets;
may you find her still standing, when you land, Sir!

BENITO.
Our Empire has lasted three hundred years,
I suppose she will last another month.
I wish I could say the same for myself. My sun is setting,
I hear the voices of the dead in this calm.

DELANO.
You hear the wind lifting;
it's bringing our two vessels together.
We are going to take you into port, Don Benito.

BENITO.
You are either too late or too early with your good
works.
Our yellow fever may break out again.
You aren't going to put your men in danger, Don Amasa?

DELANO.
My boys are all healthy, sir.

BENITO.
Health isn't God, I wouldn't trust it.

FRANCESCO.
May I fill your glass, Don Amasa?

BABU.
New wine in new bottles,
that's the American spirit, Yankee Master.
They say all men are created equal in North America.

DELANO.
We prefer merit to birth, boy.
[BABU *motions imperiously for* FRANCESCO *to leave. As
he goes, bowing to the* CAPTAINS, FOUR NEGROES *play
the* Marseillaise]
Why are they playing the *Marseillaise?*

BABU.
His uncle is supposed to have been in the
French Convention,
and voted for the death of the French King.

DELANO.
This polite and royal fellow is no anarchist!

BABU.
Francesco is very *ancien régime,*
he is even frightened of the Americans.

He doesn't like the way you treated King George.
Babu is more liberal.

DELANO.

A royal fellow,
this usher of yours, Don Benito!
He is as yellow as a goldenrod.
He is a king, a king of kind hearts.
What a pleasant voice he has!

BENITO [*Glumly*].

Francesco is a good man.

DELANO.

As long as you've known him,
he's been a worthy fellow, hasn't he?
Tell me, I am particularly curious to know.

BENITO.

Francesco is a good man.

DELANO.

I'm glad to hear it, I am glad to hear it!
You refute the saying of a planter friend of mine.
He said, "When a mulatto has a regular European face,
look out for him, he is a devil."

BENITO.

I've heard your planter's remark applied
to intermixtures of Spaniards and Indians;
I know nothing about mulattoes.

DELANO.

No, no, my friend's refuted;
if we're so proud of our white blood,
surely a little added to the blacks improves their breed.
I congratulate you on your servants, Sir.

BABU.

We've heard that Jefferson, the King of your Republic,
would like to free his slaves.

DELANO.

Jefferson has read too many books, boy,
but you can trust him. He's a gentleman and an
    American!
He's not lifting a finger to free his slaves.

BABU.

We hear you have a new capital modelled on Paris,

and that your President is going to set up
a guillotine on the Capitol steps.

DELANO.

Oh, Paris! I told you you could trust Mr. Jefferson, boy,
he stands for law and order like your mulatto.
Have you been to Paris, Don Benito?

BENITO.

I'm afraid I'm just a provincial Spaniard, Captain.

DELANO.

Let me tell you about Paris.
You know what French women are like—
nine parts sex and one part logic.
Well, one of them in Paris heard
that my ship was the *President Adams*. She said,
"You are descended from Adam, Captain,
you must know everything,
tell me how Adam and Eve learned to sleep together."
Do you know what I said?

BENITO.

No, Captain.

DELANO.

I said, "I guess Eve was a Frenchwoman,
the first Frenchwoman."
Do you know what she answered?

BENITO.

No, Captain Delano.

DELANO.

She said, "I was trying to provoke a philosophical
    discussion, Sir."
A philosophical discussion, ha, ha!
You look serious, Sir. You know, something troubles me.

BENITO.

Something troubles you, Captain Delano?

DELANO.

I still can't understand those calms,
but let that go. The scurvy,
why did it kill off three Spaniards in every four,
and only half the blacks?
Negroes are human, but surely you couldn't have
    favored them

before your own flesh and blood!

BENITO.

This is like the Inquisition, Captain Delano.
I have done the best I could.
    [BABU *dabs* BENITO's *forehead with cider*]

BABU.

Poor, poor Master; since Don Aranda died,
he trusts no one except Babu.

DELANO.

Your Babu is an uncommonly intelligent fellow;
you are right to trust him, Sir.
Sometimes I think we overdo our talk of freedom.
If you looked into our hearts, we all want slaves.

BENITO.

Disease is a mysterious thing;
it takes one man, and leaves his friend.
Only the unfortunate can understand misfortune.

DELANO.

I must return to my bosun;
he's pretty green to be left alone here.
Before I go I want to propose a last toast to you!
*A good master deserves good servants!*
    [*He gets up. As he walks back to* PERKINS, *the scrim
    curtain falls, concealing* BENITO *and* BABU]
That captain must have jaundice,
I wish he kept better order.
I don't like hitting menials.

PERKINS.

I've done some looking around, Sir. I've used my eyes.

DELANO.

That's what they're for, I guess. You have to watch
    your step,
this hulk, this rotten piece of finery,
will fall apart. This old world needs new blood
and Yankee gunnery to hold it up.
You shouldn't mess around, though, it's their ship;
you're breaking all the laws of the sea.

PERKINS.

Do you see that man-shaped thing in canvas?

DELANO.
    I see it.

PERKINS.
    Behind the cloth, there's a real skeleton,
    a man dressed up like Don Benito.

DELANO.
    They're Catholics, and worship bones.

PERKINS.
    There's writing on its coat. It says,
    "I am Don Aranda," and, "Follow your leader."

DELANO.
    Follow your leader?

PERKINS.
    I saw two blacks unfurling a flag,
    a black skull and crossbones on white silk.

DELANO.
    That's piracy. We've been ordered
    to sink any ship that flies that flag.
    Perhaps they were playing.

PERKINS.
    I saw King Atufal throw away his chains,
    He called for food, the Spaniards served him two pieces
        of pumpkin,
    and a whole bottle of your cider.

DELANO.
    Don Benito has the only key to Atufal's padlock.
    My cider was for the captain's table.

PERKINS.
    Atufal pointed to the cabin where you were dining,
    and drew a finger across his throat.

DELANO.
    Who could want to kill Amasa Delano?

PERKINS.
    I warned our men to be ready for an emergency.

DELANO.
    You're a mind reader,
    I couldn't have said better myself;
    but we're at peace with Spain.

PERKINS.

> I told them to return with loaded muskets
> and fixed bayonets.

DELANO.

> Here comes Benito. Watch how I'll humor him
> and sound him out.
> Feel the breeze! It holds and will increase.
>> [BABU *brings out* BENITO's *chair.* BENITO *sits in it*]
> My ship is moving nearer. Soon we will be together.
> We have seen you through your troubles.

BENITO.

> Remember, I warned you about the yellow fever.
> I am surprised you haven't felt afraid.

DELANO.

> Oh, that will blow away.
> Everything is going to go better and better;
> the wind's increasing, soon you'll have no cares.
> After the long voyage, the anchor drops into the harbor.
> It's a great weight lifted from the captain's heart.
> We are getting to be friends, Don Benito.
> My ship's in sight, the *President Adams!*
> How the wind braces a man up!
> I have a small invitation to issue to you.

BENITO.

> An invitation?

DELANO.

> I want you to take a cup of coffee
> with me on my quarter deck tonight.
> The Sultan of Turkey never tasted such coffee
> as my old steward makes. What do you say, Don Benito?

BENITO.

> I cannot leave my ship.

DELANO.

> Come, come, you need a change of climate.
> The sky is suddenly blue, Sir,
> my coffee will make a man of you.

BENITO.

> I cannot leave my ship.
> Even now, I don't think you understand my position here.

DELANO.
   I want to speak to you alone.
BENITO.
   I am alone, as much as I ever am.
DELANO.
   In America, we don't talk about money
   in front of servants and children.
BENITO.
   Babu is not my servant.
   You spoke of money—since the yellow fever,
   he has had a better head for figures than I have.
DELANO.
   You embarrass me, Captain,
   but since circumstances are rather special here,
   I will proceed.
BENITO.
   Babu takes an interest in all our expenses.
DELANO.
   Yes, I am going to talk to you about your expenses.
   I am responsible to my owners for all
   the sails, ropes, food and carpentry I give you.
   You will need a complete rerigging, almost a new ship,
      in fact,
   You shall have our services at cost.
BENITO.
   I know, you are a merchant.
   I suppose I ought to pay you for our lives.
DELANO.
   I envy you, Captain. You are the only owner
   of the *San Domingo*, since Don Aranda died.
   I am just an employee. Our owners would sack me,
   if I followed my better instincts.
BENITO.
   You can give your figures to Babu, Captain.
DELANO.
   You are very offhand about money, Sir;
   I don't think you realize the damage that has been done
      to your ship.
   Ah, you smile. I'm glad you're loosening up.
   Look, the water gurgles merrily, the wind is high,

a mild light is shining. I sometimes think
such a tropical light as this must have shone
on the tents of Abraham and Isaac.
It seems as if Providence were watching over us.

PERKINS.

There are things that need explaining here, Sir.

DELANO.

Yes, Captain, Perkins saw some of your men
unfurling an unlawful flag,
a black skull and crossbones.

BENITO.

You know my only flag is the Lion and Castle of Spain.

DELANO.

No, Perkins says he saw a skull and crossbones.
That's piracy. I trust Perkins.
You've heard about how my government blew
the bowels out of the pirates at Tripoli?

BENITO.

Perhaps my Negroes . . .

DELANO.

My government doesn't intend
to let you play at piracy!

BENITO.

Perhaps my Negroes were playing.
When you take away their chains . . .

DELANO.

I'll see that you are all put back in chains,
if you start playing pirates!

PERKINS.

There's something else he can explain, Sir.

DELANO.

Yes, Perkins saw Atufal throw off his chains
and order dinner.

BABU.

Master has the key, Yankee Master.

BENITO.

I have the key.
You can't imagine how my position exhausts me, Captain.

DELANO.

I can imagine. Atufal's chains are fakes.

You and he are in cahoots, Sir!

PERKINS.

They don't intend to pay for our sails and service.

They think America is Santa Claus.

DELANO.

The United States are death on pirates and debtors.

PERKINS.

There's one more thing for him to explain, Sir.

DELANO.

Do you see that man-shaped thing covered with black
     cloth, Don Benito?

BENITO.

I always see it.

DELANO.

Take away the cloth. I order you to take away the cloth!

BENITO.

I cannot. Oh, Santa Maria, have mercy!

DELANO.

Of course, you can't. It's no Virgin Mary.

You have done something terrible to your friend,
     Don Aranda.

Take away the cloth, Perkins!

     [*As* PERKINS *moves forward,* ATUFAL *suddenly stands
     chainless and with folded arms, blocking his way*]

BABU [*Dancing up and down and beside himself*].

Let them see it! Let them see it!

I can't stand any more of their insolence;

the Americans treat us like their slaves!

     [BABU *and* PERKINS *meet at the man-shaped object
     and start pulling away the cloth.* BENITO *rushes be-
     tween them, and throws them back and sprawling
     on the deck.* BABU *and* PERKINS *rise, and stand
     hunched like wrestlers, about to close in on* BENITO,
     *who draws his sword with a great gesture. It is only a
     hilt. He runs at* BABU *and knocks him down.* ATUFAL
     *throws off his chains and signals to the* HATCHET-
     CLEANERS. *They stand behind* BENITO *with raised
     hatchets. The* NEGROES *shout ironically, "Evviva Beni-
     to!"*]

You too, Yankee Captain!

If you shoot, we'll kill you.

DELANO.

If a single American life is lost,
I will send this ship to the bottom,
and all Peru after it.
Do you hear me, Don Benito?

BENITO.

Don't you understand? I am as powerless as you are!

BABU.

He is as powerless as you are.

BENITO.

Don't you understand? He has been holding a knife at
my back.
I have been talking all day to save your life.

BABU [*Holding a whip*].

Do you see this whip? When Don Aranda was out
of temper,
he used to snap pieces of flesh off us with it.
Now I hold the whip.
When I snap it, Don Benito jumps!
[*Snaps the whip*. DON BENITO *flinches*]

DELANO [*Beginning to understand*].

It's easy to terrorize the defenseless.

BABU.

That's what we thought when Don Aranda held the whip.

DELANO.

You'll find I am made of tougher stuff than your
Spaniards.

ATUFAL.

We want to kill you.

NEGROES.

We want to kill you, Yankee Captain.

DELANO.

Who could want to kill Amasa Delano?

BABU.

Of course. We want to keep you alive.
We want you to sail us back to Africa.
Has anyone told you how much you are worth, Captain?

DELANO.

I have another course in mind.

BABU.

Yes, there's another course if you don't like Africa, there's another course.

King Atufal, show the Yankee captain
the crew that took the other course!

[*Three dead* SPANISH SAILORS *are brought on stage*]

ATUFAL.

Look at Don Aranda?

BABU.

Yes, you are hot-tempered and discourteous, Captain.

I am going to introduce you to Don Aranda.

You have a new command, Captain. You must meet your new owner.

[*The black cloth is taken from the man-shaped object and shows a chalk-white skeleton dressed like* DON BENITO]

Don Amasa, Don Aranda!

You can see that Don Aranda was a white man like you, because his bones are white.

NEGROES.

He is a white because his bones are white!

He is a white because his bones are white!

ATUFAL [*Pointing to the ribbon on the skeleton's chest*]

Do you see that ribbon?

It says, "Follow the leader."

We wrote it in his blood.

BABU.

He was a white man
even though his blood was red as ours.

NEGROES.

He is white because his bones are white!

BABU.

Don Aranda is our figurehead,
we are going to chain him to the bow of our ship
to scare off devils.

ATUFAL.

This is the day of Jubilee,
I am raising the flag of freedom!

NEGROES.

Freedom! Freedom! Freedom!

[*The black skull and crossbones is raised on two poles. The* NEGROES *form two lines, leading up to the flag, and leave an aisle. Each man is armed with some sort of weapon*]

BABU.

Spread out the Spanish flag!

[*The Lion and Castle of Spain is spread out on the deck in front of the skull and crossbones*]

The Spanish flag is the road to freedom.

Don Benito mustn't hurt his white feet on the splinters.

[*Kneeling in front of* BENITO]

Your foot, Master!

[BENITO *holds out his foot.* BABU *takes off* BENITO's *shoes*]

Give Don Benito back his sword!

[*The sword-hilt is fastened back in* BENITO's *scabbard*]

Load him with chains!

[*Two heavy chains are draped on* BENITO's *neck. The cane and ball are handed to him*]

Former Captain Benito Cereno, kneel!

Ask pardon of man!

BENITO [*Kneeling*].

I ask pardon for having been born a Spaniard.

I ask pardon for having enslaved my fellow man.

BABU.

Strike off the oppressor's chain!

[*One of* BENITO's *chains is knocked off, then handed to* ATUFAL, *who dashes it to the deck*]

Former Captain Benito Cereno,

you must kiss the flag of freedom.

[*Points to* DON ARANDA]

Kiss the mouth of the skull!

[BENITO *walks barefoot over the Spanish flag and kisses the mouth of* DON ARANDA]

NEGROES.

*Evviva Benito! Evviva Benito!*

[*Sounds are heard from* PERKINS, *whose head has been covered with the sack*]

ATUFAL.

The bosun wants to kiss the mouth of freedom.

BABU.

March over the Spanish flag, Bosun.

[PERKINS *starts forward*]

DELANO.

You are dishonoring your nation, Perkins!

Don't you stand for anything?

PERKINS.

I only have one life, Sir.

[*Walks over the Spanish flag and kisses the mouth of the skull*]

NEGROES.

*Evviva* Bosun! *Evviva* Bosun!

DELANO.

You are no longer an American, Perkins!

BABU.

He was free to choose freedom, Captain.

ATUFAL.

Captain Delano wants to kiss the mouth of freedom.

BABU.

He is jealous of the bosun.

ATUFAL.

In the United States, all men are created equal.

BABU.

Don't you want to kiss the mouth of freedom, Captain?

DELANO [*Lifting his pocket and pointing the pistol*]

Do you see what I have in my hand?

BABU.

A pistol.

DELANO.

I am unable to miss at this distance.

BABU.

You must take your time, Yankee Master.

You must take your time.

DELANO.

I am unable to miss.

BABU.

You can stand there like a block of wood

as long as you want to, Yankee Master.

You will drop asleep, then we will tie you up,
and make you sail us back to Africa.

> [*General laughter. Suddenly, there's a roar of gun-
> fire. Several* NEGROES, *mostly women, fall.* AMERICAN
> SEAMEN *in spotless blue and white throw themselves
> in a lying position on deck.* MORE *kneel above them,
> then* MORE *stand above these. All have muskets and
> fixed bayonets. The First Row fires. More* NEGROES
> *fall. They start to retreat. The Second Row fires.
> More* NEGROES *fall. They retreat further. The Third
> Row fires. The Three* AMERICAN LINES *march forward,
> but all the* NEGROES *are either dead or in retreat.* DON
> BENITO *has been wounded. He staggers over to* DELANO
> *and shakes his hand*]

BENITO.

You have saved my life.
I thank you for my life.

DELANO.

A man can only do what he can,
We have saved American lives.

PERKINS [*pointing to* ATUFAL'S *body*]

We have killed King Atufal,
we have killed their ringleader.

> [BABU *jumps up. He is unwounded*]

BABU.

I was the King. Babu, not Atufal,
was the king, who planned, dared and carried out
the seizure of this ship, the *San Domingo.*
Untouched by blood myself, I had all
the most dangerous and useless Spaniards killed.
I freed my people from their Egyptian bondage.
The heartless Spaniards slaved for me like slaves.

> [BABU *steps back, and quickly picks up a crown from
> the litter*]

This is my crown.

> [*Puts crown on his head. He snatches* BENITO'S *rattan
> cane*]

This is my rod.

> [*Picks up silver ball*]

This is the earth.

[*Holds the ball out with one hand and raises the cane*]

This is the arm of the angry God.

[*Smashes the ball*]

PERKINS.

Let him surrender. Let him surrender.

We want to save someone.

BENITO.

My God how little these people understand!

BABU.

[*Holding a white handkerchief and raising both his hands*]

Yankee Master understand me. The future is with us.

DELANO [*Raising his pistol*].

This is your future.

[BABU *falls and lies still.* DELANO *pauses, then slowly empties the five remaining barrels of his pistol into the body. Lights dim*]

**CURTAIN**

# HOGAN'S GOAT

*by William Alfred*
*A. M. D. G.*
*for*
*John and Máire Sweeny*
*with love*

*First production, November 11, 1965,*
*American Place Theatre, New York,*
*with the following cast:*

MATTHEW STANTON, LEADER OF THE SIXTH WARD OF
   BROOKLYN, *Ralph Waite*

KATHLEEN STANTON, HIS WIFE, *Faye Dunaway*

JOHN "BLACK JACK" HAGGERTY, ASSISTANT WARD
   LEADER, *Roland Wood*

PETEY BOYLE, A HANGER-ON OF STANTON'S,
   *Cliff Gorman*

BESSIE LEGG, A BACK-ROOM GIRL, *Michaele Myers*

MARIA HAGGERTY, "BLACK JACK'S" WIFE, THE STANTONS'
   JANITOR, *Grania O'Malley*

FATHER STANISLAUS COYNE, PASTOR OF ST. MARY STAR
   OF THE SEA, *Barnard Hughes*

FATHER MALONEY, PASTOR OF THE ALL-NIGHT PRINTERS'
   CHURCH, *John Dorman*

EDWARD QUINN, MAYOR OF BROOKLYN, *Tom Ahearne*

JAMES "PALSY" MURPHY, BOSS OF THE CITY OF BROOK-
   LYN, *Conrad Bain*

BILL, A HANGER-ON OF QUINN'S, *Luke Wymbs*

ANN MULCAHY, FATHER COYNE'S HOUSEKEEPER,
   *Agnes Young*

JOSEPHINE FINN, MARIA HAGGERTY'S NIECE,
      *Tresa Hughes*

BOYLAN, A POLICEMAN, *Tom Crane*

A DOCTOR, *David Dawson*

CONSTITUENTS: *Stan Sussman,* piano; *Eileen Fitzpat-
   rick, Jack Fogarty, John Hoffmeister, Monica Mac-
   Cormack, Michael Murray, Bruce Waite, Albert
   Shipley*

Almost all of the place names in this play really exist; but none of these characters has ever lived except in my own mind. Any resemblance to any person living or dead is purely coincidental.

# Act one

*Ten o'clock, the evening of Thursday, April 28, 1890. The parlor of Matthew Stanton's flat on the second floor of his house on Fifth Place, Brooklyn. The set is on two levels, the lower level containing the kitchen of the Haggertys, which is blacked out. To stage right there is a steep, narrow staircase. Enter* MATTHEW STANTON, *carrying a bottle of champagne. He is a handsome, auburn-haired man in his late thirties, dressed carefully in a four-buttoned suit of good serge, and a soft black hat. He bounds up the stairs and into his flat, and throws his hat on a chair and hides the bottle of champagne behind the sofa. The furnishings of the room are in period: the chairs are tufted and fringed, the mantelpiece covered with a lambrequin, the window heavily draped.*

STANTON.

    Katie? Katie! Where the devil are you?

    Come on out in the parlor.

        [*Enter* KATHLEEN STANTON, *closing the door behind her. She is tall and slim and dressed in a black broadcloth suit which brings out the redness of her hair and the whiteness of her skin*]

KATHLEEN.

    I wish you wouldn't take those stairs so fast;

    They're wicked: you could catch your foot and fall—

    I had a bit of headache and lay down.

    Why, Mattie darling, what's the matter with you?

    You're gray as wasps' nests.

STANTON.

    I'm to be the mayor!

No more that plug who runs the Court Café
And owes his ear to every deadbeat sport
With a favor in mind and ten cents for a ball,
But mayor of Brooklyn, and you the mayor's lady.
They caught Ned Quinn with his red fist in the till,
The Party of Reform, I mean, and we
"Are going to beat their game with restitution
And self-reform." Say something, can't you, Kate!

> [KATHLEEN *sits down heavily, and puts her hand to her temple*]

KATHLEEN.
   Oh, Mattie, Mattie.
STANTON.
   Jesus! Are you crying?
   I've what I wanted since I landed here
   Twelve years ago, and she breaks into tears.
KATHLEEN.
   It's that I'm—
STANTON.
   What? You're what?
KATHLEEN.
   Afraid.
STANTON.
   Kathleen,
   Now please don't let's go into that again.
KATHLEEN.
   Would you have me tell you lies?
STANTON.
   I'd have you brave.

> [KATHLEEN *rises angrily, and strides towards the bedroom*]

   Where are you going, Kate? To have a sulk?
   Wait now, I'll fix a sugar teat for you.
   Unless, of course, you'd rather suck your thumb,
   Brooding in your room—
KATHLEEN.
   I have the name!
   As well to have the game!
STANTON.
   It's riddles, is it?

KATHLEEN.

Riddles be damned! You think me idiotic;
I might as well fulfill your good opinion—
[STANTON *walks towards her*]
Come near me, and I'll smash your face for you.
[STANTON *embraces her*]

STANTON.

You're terrible fierce, you are. I wet me pants.

KATHLEEN.

You clown, you'll spring my hairpins. Mattie, stop.

STANTON.

Are these the hands are going to smash my face?
They're weak as white silk fans . . . I'm sorry, Kate:
You made me mad. And you know why?

KATHLEEN.

I do.
You're as afraid as I.

STANTON.

I am. I am.
You know me like the lashes of your eye—

KATHLEEN.

That's more than you know me, for if you did,
You'd see what these three years have done to me—
[STANTON *breaks away from her*]
Now it's my turn to ask you where you're going.

STANTON.

I begged you not to bring that up again.
What can I do?

KATHLEEN.

You can tell Father Coyne,
And ask him to apply for dispensation,
And we can be remarried secretly.

STANTON.

Now?

KATHLEEN.

Yes, Matt, now. Before it is too late.
We aren't married.

STANTON.

What was that in London,
The drunkard's pledge I took?

KATHLEEN.

  We're Catholics, Matt.
  Since when can Catholics make a valid marriage
  In a city hall? You have to tell the priest—

STANTON.

  Shall I tell him now? Do you take me for a fool
  To throw away the mayor's chair for that?

KATHLEEN.

  I slink to Sunday Mass like a pavement nymph.
  It's three years now since I made my Easter Duty,
  Three years of telling Father Coyne that we
  Receive at Easter Mass in the Cathedral,
  Mortal Sin on Mortal Sin, Matt. If I died,
  I'd go to Hell—

STANTON.

  I think the woman's crazy!

KATHLEEN.

  Don't you believe in God?

STANTON.

  Of course, I do.
  And more, my dear, than you who think that He
  Would crush you as a man would crush a fly
  Because of some mere technical mistake—

KATHLEEN.

  Mere technical mistake? It's that now, is it?
  A blasphemous marriage, three years' fornication,
  And now presumption—Technical mistake!
    [KATHLEEN *takes a cigarette out of a box on the table
    and lights it*]

STANTON.

  I wish you wouldn't smoke them cigarettes.
  High-toned though it may be in France and England,
  It's a whore's habit here. [*Pause*]

KATHLEEN.

  "Those cigarettes."
  Don't try to hurt me, Matt. You know you can,
  As I know I can you.

STANTON.

  What do you want!

KATHLEEN.

    I want to be your wife without disgrace.
    I want my honor back. I want to live
    Without the need to lie. I want you to keep faith.

STANTON.

    Not now! Not now!

KATHLEEN.

    You've said that for three years.
    What is it you're afraid of?

STANTON.

    Losing out.
    You do not know these people as I do.
    They turn upon the ones they make most of.
    They would on me, if given half a chance.
    And if it got around that we were married
    In an English City Hall, lose out we would.

KATHLEEN.

    Matt, losing out? What profit for a man
    To gain the world, and lose his soul?

STANTON.

    His soul!
    That's Sunday school! That's convent folderol,
    Like making half-grown girls bathe in their drawers
    To put the shame of their own beauty in them,
    And break their lives to bear the Church's bit.
    We are not priests and nuns, but men and women.
    The world religious give up is our world,
    The only world we have. We have to win it
    To do the bit of good we all must do;
    And how are we to win the world unless
    We keep the tricky rules its games are run by?
    Our faith is no mere monastery faith.
    It runs as fast as feeling to embrace
    Whatever good it sees. And if the good
    Is overgrown with bad, it still believes
    God sets no traps, the bad will be cut down,
    And the good push through its flowering to fruit.
    Forget your convent school. Remember, Katie,
    What the old women in the drowned boreens
    Would say when cloudbursts beat their fields to slime,

And the potatoes blackened on their stalks
Like flesh gone proud. "Bad times is right," they'd say,
"But God is good: apples will grow again."
What sin have we committed? Marriage, Kate?
Is that a sin?

KATHLEEN.

It is with us.

STANTON.

Because
You feel it so. It isn't. It's but prudence.
What if they should make a scandal of us?

KATHLEEN.

Could we be worse off than we are?

STANTON.

Kathleen!

KATHLEEN.

Could we be worse off than we are, I said?

STANTON.

Could we! We could. You don't know poverty.
You don't know what it is to do without,
Not fine clothes only, or a handsome house,
But men's respect. I do. I have been poor.
"Mattie, will you run down to the corner,
And buy me some cigars" or "Mattie, get
This gentleman a cab." Nine years, I served
Ned Quinn and Agnes Hogan, day by day,
Buying my freedom like a Roman slave.
Will you ask me to put liberty at stake
To ease your scrupulous conscience? If you do,
You're not the woman that I took you for
When I married you. Have you no courage, Kate?

KATHLEEN.

Will you lecture me on courage? Do you dare?
When every time I walk those stairs to the street
I walk to what I know is an enemy camp.
I was not raised like you. And no offense,
Please, Mattie, no offense. I miss my home.
Whore's habit it may be to smoke, as you say,
But it brings back the talk we used to have
About old friends, new books, the Lord knows what,

On our first floor in Baggot Street in Dublin.
This following you think so much about,
We live in Mortal Sin for fear you'll lose it,
I never knew the likes of them to talk to,
Person to person. They were cooks and maids,
Or peasants at the country houses, Matt.
All they can find to talk of, servants' talk,
Serfs' talk, eternal tearing down.
I'm like a woman banished and cut off.
I've you and May in the flat downstairs. That's all.
Don't tell me I don't know what poverty is.
What bankruptcy is worse than loneliness.
They say the sense of exile is the worst
Of all the pains that torture poor damned souls.
It is that sense I live with every day.

STANTON.

Are you the only exile of us all?
You slept your crossing through in a rosewood berth
With the swells a hundred feet below your portholes,
And ate off china on a linen cloth,
With the air around you fresh as the first of May.
I slept six deep in a bunk short as a coffin
Between a poisoned pup of a seasick boy
And a slaughtered pig of a snorer from Kildare,
Who wrestled elephants the wild nights through,
And sweated sour milk. I wolfed my meals,
Green water, and salt beef, and wooden biscuits,
On my hunkers like an ape, in a four-foot aisle
As choked as the one door of a burning school.
I crossed in mid-December: seven weeks
Of driving rain that kept the hatches battened
In a hold so low of beam a man my height
Could never lift his head. And I couldn't wash.
Water was low; the place was like an icehouse;
And girls were thick as field mice in a haystack
In the bunk across. I would have died of shame,
When I stood in the landing shed of this "promised land,"
As naked as the day I first saw light,
Defiled with my own waste like a dying cat,
And a lousy red beard on me like a tinker's,

While a bitch of a doctor, with his nails too long,
Dared tell me: "In Amurrica, we bathe!"
I'd have died with shame, had I sailed here to die.
I swallowed pride and rage, and made a vow
The time would come when I could spit both out
In the face of the likes of him. I made a vow
I'd fight my way to power if it killed me,
Not only for myself, but for our kind,
For the men behind me, laughing out of fear,
At their own shame as well as mine, for the women,
Behind the board partition, frightened dumb
With worry they'd be sent back home to starve
Because they'd dirty feet. I was born again.
It came to me as brutal as the cold
That makes us flinch the day the midwife takes
Our wet heels in her fist, and punches breath
Into our dangling carcasses: Get power!
Without it, there can be no decency,
No virtue and no grace. I have kept my vow.
The mayor's chair is mine but for the running.
Will you have me lose it for your convent scruples?
   [*Pause*]

KATHLEEN.

You never told me that about your landing.

STANTON.

There's many things I never told you, Kate.
I was afraid you'd hold me cheap.

KATHLEEN.

Oh, Mattie,
Don't you know me yet?

STANTON.

Stand by me.
Stand by me, Kate. The next four days count hard.
By Sunday next, I'll have won all or lost.

KATHLEEN.

What's Sunday next?

STANTON.

The Clambake for Quinn's birthday:
We're to make things up between us and make the announcement

On the steamer voyage to Seagate Sunday evening.
Stand by me, Kate. As sure as God's my judge
The minute I get into City Hall
The first thing I will do is call the priest.
And ask him to make peace with God for us.
Stand by me, Kate.

KATHLEEN.

I will though it costs my life. [STANTON *kisses her*]

STANTON.

God stand between us and all harm! There now!
I've wiped those words from your lips.—Oh, where's my mind!
I've brought champagne, and it's as warm as tears.
Go get the glasses.

　　[KATHLEEN *takes two glasses down from a cupboard.*
　　STANTON *opens the champagne and pours it. They
　　touch glasses*]

Let the past be damned,
The dead bury the dead. The future's ours.

CURTAIN

# Act two

*Eleven o'clock the same night. The back room of Stanton's Saloon, the Court Café. To stage left, glass-paned double doors cut the room off from the bar, from which a hum of voices can be heard. To stage right, the Ladies' Entrance. Next to it, a square piano with a pot of dead fern on it. Around the room, squat round tables and bent iron chairs. Stage center, around one of the tables, with whiskeys in front of them, three people. At the head,* JOHN "BLACK JACK" HAGGERTY, *in his late sixties, wearing his Sunday clothes, his hair parted in the middle and swagged over his eyebrows in dove's wings, his handlebar mustache repeating the design. Both hair and mustache are dyed an improbable black. To Haggerty's left,* PETEY BOYLE, *a young tough in his twenties, his heavy hair parted in the middle and combed oilily back, the teeth marks of the comb still in it. His rachitic frame is wiry as a weed; and he is dressed in a Salvation Army suit that droops in the seat, balloons at the knees and elbows. Next to Boyle, but facing the audience,* BESSIE LEGG, *a blond girl in her late twenties or early thirties, her hair in a pompadour under a Floradora hat that looks like an ostrich nest, a long feather boa on, together with many strands of glass beads, and rings on every finger but her thumbs, all cheap. Her doll's face is a bit crumpled, but there is no petulance in it, merely jocose self-indulgence. There is a crêpe-paper shamrock tacked to the piano, and four sprung tapes of green and gold crêpe paper run from the corners of the room and belly over the table in a haphazardly celebrative way.*

HAGGERTY.

> That Walsh from Albany was no man's fool.
> The first thing that he asked about was Ag Hogan,
> And then about Matt's temper, you know, the time
> He nearly broke Tim Costigan in two
> For calling him Hogan's Goat. But at last we cleared
>     Matt.

BOYLE.

> Bess, Black Jack thinks the nomination'll stand!

HAGGERTY.

> Stop your tormenting, Petey. Of course, it will.
> Amn't I Assistant Leader of this Ward
> And head of the Matthew Stanton Association?
> And isn't Palsy Murphy Boss of Brooklyn
> And head of the Edward Quinn Association?
> Walsh said that Father Coyne and the both of us
> Would constitute a due and legal caucus;
> And he's the representative of the Party,
> He ought to know.

BESSIE.

> Yeah? When does Quinn find out?

HAGGERTY.

> Tomorrow morning. It has to be told him fast.
> We're to break the news Matt's nominated Sunday
> At the Clambake for Quinn's birthday down in Seagate.

BOYLE.

> Is both Associations going on this Clambake?

HAGGERTY.

> Yes. Murphy's got the job of telling Quinn
> And getting him to make things up with Matt.

BOYLE.

> That's a moonlight voyage we'll all be seeing stars.
> It'll make the riot on the *Harvest Queen,*
> When that Alderman knifed that guy in '87,
> Look like a slapping match in St. Mary's schoolyard.
> Quinn ain't never giving up to no Stanton
> In no four days.

BESSIE.

> Dust off your steel derby,
> Or your head will be all lumps like a bag of marbles.

BOYLE.
> You tell him, kid. I'll hold the baby.

HAGGERTY.
> Lord!
> What a pair of lochremauns! That's why Murphy's Boss:
> He could talk a Hindu out of a tiger's mouth.
> He'll find some cosy way to break the news,
> And Quinn will purr like a kitten.

> > [*Enter* MARIA HAGGERTY *through the Ladies' Entrance.
> > She is a tall, raw-boned woman in her late sixties, with
> > loose-stranded iron-gray hair pulled back around a
> > center part in a tight bun. She wears a rusty black
> > toque, and a long black woolen coat with a frayed
> > hem, and is carrying a large handbag, which she sets
> > down on the floor as she settles wearily into the chair
> > to stage right of* HAGGERTY, *her husband*]

MARIA.
> Ah, there you are!
> How are you, Mrs. Legg? How are you, Petey?
> I thought you might be waiting here for Matt,
> When Josie told me. Why is it so secret?

HAGGERTY.
> It won't be secret long with Josie Finn
> Trumpeting it from here to Fulton Ferry
> Like an elephant in heat. Quinn doesn't know yet.
> That's why it's so secret.

MARIA.
> What's that you're drinking?

HAGGERTY.
> Whiskey and water, May.

MARIA.
> Give Ma a swallow.

HAGGERTY.
> Great God in Heaven, drink it all, why don't you!
> We're met to celebrate Matt Stanton's luck.
> Corner-boy Boyle and Bessie the balloon brain
> See trouble in store undreamed by Albany,
> And my wife drags in here with a puss on her
> Like a lead-horse on a hearse. What's the matter with
> you?

MARIA.

    I'm sure I'm glad for Matt's sake. He's worked hard,
    And he's been good, giving us the flat and all.
    But in a way, you know, Ned Quinn is right:
    Matt's hard on people, harder than he should be.
    He's a lot to answer for before he dies.

BESSIE.

    You mean Ag Hogan?

MARIA.

    Yes, I do.

BESSIE.

    Poor girl.
    When I was there this morning, she looked awful.

MARIA.

    She'll never live to comb out a gray head.
    I've just now come from giving her her tea,
    In that coffin of a furnished room in Smith Street.
    I looked at the cheesecloth curtains hung on strings;
    And I thought of all those velvet-muffled windows,
    Those carpets red as blood and deep as snow,
    Those tables glistening underneath the lamps
    Like rosy gold, in her big house in Seagate.
    And I said to myself, if it weren't for Agnes Hogan,
    Matt would be a grocery clerk at Nolan's,
    And not the owner of the Court Café.
    And candidate for mayor; and there she lies,
    Flat on her back with two beanbags of buckshot
    On her shriveled breasts, to chain her to the mattress,
    As if she could move, her eyes in a black stare
    At the white paint peeling off that iron bedstead,
    Like scabs of a rash; and he never once comes near her,
    For fear, I suppose, they'd call him Hogan's Goat,
    And his missis might find out about their high jinks.
    And yet if Matt were any kind of man,
    Wouldn't he go and take her in his arms,
    And say, "You hurt me bad three years ago;
    But I hurt you as bad. Forgive and forget."
    Maybe it's because the girl's my niece,
    But I think I'd feel the same if she were not.

HAGGERTY.

Be that as may be, what has passed between them
Is their affair. It isn't ours to judge,
Especially after all Matt's done for us—
And you'll set this one thinking how Tom Legg
Left her in the lurch in Baltic Street,
And spraying us all like a drainpipe in a downpour,
If you keep up that way. Sure, what's past is past.
What can't be remedied must be endured.

BESSIE.

Say, listen here, Napoleon the Turd,
Legg never found me in bed with no one,
Like Matt done Ag, if that's what you're implying.

HAGGERTY.

How could he, when he worked in the subway nights,
And was so blind he couldn't tie his shoes
Without his nose to the eyelets, his rump in the air,
Like a startled ostrich.

BESSIE.

Say that again, I dare you!

HAGGERTY.

No matter now. It served what it was meant to:
Better glares than tears—

> [*A loud shout from the bar. Applause, cheers and
> singing. Enter* STANTON *from the bar with a crowd
> around him, singing. The four at the table join in*]

EVERYBODY.

He'll make a jolly good mayor!
He'll make a jolly good mayor!
He'll make a jolly good mayor!
Which nobody can deny!

HAGGERTY.

Speech, Mattie, speech!

STANTON.

Thanks all! What will I say!
It's me who should be singing songs to you,
Not you to me. And I don't know how you've learned
That I'm to run for mayor. It's a secret.
Ask the man who told you if it isn't,
Jack Haggerty—[*Applause*]

When I returned from England
Three years ago with my new wife, I thought
My chances to get back into the Party
Were gone for good. Yet in those three short years
You stuck by me so fast, the Party made me
Leader of the Ward in which the mayor
I had a falling-out with lives; and now
You're bent on giving me his place.
Ned Quinn—

> [*Booing and hissing.* PETEY BOYLE *jumps on a table,
> puts one fist on his hip, throws his head back insolent-
> ly, and sings, in a nasal imitation of John McCormack.
> Enter* FATHER COYNE, *unnoticed, through the Ladies'
> Entrance, wearing his biretta and an old black over-
> coat shorter than his cassock*]

BOYLE.

Is it Ned Quinn you mean? }
Says the Shan Van Vocht, }   *repeat*
He's in Fogarty's shebeen
Drinking bourbon with some quean,}   *repeat*
Says the Shan Van Vocht.
Let him drink it to the dregs,}
Says the Shan Van Vocht. }   *repeat*
For the goose that lays gold eggs
Lays no more for hollow legs, }   *repeat*
Says the Shan Van Vocht.

> [*Applause and laughter.* BOYLE *motions for silence and
> sings*]

BOYLE.

Go and tell that swindler! [BOYLE *points to* HAGGERTY]

HAGGERTY.

Go and tell that swindler! [HAGGERTY *points to* BESSIE]

BESSIE.

Go and tell that swindler!

BOYLE.

What the Shan Van Vocht has said! [BOYLE *apes a choir
director*]

EVERYBODY.

What the Shan Van Vocht has said!

> [*Laughter and applause.* FATHER COYNE *angrily jostles*

*his way to stage center, the people shamefacedly mak-
ing way for him*]

FATHER COYNE.

For shame! For shame! Have you no charity?
Don't turn upon the man, but on his sin.

HAGGERTY.

Father! Sit down. I thought you'd be in bed.

FATHER COYNE.

I couldn't sleep. I thought I'd come by here
And have a word with Matt alone.

BOYLE.

A word or a drink?

FATHER COYNE.

What's that you say, Pete Boyle? Speak up, why don't
   you,
And show them how malicious you can be,
And you so drunk!

BOYLE.

I didn't mean no harm.

FATHER COYNE.

You meant no harm! You're all of you alike.
You talk to preen your wit or flex your pride,
Not to lay bare your hearts or tell God's truth.
Words have more force than blows. They can destroy.
Would you punch an old man's face to test your arm?
Answer me, Pete Boyle.

BOYLE.

You know I wouldn't.

FATHER COYNE.

You did as much to me.

BOYLE.

I'm sorry, Father.

FATHER COYNE.

I hope you are, my son. Don't look so pious,
The rest of you. You're just as bad as him,
Dancing around the ruin of Quinn's name
Like a pack of savages. Do you know the story
The Rabbis set down centuries ago
Beside the part in Exodus where the Jews
Are shown exulting over the drowned troops

Of Pharaoh on the shores of the Red Sea?
The angels, says the story, joined their voices
With those of the men below. And God cried out:
"What reason is there to hold jubilee?
The men of Egypt are my children too!"
The men of Egypt were God's enemies,
And Edward Quinn's your friend, may God forgive you!

STANTON.

That kind of justice is too heavenly
For us on earth. If we condone Ned Quinn,
Don't we condone corruption with him, Father?

FATHER COYNE.

You know, don't you, a man can commit theft,
And yet not be a thief by nature, Matt?
Corruption sometimes saps the choicest men;
Sometimes it is disordered sweetness drives
A man to act contrary to what's right.
Collusion can arise from faithfulness,
And graft from bankrupt generosity.
You know I'd never ask you to condone that.
But once he's made the city restitution,
The loss of office is enough chastisement
For Edward Quinn. You must not banish him.
What purpose would it serve to break a man
Who's slaved for Church and people thirty years?

STANTON.

What purpose would it serve? 'Twould end corruption.
Corruption, Father, may be, as you say,
Disordered sweetness sometimes, but in men
Who govern others, can we risk disorder
To save the heart it works its ferment on?
A man may cut away the seething bruise
That festers in good fruit or even flesh.
The heart's corruption poisons surgery.
The pulse of it is rapid. It pollutes
Like ratbite, and like ratbite spawns
Plagues to charge whole graveyards.
Isolate its carriers fast, I say. Disown them,
Before they can infect us with the pox
We came across the ocean to avoid,

Liberty gone blind, the death of honor!—
Would you have the big men of this city say
That they were right in keeping us cheap labor,
Because we are not fit for nobler service,
We dirty what we touch? Say that they will,
And with full right. unless we dare cut free
From these enfeebling politics of pity,
And rule the city right. Ned Quinn must go—[*Applause*]

HAGGERTY.

Hurray for Stanton! The man is right, God bless him.
What answer, Father, can you make to that?

FATHER COYNE.

What answer, Black Jack, but the same old answer?
Judge not, Matt Stanton, lest yourself be judged;
Beware, Matt Stanton, lest in pointing out
The mote within your neighbor's watering eye,
You overlook the beam that blinds your own.

STANTON.

I meant no disrespect. Forgive me, Father.

FATHER COYNE.

Do not delude yourself it is offense
Has made me quote the Scripture to you, man.
I dare not take offense. My task is love.
I have no passion save the one for souls.
*Salus suprema lex*, remember that,
Salvation is the law that must come first.
My cure includes both you and Edward Quinn.
Because it does, I have to warn you. Matt,
Do not mistake vindictiveness for justice.
I hope you take my meaning. Do you?

STANTON.

Yes.
I'll make no move against Ned Quinn, I promise,
Unless he moves against me first.

FATHER COYNE.

Good, Matt.

STANTON.

For your penance, Petey, draw the priest a beer.

FATHER COYNE.

I won't tonight, Matt, thank you. I've a matter

I'd like to talk to you about alone.

STANTON.

Sure, Father—Out, the lot of you, to the bar.
The drinks are on the house.

HAGGERTY.

Stanton abu, boys.

BOYLE.

Let the Jickies and the Prods,
Says the Shan Van Vocht,
Look down on us like gods,
Says the Shan Van Vocht.
We've got Stanton, damn the odds,
Says the Shan Van Vocht.

[*Exit* EVERYBODY *cheering. Pause*]

FATHER COYNE.

It's no good being delicate. If I tried,
I'd put your eye out, Matt, or break your bones.
I'll just come out and say it: go see Ag.

STANTON.

Agnes Hogan, Father?

FATHER COYNE.

Agnes Hogan.
What other Ag would I mean?

STANTON.

I can't do that.

FATHER COYNE.

You can't or you won't?

STANTON.

One knock at Aggie's door,
And Josie Finn would be scissoring down Fifth Place
With the wind in tatters around her, and at Kate's ear
Before the latch was lifted. It would all come out—

FATHER COYNE.

It should have come out long since. Ag's dying, Matt.
Tell Kate about her, and go.

STANTON.

Whose fault she's dying?
Did you ever know her stop when the thirst was on her?
Who poured that whiskey down her fourteen months
Until the lungs were tattered in her breast?

Who landed her in Saranac? [*Pause*]
She was always like that.
Whiskey, or clothes, or diamonds . . . or men!
You can say what you want of Jo Finn and her tongue,
If it wasn't for her, I'd never have found out
I was the goat for fair.

FATHER COYNE.

Ag was fully clothed.
And so was Quinn.

STANTON.

You didn't see them, Father.
They were leg in leg when Josie brought me in.
Asleep, I grant you, but his ham of a hand
Was tangled in the fullness of her hair—

FATHER COYNE.

You told me that long since. What's done is done.
Don't let the woman die unreconciled.
Tell Kate, and go to see her.

STANTON.

Yes but—

FATHER COYNE.

What?
What can I know of love, a celibate,
Numb as a broomstick in my varnished parlor,
With my frightened curate jumping at each word,
And Ann Mulcahy to do my housekeeping
Without a whimper of complaint. What can I know?
Putting aside the fact that priesthood's marriage
To a Partner Who is always right, I know
If you don't tell Kate, there are others will,
Before the ink is dry on the campaign posters,
And that would be disastrous—

STANTON.

Tell her what!

FATHER COYNE.

Don't take that tone with me.

STANTON.

I lived with her?
Shall I tell my wife I serviced Ag three years?

FATHER COYNE.

If you're trying to shock me, Matt, you're being simple.
For forty years, no Saturday's gone by,
I have not sat alone from three to nine
In my confessional, and heard men spill
Far blacker things than that. Man, use your reason!

STANTON.

I loved Ag, and kept faith.

FATHER COYNE.

Who says you didn't?

STANTON.

I loved her and kept faith. I did my part.
She played me false with Quinn.

FATHER COYNE.

If you loved her, Matt,
How is it that you didn't marry her,
Before she, how did you put it, played you false? [*Pause*]

STANTON.

Not to give you a short answer, Father,
But don't you think that's my affair?

FATHER COYNE.

No, Matt.

STANTON.

It's not the kind of thing you talk to priests of.

FATHER COYNE.

You're trying to make me angry, aren't you?
Since *you* won't tell *me* why, let me tell you.
You only wanted Ag for fun and games;
You didn't want her on your neck for life.
You thought she'd spoil your chances, didn't you?
Your chances for the mayor's chair? You thought,
If you married her, they'd call you Hogan's Goat
To the day you died. Your heart rejoiced when you found
The both of them in bed—

STANTON.

Are you finished, Father?

FATHER COYNE.

No, Matt. I'm not. Do you know why you're fuming?
Because you're a good man, and you feel ashamed,
Because I'm saying what you tell yourself:
Whatever wrong was done was on both sides.

The woman made you what you are today;
The woman's dying. Hogan's Goat, or not,
Pocket your pride, and tell your wife about her.
Go talk with Ag, and let her die in peace,
Or else you'll be her goat in the Bible sense,
With all her sins on your head, and the world a desert.
Do you think I like to say such things to you?
I'm trying to help you, Matt.

STANTON.

I had the right
To show her no one plays Matt Stanton false
More than one time!

FATHER COYNE.

If you'd the right, my son,
Why are you screaming at me?

STANTON.

Because you'd have me
Destroy this new life I've been three years building,
Not only for myself but for my kind,
By dragging my poor wife to the room in my heart
Where my dead loves are waked. [*Pause*]

FATHER COYNE.

Tell Kathleen, Matt.
Maybe it's that which stands between you, son,
And stiffens both your backs against each other.

STANTON.

Who dares to say that something stands between us?
That's a pack of lies!

FATHER COYNE.

Is it? Tell Katie, Matt—
   [BOYLE *bursts through the bar door*]

BOYLE.

It's Aggie Hogan, Father.
She's dying; and she won't confess to your curate.
They want you.

FATHER COYNE.

Mattie?

STANTON.

Sacred Heart of Jesus!

FATHER COYNE.

Will you come with me?

STANTON.

I will, Father. I will.

[*Exit all three through the Ladies' Entrance*]

CURTAIN

## Act three

*Midnight the same night. The all-night Printers' Church in the Newspaper Row of Brooklyn on lower Fulton Street.* STANTON *kneels on a prie-dieu with a framed baize curtain atop it.* FATHER MALONEY *sits on the other side of the prie-dieu, hearing his Confession.*

STANTON.
Bless me, Father. I have sinned. Three years.
It is three years since I made my last Confession.
I accuse myself of lying many times.
FATHER MALONEY.
How many times?
STANTON.
God knows!
FATHER MALONEY.
With a mind to harm?
STANTON.
God knows!
FATHER MALONEY.
Take hold of yourself. What ails you!
STANTON.
I did a woman wrong. Tonight she died.
Tomorrow is her wake.
FATHER MALONEY.
What kind of wrong
Is it you did her?
STANTON.
I . . .
FATHER MALONEY.
What kind of wrong?

STANTON.

    I lived with her three years before I married.

    They pulled the sheet over her face an hour ago.

    The hem of it gave. It was gray as a buried rag.

    She wouldn't have the priest. She lay there sweating,

    And they around her with their lighted candles.

    She glowered and said, "If such love was a sin,

    I'd rather not make peace with God at all."

    They pressed her hard. She shook and shook her head.

    She kept on shaking it until she died—

    Absolve her through me!

FATHER MALONEY.

    You know I can't do that.

STANTON.

    What can you do then!

FATHER MALONEY.

    Absolve *you* from *your* sin.

STANTON.

    Her sin is mine. Absolve the both of us.

FATHER MALONEY.

    Why did you leave this woman?

STANTON.

    She played me false.

    I found her in the one bed with a man—

    She stood on the wide porch with her hair down, crying.

    I walked away. I heard her screaming at me.

    She told me, go, yes go, but not to come back. Never.

    She'd rip the clothes she bought me into threads

    And throw them in the fire. She'd burn my letters,

    And every bit of paper that I'd put my name to.

    And she did . . . I'm sure she did. She was wild by nature.

    But tonight . . . when I came back . . . she stretched out her hands

    Like a falling child . . .

FATHER MALONEY.

    Go on.

STANTON.

    And I turned away—

    I cannot rest with thinking of her face

And that black look of stubborn joy on it.

FATHER MALONEY.

Well for you, you can't rest. She died in the Devil's arms
In a glory of joy at the filthy shame to her flesh
You visited on her, and like all the rest,
You come to a strange priest outside your parish
In the mistaken hope he will not judge you,
But give you comfort when you need correction.
What about this other one you took up with
When you threw the dead one over?—

STANTON.

Jesus, Father!

FATHER MALONEY.

Don't take the name of the Lord in vain to me!

STANTON.

I don't know why I came here in the first place.

FATHER MALONEY.

You came here for forgiveness—

STANTON.

From the likes of you!
For thirty years I've put up with your kind.
Since my First Communion. Saturday Confession!
Spayed mutts of men, born with no spice of pride,
Living off the pennies of the poor,
Huddled in their fat in basement booths,
Calling the true vaulting of the heart
Towards its desire filth and deviation,
Dragging me, and all unlike you down—

FATHER MALONEY.

Whatever a noble creature like yourself
May think of me, I'm here to do God's work;
And since that begins with dragging you down to the earth
We all have come from and must all return to,
Drag you down I will. God lifts none but the humble—

STANTON.

The pride steams off you like the stink of cancer,
And you sit there and preach humility!

FATHER MALONEY.

Take care! I will deny you absolution.

STANTON.
>What harm! Who can absolve us but ourselves!
>I am what I am. What I have done, I'd cause for.
>It was seeing what life did to her unmanned me;
>It was looking in her eyes as they guttered out
>That drove me here like a scared kid from the bogs
>Who takes the clouds that bruise the light for demons.
>But thanks to the words from the open grave of your
>>mouth
>I see that fear for the wind in fog that it is
>And it is killed for good. I'm my own man now.
>I can say that for the first time in my life.
>I'm free of her; and I'm free of you and yours.
>Come what come may to me, from this day forward,
>I'll not fall to my knees for man or God.
>>[STANTON *rises, and quickly strides out.* FATHER MA-
>>LONEY *rises*]

FATHER MALONEY.
>Will you dare to turn your back on the living God!

**CURTAIN**

# Act four

*Ten o'clock, Friday morning, April 29, 1890. The back room of Fogarty's Saloon.* JAMES "PALSY" MURPHY *sits at a chair pushed well back from a table, apprehensively holding a sheaf of papers in his hand. He is a florid, rather stout man in his late fifties, with black hair* en brosse, *graying at the temples.* MAYOR EDWARD QUINN *stands facing* MURPHY *like a statue of a lawyer in a park. He is a tall, husky, big-boned man in his seventies, bald, but with hair growing out of his ears. He is dressed in rumpled morning clothes.*

QUINN.
  Does Matthew Stanton think he can oust me
  By hole-in-corner meetings in school halls,
  With craw thumpers and Sunday-pass-the-plates,
  Black Jack the plug and the ga-ga Parish Priest
  Both nodding yes to everything he says
  Like slobbering dummies?—What is it that he said?
MURPHY.
  Do you want to hear?
QUINN.
  Would I ask, James, if I didn't?
MURPHY.
  Listen then. I have . . . full notes on it.
  I took down everything that Stanton said.
QUINN.
  Read it. Read it. Do you want applause?
MURPHY.
  No, Ned: attention. Here: "My dear old friends,
  When Father Coyne asked me to speak to you,
  He said it was about Ag Hogan's bills,

A gathering to help raise funds to pay them.
I never thought the purpose of this meeting
Would be political"—
QUINN.
  "I never thought
The purpose of this meeting"—Father Coyne!
I roofed his sieve of a church and glazed it too;
And put a tight new furnace in its cellar.
There's not a priest you can trust!
MURPHY.
  Will you listen, Ned!
QUINN.
  I'm listening. Go on.
MURPHY.
  "The Party of Reform"—
QUINN.
  "The Party of Reform"! Ah, yes, reform!
A Lutheran lawyer with a flytrap mouth
And a four-bit practice of litigious Swedes
In a closet rank as rats down by the river!
A lecherous broker with a swivel eye
You wouldn't trust with Grandma in a hack!
A tear-drawers arm in arm with a gaping bollocks!
MURPHY.
  Will you quit your interrupting!
QUINN.
  Read on. Read on.
MURPHY.
  "The Party of Reform has in its hands
Sworn affidavits on the city books"—
QUINN.
  Got by collusion and by audits forged
As the certificates above their parents' beds!—
MURPHY.
  "The Party of Reform has in its hands
Sworn affidavits on the city books,
Drawn up from careful audit, and declaring
A hidden deficit of fifteen thousand"—
QUINN.
  Of fifteen thousand! The unfortunates!

They couldn't even get that business right.
It's twenty thousand. Palsy, if it's a cent! [*Glum pause*]
I'm in the treasury for twenty thousand. [*Pause*]

MURPHY.

"You say they will expose us to the public,
Unless we guarantee that Edward Quinn
Resigns as candidate in the next election"—

QUINN.

See, that's Matt's game. He's out to get my job;
But he's not the guts to grab it like a man.
Will you listen to the cagey way he puts it:
"*You* say *they* will expose *us* to the public!"
As sneaky as a rat in a hotel kitchen.
Don't you see the cunning of it, James? The craft?
It's not my job he wants, but to save the Party!
And all I did for him. I made him, James.
I picked him up when he first came to me,
Twelve years ago, when he was twenty-five
And lost his job for beating up that grocer.
He'd no knees in his pants; his coat was slick
With grease as a butcher's thumb. He was skin and bones.
I was sitting here in Fogarty's back room,
With poor Ag Hogan codding me, when he
Burst in the door, and asked me for my help.
"I'll do anything that's honest, Mr. Quinn,"
Is what he says. He had that crooked grin—
It reminded me of Patrick that's long dead,
Patrick, my poor brother—

MURPHY.

Go on, now, Ned!
Leave out the soft-soap. He'd a crooked grin
You knew would serve you well among the women—

QUINN.

I should have said, "Go now, and scare the crows,
Raggedy-arse Keho; that's all you're good for!"
But, no, there was that grin; and Ag said, "Take him."
She loved him, the poor slob, from the day she saw him,
Fat good it did her. "You can put him on
With Judge Muldooney," says she; "take him, Ned,

God will bless us for it. . . ." [*Pause*]
Aggie's dead, James. Dead.
MURPHY.
Yes, Ned. She is.
QUINN.
Did Stanton get to see her? [*Pause*]
Did he?
MURPHY.
Yes.
QUINN.
She wouldn't let me in. [*Pause*]
MURPHY.
I'm sorry, Ned.
QUINN.
And Stanton's high-toned wife?
What did she say when she found out about them?
MURPHY.
She didn't, Ned. She knows that Ag helped Matt,
But nothing else.
QUINN.
Ah, nothing else? I see.
Where was I, Palsy?
MURPHY.
"All I done for him,"
Fifth book, tenth chapter—
QUINN.
Go to hell, James Murphy.
You think it's funny, do you? I'll give you fun.
If it's jail for me, you know, it's jail for you.
No hundred-dollar suits and fancy feeds
With tarts in Rector's drinking cold champagne
From glasses bright as ice with hollow stems,
But tea from yellowed cups and Mulligan
Foul as the odds and ends they make it from.
MURPHY.
Sure, they'll send us puddings.
QUINN.
Are you mad, or what?
I tell you, I'm in danger. I'm in danger.

Don't shake your head. They're spoiling for the kill.
It's in their blood.

MURPHY.

Whose blood?

QUINN.

Whose blood but our own.
They turn upon the strong, and pull them down,
And not from virtue, James, but vicious pride.
They want to hold their heads up in this city,
Among the members of the Epworth League,
The Church of Ethical Culture and the Elks,
That's why they're taking sides with Ole Olson,
Or whatever the hell his name is, and that whore
From Wall Street in the clean pince-nez. For thirty years
I've kept their heads above the water, James,
By fair means or by foul. Now they've reached the shore
They'd rather not remember how they got there.
They want to disown me. They're a faithless lot,
And Matthew Stanton is the worst of all—
Read on, why don't you? What's the matter with you?
  [*Pause*]

MURPHY.

"I would not stand in this school hall before you
If Edward Quinn had not, in his full power,
Made of me what I am. I cannot think,
Since you have shared his generosity
As long as I, that you are asking me
To help you pull him down"——

QUINN.

Good Jesus, James!

MURPHY.

"The way to cope with the Party of Reform's
To raise the funds to make Quinn's deficit up.
I pledge three thousand dollars, and I ask
Each and every one of you who can
To give as much as possible. Ned Quinn
Must not live out his final days in jail
Because he was too kindly to be wise"——

QUINN.

I want no handouts from the likes of him.

Will he pity me?

MURPHY.

What's that?

QUINN.

You heard me, James.
Will he pity me? Does he think I need his pity!
I made him, and I can unmake him too,
And make another in his place. I'm old,
I'm far too old to live on charity
From a greenhorn that I picked up in a barroom
To run my sweetheart's errands. Don't you see, James?
He took Ag from me first; that's how he started.
He ran her roadhouse for her. "He was handsome!
He'd skin like milk, and eyes like stars in winter!"
And he was young and shrewd! She taught him manners:
What clothes to wear, what cutlery to begin with,
What twaddle he must speak when introduced
To the state bigwigs down from Albany.
He told her that he loved her. She ditched me.
I'm twenty years her senior. Then that day,
That famous Labor Day three years ago,
We'd a drink or two, you know, for old times' sake,
And we passed out, and that bitch Josie Finn
Found out about us, and brought Matt in on us,
Our arms around each other like two children.
And he spat on poor Ag's carpet, called her a whore,
Me a degenerate. Three years ago,
The very year he married this Kathleen,
The Lord knows who, James, from the Christ knows
    where,
In some cosy hocus-pocus there in London,
To show Ag he could do without her. He never spoke
To Ag at all until he found her done for,
Dying lung by lung. He'd never speak to me at all
If I were not in trouble
Don't you see the triumph of it, Palsy Murphy!
He takes his vengeance in a show of mercy.
He weeps as he destroys! He's a crocodile—

MURPHY.

Ned, I . . .

QUINN.

Ned what?

MURPHY.

I hope you won't be hurt.

We on the Party board agree with Matt.

We feel the time has come for some new blood—

QUINN.

"We on the Party board agree with Matt"!

Now it comes out at last! It all comes out!

You and your pack of lies, your trumped-up story,

Pretending to be reading what he said

When you can't read a thing that hasn't pictures.

Did you think me such a boob I wouldn't know

What you and Walsh were up to here last night?

It made the rounds of the Ward by half past nine! [*Pause*]

Bismarck the diplomat! You goddamned fool,

Pouring that vat of soft-soap over me!

"Because he was too kindly to be wise"!

They'll soon be making you the editor

Of *The Messenger of the Sacred Heart.*

MURPHY.

Now, Ned—

QUINN.

"Now, Ned." "Now, Ned." Shut up, or I'll drink your
    blood.

The only thing rang true in what you said

Was Stanton's offer to be noble to me. [*Pause*]

MURPHY.

I wanted to break it easy. Matt made no offer.

The Party it is will cover you on the books.

But on one condition, Ned: you must resign.

QUINN.

*I* must resign. We'll see who backs out first.

I didn't stay the mayor of this city

For thirty years by taking orders, James.

You tell the Party board I'll rot in prison

Before I'll let Matt Stanton take my place.

You tell the Party board I'll meet the debits

The Party of Reform found in the books.

You tell the Party board they'd best not cross me.
Don't look as if you think this all is blather.
There's not a one of you I can't get at,
You least of all. Remember that, James Murphy.
How long, do you think, that knowing what I know
About your money, James, and how you got it,
The Jesuit Fathers at St. Francis Xavier's,
With all their bon-ton notions of clean hands,
Would let your boys play soldier in their yard?
Don't glare like that at me. You tell the board
What I have said. I meant it, every word.

MURPHY.
The Party will disown you!

QUINN.
Let them try!
I'll grease the palm of every squarehead deadbeat
From Greenwood Cemetery to the Narrows
Who'll stagger to the polls for three months' rent,
I'll buy the blackface vote off all the fences
Down Fulton Street from Hudson Avenue.
I'll vote from every plot in Holy Cross
With an Irish headstone on it. I'll win this fight—

MURPHY.
I'll telegraph to Albany. I warn you!

QUINN.
Damn Albany! Get out of here. Get out!
  [*Exit* MURPHY *stage left.* QUINN *walks over to the bar
  door to stage right*]
Hey, Bill.
  [*Enter* BILL, *a wiry bowlegged man about seventy who
  has the look of a drunk*]
Go down to one-o-seventy Luqueer Street,
And get me Josie Finn—On second thought,
Best wait till noon and collar me some schoolboy
To run the errand for me. If they saw you,
They'd know 'twas I that wanted her. And yes!
Send to Fitzsimmons and Rooney for a wreath,
A hundred-dollar wreath, and have them spell
This message out in them gold-paper letters

On a silk-gauze band: "For Agnes Mary Hogan,
Gone but not forgotten." Look alive!

**CURTAIN**

## Act five

*Eight o'clock the same evening. The Haggertys' kitchen, beneath the Stantons' parlor in the double set. The kitchen table and chairs are of cheap oak, varnished and revarnished until they looked charred and blistered  The chairs are unmatched, and of the "Queen Anne" style, jerry-built replicas of a bad idea of eighteenth-century furniture, with die-embossed designs on the back, their seats repaired with pressed cardboard. Behind the table stands the big coal cooking stove, jammed into the chimney. The mantelpiece is covered with newspaper cut into daggers of rough lace and filled with every kind of souvenir you could think of, yellowing letters, bills, clippings stuck behind the grimy ornaments. To stage right of the stove, an entrance into the three remaining rooms of the flat, an opening hung with a single portière of heavy, warped, faded brown velour on greasy wooden rings. Through that opening, from time to time, as the scene progresses, can be heard the sound of people saying the Rosary. The door of the flat, giving on the hall and the stairs to the Stantons' flat, is ajar; and leaned against it glitters Edward Quinn's appalling flower piece. Seated to stage left of the table is* JOSIE FINN, *a tall, rather handsome woman in her late thirties, with her black hair in a loose bun. Opposite her sits* ANN MULCAHY, *a small, plump woman with a face like a withered apple, red hair gone white, and fine searching eyes. Between them, its back to the audience, stands an empty chair. They have cups in front of them, and are waiting for the kettle to boil for the tea.*

ANN.

 I'm sure Matt will have luck for burying Ag
 And letting Maisie hold the wake downstairs here
 In his own house for all that passed between them.
  [JOSIE *nods disconsolately. Enter* PETEY BOYLE, *swaying slightly, his hat in his hands*]

BOYLE.

 I'm sorry for your trouble, Mrs. Finn.

JOSIE.

 My trouble, Petey. Trouble it is for fair.
 That's Aggie Hogan that's laid out in there,
 My dead aunt's daughter, that I haven't talked to
 For, Mother of God, I think it's three long years
 September.

BOYLE.

 If you come to crow about it,
 My ass on you then, kid—

JOSIE.

 Sir, you presume!
 John Haggerty!
  [BOYLE *scurries through the portière to the sanctuary of the coffin*]

ANN.

 Now don't be calling Jack. It will cause trouble.
 Poor Petey Boyle was always ignorant.
 He meant no harm by talking to you dirty,
 Josie dear.

JOSIE.

 It's not his talking dirty
 Made me mad. What kind of creature must he take me for,
 To come to crow at my own cousin's wake!—
 You know, Ag wouldn't see me at the last?

ANN.

 Nor would she have the priest. She was crazed with pain,
 In fever tantrums, don't you know, half dead.
 She hardly knew what she was doing.

JOSIE.

 Ann, you're a saint.

ANN.

Now, Josie, praise is poison,
Though I thank you for the kindness that's behind it.

JOSIE.

How can you live, remembering what you've done,
Unless you are a saint, or a half brute,
Like Quinn in there!

ANN.

By doing what you must;
And begging for the grace to forgive yourself
As well as others when you don't do right.
You just reminded me: I hope Ned's going soon.
It's getting on towards eight; and Matt's expected down.

JOSIE.

Oh, Quinn knows that. Sure, Quinn knows everything:
Whose money's stained, and how, and whose is not;
Who's in whose bed, and who is not, and why;
Who has a shame to hide that he can use
To coat his nest with slime against the wind!

ANN.

There's a bit of skunk in all of us, you know.
We stink when we're afraid or hurt. Ned's both.

JOSIE.

Pray for me, Ann Mulcahy. I've made a vow
On my dead mother's grave to guard my tongue
And keep my temper.

ANN.

God in Heaven help you.

JOSIE.

It's up to me, not Him.

ANN.

Ah, don't say that.
Sure, that's presumption.

JOSIE.

Then I won't say that.
But thinking back on things I've said and done,
And my knees all bunions, kneeling out Novenas,
If you think that God and all His holy angels
Can shut my mouth once anger oils the hinges,

You're more a fool than ever I took you for
When first I met you—
　　[*Enter* FATHER COYNE, *dressed in the same rusty black
　　coat and frayed biretta*]

FATHER COYNE.
　Here in the nick of time!
　Who's calling my lost parish's one saint
　A fool to her face!

JOSIE.
　Good evening to you, Father.

FATHER COYNE.
　Good evening, Mrs. Finn. I'm glad to see
　Your three hard years of war with the deceased
　Has ended in some show of gallantry.
　What was the fight about? Do you recall?

JOSIE.
　You well know that I do. But what's been has been.
　She'd have done the same for me.

FATHER COYNE.
　I'm sure she would:
　For where would be the harm in that, I ask you?
　There'd be small danger of much conversation
　To thaw your icy hearts—

ANN.
　Please, Father Coyne—

FATHER COYNE.
　Dear God, forgive me. I forgot you, Ann.
　It's like me to fly out at Mrs. Finn
　With the one soul left here I could scandalize
　From Dwight Street to the steps of City Hall.
　I'll be as gracious as St. Francis Sales
　To make it up to you, Ann—Now, Mrs. Finn,
　And how have you been ever since?

JOSIE.
　Since when?

FATHER COYNE.
　Since Easter Sunday three long years ago,
　The last time that I saw you in my church!

JOSIE.
　There's other churches!

FATHER COYNE.

Yes, but not this parish;
And that's where you belong—
[ANN *touches* FATHER COYNE *on the sleeve and looks into his eyes*]
I'm a sinful man.
Pray for me, Ann Mulcahy. I'll begin the beads,
Before I throw my forty years of prayer
Into the pits of Hell to best a slanderer.
Will you come with me?

ANN.

In a minute, Father.
The kettle's on the boil.
[*Exit* FATHER COYNE *through the portière. Pause*]

JOSIE.

I have the name;
As well to have the game!

ANN.

He meant no harm.
He's torn apart with trying to talk sense
To poor Ag dying; and he struck at you
Because you brought the days back Ag was well. [*Pause*]
Will you wet the tea, while I go in and ask
If Ned Quinn can't be hurried just a bit.
I'm destroyed with worrying that Matt will come.
[*Exit* ANN. *Sound of Rosary.* JOSIE *rises, and brews the tea in a large earthenware pot. Enter* QUINN *quietly through the portière. Sound of Rosary.* JOSIE *looks up from the stove, directly at him, then away. Most of their conversation is carried on with averted faces*]

QUINN.

Why have they put that wedding ring on Ag? [*Pause*]

JOSIE.

She asked them to. She said it was her mother's. [*Pause*]

QUINN.

What harm would there be in it, I'd like to know!

JOSIE.

You'd like to know? You know damned well what harm.
I told you no this afternoon. I meant it.
Am I your cat's-paw, do you think, Ned Quinn,

To pull your poisoned chestnuts from the fire
And feed them to your foes? I told you. No.

QUINN.

You didn't think that way the day you led him
Into the room where her that's dead in there
lay in my arms as guiltless as a baby
In a fit of drunken warmth she took for love!

JOSIE.

More shame to me I didn't think that way!
She was my own blood, and she loved the man;
And I tried to get between them, and broke her heart.
It's all my fault that she lies dead in there,
No one's but mine. And she was good to me,
And I betrayed her—Ned, she wouldn't see me.
She wouldn't let me in the room at the last.
They say she'd not confess her life with Matt;
They say she would not call that life a sin. [*Pause*]
I'll never interfere that way again.
If it were not for me, they'd have been married,
And there'd have been no sin. Has Ag gone to Hell?
Do you think that, Ned? For that would be my fault.
Have I destroyed her life forever, Ned,
In this world and the next? [*Pause*]

QUINN.

You're talking blather.
Ach, God's more merciful than Father Coyne,
Be sure of that, or we'd have been roasted black,
The whole damned lot of us, long since. [*Pause*]
Come on.
Wouldn't you like to make it up to Ag, Jo?
Do something for her dead? That's all I'm asking.
Shouldn't Matt pay for what he did to her?
All that you'd need to say's a single sentence,
When the Lady Duchess Kathleen Kakiak
Descends in visitation: "Mrs. Stanton,
Sure, God will bless you for your charity."
"My charity?" she'll ask. You'll say, "You know,
Ag having lived with Matt three years and all."
That's all you'd have to say.

JOSIE.

    What am I, Ned,
    That you take me for a fool and villain both?
    Don't talk to me about your broken heart,
    And how you feel you owe poor Ag revenge!
    If she had wanted that, would she have died
    Without the sacraments to spare Matt pain?
    I know you want to drive Matt from the running
    And that you'd stop at nothing short of murder
    For one more term as lord of City Hall.
    Best give it up, Ned. Fast. It will destroy you.

QUINN.

    Give what up, Jo?

JOSIE.

    Your pride. Your murderous pride.

QUINN.

    I don't know what you mean by that at all.
    They're out to get me, Jo. I have to fight.
    They telephoned today at half past three:
    "Albany says resign or they'll destroy you!"
    I had to send a letter to that bastard
    Throwing in the sponge. But I'm not through yet;
    And I'll win out. I always have before.
    But if I go down, I won't go down alone.
    You may call that pride, if you like. I call it honor.

JOSIE.

    No, Ned. Not honor, I know. Pride kept me from her.
    I'd not admit the wrong was on my side,
    And her with the blood of her heart on her shaking chin
    In that icebox of a hallroom down in Smith Street,
    The wall at her nose. Oh, Sacred Heart of Jesus,
    I should have flung myself on the oilcloth floor
    And not got up until she gave me pardon.
    She'd have laughed at me, and called me a young whale,
    Or some such nonsense. She'll never laugh again. . . .
    What must Matt feel?

QUINN.

    Good riddance to bad rubbish
    Is what he feels!

JOSIE.

> You never knew Matt, Ned,
> If you think that.

QUINN.

> I knew him well enough!—
> You're still in love with him—

JOSIE.

> What's that to you!

QUINN.

> And him with the worst word in his mouth for you,
> As he always has had!

JOSIE.

> I don't believe you, Ned

QUINN.

> Ah, well. Ah, well. No one believes me now.
> Stanton's your god; and that's just as it should be.
> You're traitors all, as fickle as the sunlight
> On April Fools' Day. But there'll come a time
> You'll say Ned Quinn was right.

JOSIE.

> What kind of thing
> Is it he says of me?

QUINN.

> No matter, now.
> You'd not believe me if I told it to you.

JOSIE.

> What does he say? [*Pause*]

QUINN.

> For one thing that you're two-faced,
> And well enough, since the face that you were born with's
> Like a madman's arse.

JOSIE.

> You son of a bitch, Ned Quinn,
> That sounds like you, not him.

QUINN.

> Have it your own way.
> I'm old, you know; I'm all dustmice upstairs.
> It's hard for me to lay my mind on recollections.
> Yet it seems to me I can recall a toast
> Matt drank his birthday night at Villepigue's

Two weeks before we had that fight in Seagate. . . .
He stood there fingering that green silk tie
That you embroidered those gold shamrocks on—

JOSIE.

How do you know that I gave Matt that tie?

QUINN.

He told me when he gave the tie to Petey—

JOSIE.

You made that up! [*Pause*]

QUINN.

He lifted up his glass,
And laughed, and said: "Confusion to the devil
That's bent Jo Finn as fast around my neck
As a coop around a barrel; and her legs as loose
As her lying tongue"—

JOSIE.

God's curse on you for that!

QUINN.

God's curse on me? I'm only telling truth.
Come to your senses, woman. He played me false.
And Ag. And her he's married to, Kathleen.
What makes you think you are the bright exception?

JOSIE.

Because I know him for a good man, Ned.
And not a poisonous old woman of a thief,
Destroying names to keep himself in office—

QUINN.

A thief, am I! I'll get what I want without you;
And when Stanton plays you false, don't whine to me.
[*Enter* KATHLEEN, STANTON, *and* MURPHY. MURPHY *is
carrying a case of liquor, which he sets on the chair
nearest him, his eyes fixed on* QUINN *and* STANTON *confronting each other*]

STANTON.

I will not play her false, nor will I you. . . .
I got your letter; and I thank you for it.
I'm sorry that my winning means your loss.
[*Pause.* QUINN *glares at* STANTON, *then takes a step towards the door*]

MURPHY.

Wait, Ned!

STANTON.

I swear, I'll see you through this trouble.

I want to be your friend again. Shake hands.

Come on, man. And what better place than here.

I'm sure Ag would have wanted it. Come on—

QUINN.

Good God! The goat can talk. When Ag was living, though,

You rarely met the livestock in the house!

[STANTON *hurls himself at* QUINN, *and takes him by the throat.* KATHLEEN *screams.* JOSIE *and* MURPHY *rush to get between them*]

STANTON.

I'll kill him!

MURPHY.

Hold him back. Go on, Ned. Go.

Remember Ag, Matt. Please. No disrespect.

[MURPHY *is holding* STANTON's *arms.* QUINN, *disengaging himself from* JOSIE, *blackly looks* STANTON *up and down, and spits in his face. It takes both* MURPHY *and* KATHLEEN *to hold* STANTON *back.* QUINN *watches the struggle. Exit* QUINN *slowly.* JOSIE *fetches a rag, and hands it to* STANTON. *He wipes the spittle off his face and coat*]

JOSIE.

Pay him no heed, Matt. Sure, what need have you

To care what a thief thinks who's been found out—

STANTON.

I'll thank you to keep out of this, Jo Finn.

You always were a one for interfering.

JOSIE.

Why take things out on me? It was he spit at you.

KATHLEEN.

Mattie, Mattie, are you crazed or what?

You've hurt the woman's feelings.

STANTON.

Kate, come ahead.

Where are the Haggertys?

JOSIE.

Inside with the rest.

Inside in the parlor.

[STANTON *takes* KATHLEEN *by the arm, but she holds back*]

KATHLEEN.

Matt, beg her pardon.

STANTON.

For what? For what? Don't waste your sympathy

On that one. And stay clear of her as can be:

She has a wicked tongue. Watch out for her—

KATHLEEN.

The woman heard you!—

STANTON.

Devil a bit I care!

Will you come into the parlor!

KATHLEEN.

Matt, she's crying.

[STANTON *strides over towards* JOSIE, *awkward with remorse*]

STANTON.

Josie—

JOSIE.

Never mind. I heard you, Matt.

STANTON.

The devil

Take you then, for your big ears!

JOSIE.

The devil take me, Matt.

KATHLEEN.

Please, Mrs. Finn—

JOSIE.

Go in now to the wake,

And let me be!

[*Pause.* MURPHY *shakes his head, and motioning* KATHLEEN *towards the portière, holds it up for her. Exit* KATHLEEN, STANTON, *and* MURPHY. JOSIE *walks to the table and picks up the rag which* STANTON *used to wipe the spittle off himself. In a spasm of rage, she*

*tears it in two and throws it on the floor. Enter* MARIA
  HAGGERTY]

MARIA.
  What's this that Mrs. Stanton's after saying
  About a fight between her man and you?

JOSIE.
  I'm not the kind that would demean myself
  By having words with the likes of him, Maria.

MARIA.
  The likes of him? What is this all about?
  I've never heard you talk that way of Matt.

JOSIE.
  I never found him out until just now.
  He treated me like dirt. And who is he
  To be so high and mighty—Hogan's Goat,
  A fancy boy made good! Ag's fancy boy!

MARIA.
  You shut your mouth, or I will shut it for you.
  Matt's broken up because of Aggie's death;
  That's why he lost his temper. That and Quinn,
  Bad luck be with the day I let him in here.
  I'll not have you make trouble for Matt, Jo.
  I want you to come into the parlor now
  And take Matt's hand.

JOSIE.
  It's he should take my hand.

MARIA.
  Will you come in, if he comes out to you first?
    [*Enter* KATHLEEN *softly behind* MARIA]

JOSIE.
  I'll make no promises.
    [*Pause.* KATHLEEN *puts her black-gloved hand on*
    MARIA's *shoulder.* MARIA *starts, and acknowledges her*
    *with nervous heartiness*]

MARIA.
  Why, Mrs. Stanton!

KATHLEEN.
  I'd like to talk to Mrs. Finn alone. [*Pause*]
  Maria? Just a moment or two. Alone.
    [*Exit* MARIA *reluctantly*]

Mrs. Finn, please. Matthew meant no harm . . .
He has a dreadful temper. You know that.
And he's like a scalded cat since yesterday
When he got the news that Agnes Hogan died. [*Pause*]
He told me just how much she'd meant to him
When he was starting out on his career.
You know that better, maybe, than myself—

JOSIE.

He told you that, did he! Did he tell you how
He lived with her three years in a state of sin
In a love nest of a roadhouse down in Seagate?
And the devil take the talk! Did he tell you, too,
She drank herself consumptive for his sake
Because he threw her over three years since,
When he'd got all he wanted from her, missis,
And married you—

[KATHLEEN *gasps and runs out the door.* JOSIE *looks
straight ahead into the air before her face, brings both
hands to her forehead with a slap, and sits swaying in
her chair*]

CURTAIN

## Act six

*Eleven o'clock the same evening. The Stantons' flat. Before the curtain rises, the sound of a scuffle and a cry.* KATHLEEN *stands, tight with fury, a large silver hand mirror, which she has just struck* STANTON *with, in her hand.* STANTON *sits on the edge of the couch, a handkerchief to his fore-head, which is bleeding slightly.* KATHLEEN *turns her gaze from* STANTON *to the floor. With that sudden recession of energy which follows drunken violence, she sways and slumps, the hand with the mirror in it hanging slackly at her side. She kicks at the fragments of the mirror with the toe of her shoe, as if she were puzzled by them. She is very drunk, but on brandy; that is, her mind is sharper than it would seem to be.*

KATHLEEN.
    The mirror's broken.
STANTON.
    Yes, that means bad luck.
KATHLEEN.
    I know it does. But now I can see plain,
    Just as it says in First Corinthians:
    When I was a child, I saw as a child does,
    Saw what I loved as in a mirror darkly,
    But now I see his face—
STANTON.
    This night of all nights!
    When I have Quinn's note resigning in my hand!
    The bitch of a Josie Finn with her snake's tongue!—
    Where have you been till now? Where did you get it?

KATHLEEN.

Did I get what, Matt?

STANTON.

The drink that's crazed you.

KATHLEEN.

In your own back room with a woman named Miss Legg.
Miss Bessie Legg. She'd yards and yards of beads on,
And a hat like a berry patch attacked by magpies,
And a fancy neckpiece like twelve Persian cats
All tied together. You'd think she'd blow away
At the first breeze with all those feathers on her.

STANTON.

How could you do a thing like that to me?
Get paralyzed for everyone to gawk at,
And with the district whore?

KATHLEEN.

She's that, is she?
Birds of a feather flock together, Matt,
And whore will meet with whore. That's what I am.
We aren't married. We aren't. You know that.
Isn't it the same as you and Agnes?

STANTON.

Jesus, Katie! [*Pause*]

KATHLEEN.

Are you hurt bad, Matt?

STANTON.

It's nice of you to ask. [KATHLEEN *flies at him*]

KATHLEEN.

You son of a bitch, I'll kill you.
    [STANTON *pinions her arms. She drops the mirror.
    What began as battle ends as embrace*]
Mattie, Mattie.

STANTON.

Oh, Katie, what's the matter with us both!

KATHLEEN.

What can a woman say when she learns the man
She left her country and her God to marry
Has married her to show his cast-off mistress
That he can do without her, or even worse,
Only to earn his good name back again?

STANTON.

I married you because I love you, Kate.

KATHLEEN.

Then why was I the one soul in this city
Who didn't know of you and Agnes? Why?

STANTON.

I didn't want to hurt you.

KATHLEEN.

Well, you have—
How do I know you won't abandon me
If I don't get you what you want from life?

STANTON.

Don't say such things.

KATHLEEN.

No wonder they seemed strange,
Your what-d'ya-callem's, your constituents:
They none of them could look me in the face
For fear they might let on. Didn't Bessie Legg
Tell me she thought the only reason Agnes Hogan
Went to bed with Quinn was to prove to herself
That there was someone loved her, when she saw
Your feelings for her dying like wet coal,
And realized she'd lost you? How do I know
The same thing will not happen to myself;
And people won't be saying a year from now,
Kate went the same way as the poor dead whore?

STANTON.

Kate. Don't call her that.

KATHLEEN.

Why not? Don't they?

STANTON.

They don't. And don't you call her out of name.
You never knew her. And the talk you've heard
Has been about her as she was in public,
Stripping the heavy diamonds off her fingers
To keep the party going one more hour.
I knew what lay behind it. It was mine:
Her will to fullness. She contained a man
As the wind does, the first giddy days of spring,
When your coat blows open, and your blood beats hard,

As clear as ice, and warm as a chimney wall.
'Twas she first gave me heart to dare be free.
All threats turned promise when she talked to you.
With her on your arm, you saw your life before you
Like breast-high wheat in the soft dazzle of August.
She had a way of cupping her long hands
Around my bulldog's mug, as if I were
Some fancy fruit she'd bought beyond her means,
And laughing with delight. She put nothing on
She did not feel, and felt with flesh and soul.
I don't believe she knew what shame might be.
You could not resist her. *I* could not. I tried.
I was twenty-five years old, when first I met her.
I'd never . . .

KATHLEEN.

What?

STANTON.

I was what you'd call a virgin. . . .

KATHLEEN.

The saints preserve us!

STANTON.

Yes, it's funny now;
It wasn't funny then. [*Pause*]
It was she wooed me.
It seemed—Lord knows, I don't—unnatural.
She was ten years my senior. But, oh, Kate,
To look at her downstairs, you'd never know
What once she was! Her hair was bronze and silver
Like pear trees in full bloom, her eyes were opal,
Her skin was like new milk, and her blue veins
Trembled in the shimmer of her full straight neck
Like threads of violets fallen from her hair
And filliped by the breeze. She bought me presents:
A handmade vest of black brocaded silk,
A blond Malacca cane with a silver head
Cast like an antique statue, the Lord knows what,
There were so many of them. And she'd cock
That angel's head of hers, and tell me:
"You look like such a slob, Matt, I took pity
And bought you something nice. You can pay me back . . .

Some day." [*Pause*]
I took them not to hurt her, Kate;
And when she asked me would I work for her,
Would I run the gaming rooms in Seagate for her,
And keep her out of trouble, I said yes;
And when she asked me would I be her man,
I'd have said yes, but I could scarcely breathe
Between the want and fear of her. I nodded—
I never knew a man say no to her
Until I did myself that Labor Day
I found her in the one bed with Ned Quinn.
I looked her in the eyes, and I said, "No!
I'll play the fancy boy to you no more." [*Pause*]
That's what I was, Kathleen, Ag's fancy boy,
I was Hogan's Goat to everyone, Ag's stud.
All my high hopes for power and for office
Fell down around my ears like a spavined roof
When I first heard them call me that—And, Kate,
When it comes to feelings, there was my side too:
I might have been some tethered brute in the yard
The way she acted. That last year she seemed bent
On driving home to me she was all I had,
Without her, I was nothing—Even after Newark,
She never changed—

KATHLEEN.

What happened in Newark?—

STANTON.

Nothing!
I don't know why I brought it up in the first place.
We had a fight. I left her. I went to Newark.
She followed me. We made it up. That's all.
Let's not talk about it. It brings things back.

KATHLEEN.

You loved her, didn't you? You love her still.

STANTON.

Ag's dead, Kathleen. How can you love a corpse?
And in my heart she's been that these three years—
Part of me lay dead as a horse in the street
In that house in Seagate, till I met you in London.
It was as if God had sent me down an angel

To bring me back from the grave. That's why I asked you
To marry me in that London City Hall
Without the eight weeks' wait to cry the banns,
And come back with me right away. I was afraid,
I was afraid I'd lose you, if I left
And waited here for you till the banns were cried—
I swear to you, on my dead mother's grave,
As soon as the election's past, we'll marry
Right in St. Mary's Church, and damn the gossip! [*Pause*]
I didn't tell you—

KATHLEEN.

Why?—

STANTON.

I was ashamed
That I was ever young. I wanted you
To think I knew my way around from birth.

KATHLEEN.

Lord help us!

STANTON.

And somehow, even more, I was ashamed
That I had let her woo me like a girl,
And I could not resist her or say no
For three long years. It was that slavery
I was ashamed of most—

KATHLEEN.

That slavery,
My dear, is love—

STANTON.

What is it you just said?

KATHLEEN.

I'm terrible drunk.

STANTON.

Sure, don't I know that!
And if you weren't, Kate, you'd be a widow.
You'd have brained me good and proper with that mirror,
If your eye had not been blurred—

KATHLEEN.

But I see plain!

STANTON.

Come, Katie, let me help you into bed—

KATHLEEN.
You never came to look for me, did you?

STANTON.
I did. I couldn't find you.

KATHLEEN.
Tell the truth!
You were too proud. You sat up here and waited.
You knew I would come back like a hungry cat,
Like Agnes Hogan! Call to her, why don't you?
She'll stiffen in the coffin at your voice
And drag herself up those dark stairs outside
On her bare feet! They never put shoes on them.
She's back to where she was before in Ireland:
The dirt will clog her toes!

STANTON.
Oh, Jesus, Katie!

KATHLEEN.
Don't you understand me, Mattie?

STANTON.
Come on now, Kate.
The fire's sunk. You'll catch your death of cold,
If you keep up this way. Kate, come on to bed.

KATHLEEN.
No, never!

STANTON.
Katie, Katie, what's the matter!

KATHLEEN.
I looked at her downstairs. I feel afraid.
They say death visits three before it's done.
I looked at her sewn lips, her spotted hand
With the wedding ring you never gave her on it.
They said it was her mother's. Poor Aggie, Matt!
Poor you and me!
   [*Pause.* STANTON *covers his face with his hands and
   falls to the couch.* KATHLEEN *suddenly throws herself
   on her knees, and embraces him around the waist*]
I don't want liberty!
Don't leave me, Mattie, please. I feel afraid.
   [STANTON *uncovers his face, cups the back of her head
   in his hand, and kisses her temples*]

STANTON.

Toc-sha-shin-inish, my darling. Don't be talking—

KATHLEEN.

It isn't God I want, it's you—

STANTON.

Sh. Sh.

KATHLEEN.

I wanted to go away, Matt; but I couldn't.
Those things you said about you and Ag Hogan,
About resenting how you felt for her,
They go for me—Oh, Matt, we're like twin children:
The pride is in our blood—I'd like to kill you,
Or die myself. Do you understand me, Matt!
Don't let me. I am sick with shame. I love you—
   [STANTON *kisses her on the mouth, lifts her to her feet,
      and helps her towards the bedroom*]

STANTON.

You're crying drunk—

KATHLEEN.

*In vino veritas:*
There's truth in drink.

STANTON.

God! Now she's quoting Latin,
And me so ignorant that all I know
Is that I'm cold and want my wife beside me
Before I can feel warm again or rest.
Ag's dead, Kate, dead.
But, Katie, we're alive.
Come with me out of the cold. Ag's gone for good.

CURTAIN

# Act seven

*Midnight the same night. The back room of Stantons' Saloon.* Stanton for Mayor *is spelled out in gold-paper letters hanging from the crêpe-paper streamers.*

BESSIE LEGG *sits at a table, looking downcast and bewildered, an empty glass before her, her back to the Ladies' Entrance. The door to the Ladies' Entrance swiftly opens a crack.* BILL *sticks his head in and withdraws it. The door swiftly closes.* BESSIE *cranes round, sees nothing, and returns to her glum daydream. Enter* QUINN *and* BILL *through the Ladies' Entrance.*

BESSIE.
Watch what the hell you're doing!
Creeping up on parties like the Blackhand!
Good Christ, it's you! What are you doing here?
You want to start a riot?

QUINN.
Go easy, Bessie,
Or you'll have them in here. I'll tell you what to do.
Go get two doubles; and tell them at the bar
You'd like to be alone in here awhile,
You have a customer.
    [QUINN *puts a ten-dollar bill on the table in front of her*]

BESSIE.
I'm through with that.

QUINN.
I'm through with that, says she, and her stairs in splinters
From the armies charging up and down them nights!
Don't sit there that way with your mouth sprung open
Like a busted letter box. Go get the drinks.

[QUINN *moves out of sight of the bar. Exit* BESSIE, *opening and closing the door as if it were mined*]

QUINN.
Keep watch outside now, Bill. Give the door a kick
If you see that bastard coming. If the trunk is there,
And the box is in it, I'll pass you out the key.

[*Exit* BILL *through the Ladies' Entrance.* QUINN *walks around the room as if examining it before taking it over. Kick at the bar door.* QUINN *starts, looks towards the Ladies' Entrance, then back at the bar door. When he sees that someone is opening the door for* BESSIE, *he draws back into the shadows. Enter* BESSIE *with two double whiskeys in her hand*]

BESSIE.
When I say private, I mean private, Percy.
Din't your mother teach you manners—Thanks for nothing!
Pinching a person when a person's helpless!
Shut the door or you'll get a bourbon eyewash.

[*As the bar door shuts behind her, a* MALE VOICE *chants in falsetto*]

MALE VOICE.
Remember St. Peter's,
Remember St. Paul's,
Remember the goil
You kissed in the hall!

BESSIE.
Honest, if there ain't more snots than noses,
I'm the Mother Superior at Good Shepherd's!
Here's your lousy drinks.

[BESSIE *sets the doubles before herself and* QUINN *as she sits down. She pushes the change from the ten across the table.* QUINN *smiles, and pushes it back to her*]

That was a ten-spot.
Them drinks were forty cents.

[QUINN *smiles again, shakes his head, and motions her to take the money. She does, with a shamefaced smile, They lift their glasses to each other and drink*]

QUINN.

How are you since? . . .

BESSIE.

You didn't come here for no dish of tea.

QUINN.

As a matter of fact, I'd like to ask a favor;
And I missed you at the wake. That's why I came.

BESSIE.

You didn't miss me, kid. I didn't go.
Dead people make me nervous. What's this favor?

QUINN.

I hear you've been spelling out May Haggerty
Looking after Ag this past year, Bessie.
I wonder did Ag still have a cowhide trunk?

BESSIE.

A yellow leather trunk? She did.

QUINN.

Where is it?

BESSIE.

It's around the corner in her room in Smith Street,
The Haggertys didn't have time to cart it home.

QUINN.

There's something in it that I'd like to have,
For a keepsake, don't you know. Have you the key?

BESSIE.

The key to Ag's room? Yeah.

QUINN.

Good. Give it here.

BESSIE.

What's in this trunk you want?

QUINN.

An onyx brooch.
It was my poor old mother's. I gave it Ag
When I first met her.

BESSIE.

She ain't got that now.
I seen that tin box that she kept her things in
Two days ago. That's where May got the ring
They're burying Ag in. That was all there was,
That and some old papers—

QUINN.

   I'd like to see those too.

BESSIE.

   Why?

QUINN.

   Why! To make sure that there are no receipts there
   To fall into wrong hands.

BESSIE.

   You go ask Maisie.
   I got no right to give no key to you.
   Those things are hers now.

QUINN.

   Lord! I can't do that.
   She'd go ask Matt; and then I'd never get them!

BESSIE.

   I thought you wanted that thing that was your mother's.

QUINN.

   I do. That onyx ring.

BESSIE.

   You said a brooch.
   There's something in that box that'll cause trouble.
   I'm going to take and give the key to Matt.

QUINN.

   I wouldn't do that, child, if I were you.
   Remember what you told them in the bar,
   You wanted to be alone in here awhile,
   You had a customer? Shall I call the cop,
   What's this his name is, Boylan's on this beat,
   And have you up on lewd solicitation?
   Would you like a three months' course in sewing mailbags
   In the Women's Prison? Bessie, smarten up.
   Hand me the key.
      [BESSIE *rummages in her bag, then throws the key and*
      *the change from the drinks on the table. She rises, and*
      *walks towards the bar door*]
   Where do you think you're going?

BESSIE.

   Ain't you finished with me yet?

QUINN.

   Sit down, my dear.

You'll not leave here till the box is in my hands.
You'd be up the street and at Matt's ear in no time
Like a wasp at a pear. Sit down when I tell you to.

[BESSIE *sits down.* QUINN *opens the door to the Ladies'
Entrance. Sound of running feet.* QUINN *closes the
door, returns to the table, and sits down. He pushes
the change from the drinks back to* BESSIE]

Would you like another drink while we're waiting,
Bessie?—

BESSIE.

I wouldn't drink with you if I had the jimjams
And every crack in the wall had a rat's snout in it.

QUINN.

I know how my morality must offend
A fine upstanding woman like yourself—

[BESSIE *throws her whiskey in* QUINN'S *face, looks terrified, then bursts into tears. With great coolness,* QUINN
*pulls a large silk handkerchief out of his pocket, and
blots his face and clothing*]

You always were a great one for the crying.

BESSIE.

I guess I done some bum things in my life
But this is the first time that I ever ratted.

QUINN.

Ratted, my dear? I don't know what you mean.
I told you all I wanted was old receipts.

[*Sound of running.* BILL *runs through the Ladies' Entrance and hands* QUINN *a tin box.* QUINN *motions* BILL
*back out to keep watch. Exit* BILL. QUINN *puts the box
on the floor and kicks it. It opens. He puts the box on
the table*]

I gave that box to Ag myself. The lock
Was always window dressing. For how could I know
When there might be something here I'd like to see.
Will you look at this? A bundle of scorched letters:
Matt Stanton, Esq., Care of the Gen PO,
Newark, New Jersey. That's where Mattie went
When he slipped Ag's tether in Seagate. And look, the
    necktie

That Josie made for Matt, and a dried camellia,
And a pair of busted garnet rosaries.
And this, dear God in Heaven, look at this,
A letter with no salutation on it
In poor Ag's pothook script. It has no date.
"You're dead to me, because I'm dead myself.
I have been since you left me. If you think
I mean to cause you trouble for what you've done,
You never knew me. You've made your dirty bed.
Lie in it now till you feel the filth in your bones.
I—" No more. No more!—Ag always was too proud.
She never sent it.

BESSIE.

Put them things all back.
They don't belong to you.

QUINN.

Wait now. Wait now.
There's a trick to this false bottom. There it goes.
If it's not the kind of receipt I knew would be here!
It's charred. She meant to burn it. But you can read it.

BESSIE.

Give me them things.

QUINN.

I only want this, Bessie.
  [QUINN *puts the paper in his pocket*]
I'm through now. We can part. Don't worry, child.
I'm putting these things in the box, and Bill will return it
And lock the trunk and room behind him. But mark me.
You're not to say a thing of this to Stanton.
He's a worse suspicious nature than your own;
And we've got to come, you know, to a meeting of minds
At the Clambake on my birthday Sunday, Bessie,
Stanton and I. It would only throw him off
If he heard I had been going through Ag's things.
We wouldn't want that, Bessie; would we, child,
Any more than you'd want that stretch in jail.
I hope you take my meaning—I must leave you, Bessie.
  [QUINN *rises with the box under his arm, and moves
  towards the Ladies' Entrance*]

BESSIE.

I hope you rot in Hell!

QUINN.

You must love me, child,

That you should want my company forever.

> [*Exit* QUINN. *Sound of a hack rolling off.* BESSIE *grabs the money off the table and crumbles it up in her hands. She looks at the door and at the money. She puts the money in her bag and bursts out crying*]

**CURTAIN**

## Act eight

*Twilight, the evening of Sunday, May 1, 1890.*

*The stern of a Coney Island steamer bound for Seagate.
The lower deck is overhung with an upper, upon which
people pass from time to time. There are two oval portraits, one of* STANTON, *the other of* QUINN, *suspended
from the railings of the upper deck, above entrances to
stage right and stage left. Between them, there is a large
shield printed in bold Pontiac reading* For the Public
Good. *The shield and portraits are hung over swagged
bunting. On the lower deck, to stage right, there is a table
with a cluster of carpet-seated folding chairs around it. Set
off a little from them, its back to the table, there is a
carpet-seated armchair.*

HAGGERTY, BOYLE, *and* ANN MULCAHY *are seated at the
table.* HAGGERTY *is wearing a green-and-gold sash with* The
Matthew Stanton Association *printed on it. Enter* MARIA
HAGGERTY *with a large, loaded tea tray, which she sets on
the table. She pours and passes the tea.*

MARIA.
    One hour more, and we'll be into Seagate.
    That's what the deckhand says. I'm glad of that.
    Two hours more of sailing, I declare to God,
    And the babies all would be drunk in their carriages.
HAGGERTY
    Where's missis, May? Will I bring her tea to her?
MARIA.
    No. Let her sleep. She's dozed off in Matt's stateroom.
    The brandy must have killed the queasiness.

ANN.

    Wasn't that a grand speech Ned Quinn made

    Before Matt came, on the pier at Fulton Street,

    When he said he was glad he'd arranged the Clambake late,

    So that he could begin his voyage into the evening,

    His loyal supporters at his side to the end.

BOYLE.

    I'm coming. I'm coming.

    And my belly's full of gin.

    I hear their drunken voices calling

    Old Ned Quinn.

HAGGERTY.

    Don't dance on Quinn's grave, Petey. It's unlucky.

    We're not through this night yet.

MARIA.

    True for you there, Jack!

    They've yet to make the bad blood up between them.

    Father Coyne's been in Quinn's stateroom this past hour,

    And Palsy's been at Matt in the Saloon Bar.

    Quinn wants Mattie to come to *him;* and Matt

    Won't move an inch towards him till Quinn begs his pardon

    For spitting in his face at Aggie's wake.

HAGGERTY.

    Woman, shut up. No call to worry that much.

    If you knew politics as well as I do,

    You'd see they'll both bow down to a higher law

    Before this night is out.

BOYLE.

    St. Albany,

    Pray for us.

HAGGERTY.

    Stop your blaspheming, Petey.

    I don't mean Albany, but the public good—

       [*Enter* BESSIE LEGG, *stage right, in a rush*]

BESSIE.

    Oh, Petey. Petey. Come to the front of the boat.

    You can see the electra light from Coney there,

    And that hotel they built like a elephant.

Why don't youse all come. God, it's beautiful.

[*Exit* BOYLE *and* BESSIE, *the* HAGGERTYS *and* ANN, *stage right*]

BOYLE.

I asked me mother for fifty cents,
To see the elephant jump the fence.
He jumped so high, he touched the sky,
And never come down till the Fourt' of July.

The Fourt' of July when he crashed to earth
He landed near my fat Aunt Gert.
She says you lumpy pig-eyed skunk
Stay off that sauce if you get that drunk.

[*Sound of their laughter fading. Enter* QUINN *and* BILL, *with* FATHER COYNE *following, stage left*]

FATHER COYNE.

You'll meet with him here then?

QUINN.

Yes, Father, I will.
I'll meet with him anywhere. But he'll come to me.

FATHER COYNE.

I'll go and get him.

[*Exit* FATHER COYNE, *stage left.* QUINN *stands back and looks at the shield and posters*]

QUINN.

Look at that now, Billy.
Brooklyn, how are you! For the public good!
A whore for a mayor and a spoiled nun for his lady!
We mustn't let that happen, must we now?—
Pray lose me, Billy. Here's the lot of them.

[*Exit* BILL, *stage right. Enter* FATHER COYNE, *followed by* MURPHY *and* STANTON. STANTON *walks forward, keeping his eyes straight ahead.* QUINN *rakes all three of them with his eyes, then averts his gaze from* STANTON]

QUINN [*To* MURPHY].

If it isn't the Lord Beaconsfield of Brooklyn
With the ten thumbs of his fine Italian hands
Done up in ice-cream gloves. [*He turns suddenly to* STANTON]

How are you since?—
STANTON.

I'll speak no word until he begs my pardon.
I told you, Father. Has he grown so old and silly
He thinks men can do harm without amends!
FATHER COYNE.

Do you want him to get down on his knees to you!
He's lost enough already. Leave him his pride.
MURPHY.

The food in the mouth of the voters is at stake,
It's bread and lard for lunch for thousands, thousands,
If this election's lost; and it will be lost
Unless you join your hands and pull together.
QUINN.

For all that's passed between us, I'll shake his hand,
If he will mine.
MURPHY.

Come on now, Matt. Come on.
QUINN.

When he gets as old as I am, he'll understand
It was death I spat at that night at the wake,
And wish he'd come to terms with an old man's rage.
      [*Pause.* STANTON *suddenly grabs* QUINN's *hand.* QUINN
      *gives him a clumsy bear hug, his face appearing over*
      STANTON's *shoulder*]
STANTON.

Go on now, Ned. You're not that old. You've years.
There's years of use in you.
QUINN.

Matt boy.
MURPHY.

They say that when a man shakes hands with his foe,
A suffering soul shoots out of Purgatory
Straight into Heaven, like a lark from a cage.
FATHER COYNE.

What Council was it, Palsy, declared that dogma?
QUINN.

Sister Mary Asafoetida Doyle,
His fourth-grade teacher.

One keghead gave, and she went on her ear.
She showed us everything she had that time,
The clocks of her stockings to her knicker buttons,
Acres and acres of somersaulting drawers.
Amn't I right, Pete boy?

BOYLE.

You're right as rain.

BESSIE.

You was too young to notice.

[BOYLE *pulls the lower eyelid of his left eye down with
his left forefinger*]

BOYLE.

Do you see green?—
That was the night Matt found Ag playing tigress
To Tiger Quinn.

MARIA.

You shut your mouth, Pete Boyle.

BOYLE.

He said she broke her ass!

HAGGERTY.

That wasn't gossip.
It was a simple statement of pure fact,
To use the lawyer's parlance.

MARIA.

The lawyer's parlance!
Drink your tea, you omadhaun. You're drunk.
Shut up and drink your tea.

HAGGERTY.

"Ah, man! Proud man!
Dressed in a little brief authority"—

[MARIA *gives him what she'd call "one look"*]

I'm drinking it fast as I can! My mouth's destroyed!

BESSIE.

You should see Pete jigging. He's the best there is.
He learned me how.

BOYLE.

Get up and we'll show them, kid.

HAGGERTY.

They'll show us, will they! Stand up to me there, woman,
And show them how we won the branch and bottle

On the pounded clay of every Kerry crossroads.

[MARIA *and* HAGGERTY *begin the jig with* BOYLE *and* BESSIE *doing a little shuffle all their own.* ANN *remains seated, helpless with shamefaced laughter.* KATHLEEN *rises and, standing half in the shadows, watches them with a shy smile. They are too engrossed to notice her*]

BOYLE.

He gave it to Maisie;
It near drove her crazy,
The leg of the duck!
The leg of the duck!

[*Enter* STANTON, *searching for* KATHLEEN. *He looks amused; but when he sees* KATHLEEN, *his face blackens*]

I gave it to Bessie;
She says it was messy,
The leg of the duck!
The leg of the duck!

STANTON.

What kind of song is that in front of my wife?

HAGGERTY.

We didn't see her, Matt.

STANTON.

Are you blind or what!
You, you narrow-back plug, with your mouth of slime,
You can slather this one all that you've a mind to,
But there are others born with a little shame!—
I'd be amazed at you two, May and Jack,
If I'd not noticed the liberties you've been taking
These past few months. There'll be an end to that.

HAGGERTY.

All right. All right. There'll be an end to that. . . .
Come, May and Ann, we'd best go inside now.

BOYLE.

Wait; we'll come too. I'll lug these things for you.

[*All four move towards the exit to stage right*]

KATHLEEN.

Maria, dear, come back in a few minutes.
I need you. Please. I'm not myself at all.

MARIA.

Yes, ma'am. Yes, ma'am.

[*Exit* BOYLE *and* BESSIE, HAGGERTY *and* MARIA]

KATHLEEN.

    Beg their pardon, Mattie.

    They didn't see me; and what harm if they did,

    They were only dancing.

STANTON.

    Things have changed now, Kate.

    You have to demand respect, or you won't get it.

    From this day on, they're to learn their place and keep it.

    We're with them, but not of them. —Kate, I've won!

    Quinn and I made it up and he wants to meet you.

KATHLEEN.

    If that's what winning means, God help us both.

STANTON.

    What's the matter with you?

KATHLEEN.

    It's being aboard a ship,

    It's that, I suppose. When I watch the wake of the boat

    Spread out like a pigeon's tail with the wind going
        through it,

    I think of all that's left behind or canceled,

    And the heart of me feels pillaged in my breast.

    The farther away I go from what is past,

    The more I stiffen with the sense of danger.

    I look around me at all, and want to hold it:

    May dancing there with her back straight as a bowstring

    Despite the tug of age on all her bones,

    And the dazzle of Jack's eyes as they browsed her face,

    And Ann Mulcahy helpless with pure joy,

    And that dusty weed of a boy and Bessie Legg,

    Playing their little games like aging children.

    There's not a thing that is not riches, Mattie,

    And it all goes from us, darling, like those days

    On the boat from England, glazed with salt and sunshine,

    We melted first into light like flame and candle,

    It all goes from us. Hold me, Mattie, hold me.

    Don't thrust me from you as you just did them.

STANTON.

    Katie, I'd sooner hack the hands from my wrists

    Than thrust you from me. As for what's been lost,

God in Heaven be with the days I lay
Like a bee in a lily with the ocean's glitter
Live gold on the stateroom panels. They were good.
But what's ahead, you'll not believe till you see it.
We've won! We've won, Kate! Quinn's arranged our
    landing:
You'll be breathing music like the saints in Heaven
As you walk ashore. But let him tell it you. [STANTON
    *kisses her*]
What is that? Brandy, that I smell on you?

KATHLEEN.
I took a glass or two for the seasickness.

STANTON.
Promise me on your dead parents' grave,
You'll drink no more from this time forward, Kate.
There's no sight worse on earth than a drunken woman.
I know it to my shame, from her that's dead. [*Pause*]

KATHLEEN.
. . . I promise, Mattie. [STANTON *kisses her hand*]

STANTON.
There now. I'll get the mayor.
    [*Exit* STANTON, *stage left.* BESSIE *emerges from the
    shadows, stage right, and hurries over to* KATHLEEN]

BESSIE.
You mind if I sit down? Remember me?

KATHLEEN.
Of course, I do, Miss Legg. Please do sit down.
I'm pleased to see you.

BESSIE.
It isn't Miss. It's Mrs.

KATHLEEN.
Yes. Mrs. Legg. Of course.

BESSIE.
Was he that mad
Just for that dirty song that Petey sung,
Or was it something that Quinn said to him
That he took out on us? You know what I mean.

KATHLEEN.
No, I don't, Miss Legg. I don't know what you mean.

BESSIE.

Not Miss. It's Mrs.

KATHLEEN.

What would the mayor say?

Matt's just gone in to get him. They're friends now.

BESSIE.

They're friends now. Yeah. They're friends.

KATHLEEN.

What is it,

Please?

BESSIE.

Oh, he hurted my feelings, see, the way he talked,

And I got nervous. I'm a nervous girl.

That, and you know, what you said up my flat that night,

About there was some mix-up in the marriage.

It sounded so romantic when you said it,

"The man I left my God and country to marry."

I couldn't make it out. You was awful . . . you know.

KATHLEEN.

If I said that, I was awful drunk indeed.

You didn't believe me, did you, Mrs. Legg?

BESSIE.

Oh, no. Oh, no. But I don't know where you was

Before I went and took you up my flat.

I thought that maybe Quinn got wind of it—

KATHLEEN.

I hope you've not repeated what I said.

You haven't, have you?

   [BESSIE *rises*]

BESSIE.

Excuse me. I'll be going.

KATHLEEN.

Now don't be that way.

BESSIE.

What do you think I am,

Some kind of rat. . . . I thought you was a sport.

You're like the rest. . . . Oh, I seen you looking round

When I brought you back up my flat that night.

It's not my fault the place is such a mess.

I only rent it, see? It isn't mine.

And we only just got in when you passed out—
I mean, fell off to sleep. . . . I didn't like
To make no noise. . . . It's hard to keep things nice.
There was a time I had things beautiful.
When Legg was living with me, Legg, you know,
My husband . . . I passed the flat we used to have
On Baltic Street and Court the other day.
We lived in it two years. I kept it spotless. . . .
The windows all were dirty when I passed,
The windows of the flat we used to have,
I mean. All dirty . . . It nearly broke my heart.
I had a lovely home. I used to have . . .
Canary bird. Piano. Everything—
It's not my fault Legg left. Where he is, Christ knows.
Maybe he's dead. I hope to God he is,
May God forgive me, but I hope he is!
    [BESSIE *bursts into tears.* KATHLEEN *rises and comforts her. Enter* BOYLE, *stage right*]

KATHLEEN.
Oh, Bessie, Bessie, God in Heaven help us.

BOYLE.
Who turned on the hydrants?

BESSIE.
Hello, Petey.
Buy me a drink or something, will you, ha?

BOYLE.
Sure, kid, sure.
    [BOYLE *walks to the exit, stage right.* KATHLEEN *and* BESSIE *look at one another*]

KATHLEEN.
Goodbye.

BOYLE.
You coming, Little Eva?
    [*Exit* BOYLE. BESSIE *walks to the exit, then turns to* KATHLEEN *again*]

BESSIE.
Don't worry, missis. Don't. There ain't no call.
There ain't no one can hurt you. You're a lady.
    [*Exit* BESSIE. KATHLEEN *walks to the rail and looks at the wake of the steamer. Sound of a ship's bell. Enter*

MARIA *with a water glass of brandy*]

DECKHAND.

Seagate. Seagate. In ten minutes. Seagate.

MARIA.

I brought you this.

KATHLEEN.

I won't. I promised Matt—

MARIA.

House devil and street saint, sure, he's worse than Quinn!
He's down there now with Quinn playing king of England.
He traipses up to me in the Saloon Bar
And takes my hand and thrusts ten dollars in it.
He's not dead yet! There'll come a time he'll see
There are some things in the world you can't take back.
If I could get a job, we'd move. We would—
   [KATHLEEN *presses her fist to her mouth and sinks into
   the armchair*]
Good Jesus, Mrs. Stanton, what's the matter!
Promise or no, best have a drop of this.
   [KATHLEEN *downs half the glass of brandy*]

KATHLEEN.

Promise or no.

MARIA.

You'll feel the good of that.
   [*Pause. Sound of ship's bell and of the paddle churning
   water for the turn inshore*]

KATHLEEN.

Do you know what I am thinking about, Maria?
How it is this time of year back home in Ireland.
The foxglove has come out in the boreens,
And the seals are barking on the mossy rocks
Below Mount Brandon. On this very day,
They'll dress the loveliest girl in all the village
In a wedding gown, and lead her to the church
To put a crown of roses on the Virgin.
And all the children in Communion clothes,
White suits and dresses, smilax wreaths, pearl prayer
   books,
Will stand around her as she climbs the ladder,
And sing that song that always makes me cry:

Daughter of a mighty Father,
Maiden, patron of the May,
Angel forms around thee gather,
*Macula non est in te.*
*Macula non est in te:* Never spot was found in thee.
    [KATHLEEN *breaks into tears*]

MARIA.
    Oh, Mrs. Stanton.

KATHLEEN.
    What's the matter with me?
    My ears are ringing like a field of weeds,
    Noontime in August, when the sun's raw fire.

MARIA.
    I wonder is it flashes.

KATHLEEN.
    At my age!

MARIA.
    More likely kicks. Are you all together, missis.

KATHLEEN.
    Am I what, Maria?

MARIA.
    Have you missed your term?
    Don't bite your lip and blush. You're not a nun.

KATHLEEN.
    No, I've not missed my term.
        [*Enter* QUINN, *stage left. He stands looking over at*
        MARIA *and* KATHLEEN, *unnoticed by them at first*]

MARIA.
    Then it's the dead.

KATHLEEN.
    The dead?

MARIA.
    The dead. Who do you know needs prayers?
    They say that's how the dead call on the living,
    By whining in their blood.

KATHLEEN.
    Poor Agnes Hogan,
    The Lord have mercy on her and preserve her . . .
        [KATHLEEN *notices* QUINN]
    Don't look so troubled, May. I'm better now.

You know there's a bottle of that Worth perfume
Down in the stateroom in my reticule.
Would you bring it to me, dear, with a handkerchief.
   [*Exit* MARIA, *stage right.* QUINN *walks over to* KATH-
   LEEN]
Good evening to you, Mrs. Stanton. May I?
KATHLEEN.
   Please do, your honor.
      [QUINN *sits down*]
QUINN.
   Matt's stuck in the bar,
   Buying drinks for all the upright voters,
   So I came up alone. It would fill your eye
   To see him there. You'd think he trusted them!
KATHLEEN.
   God forbid he shouldn't trust them, Mayor.
QUINN.
   If you think, my dear, not trusting people's a sin,
   You'd best get out of politics.
KATHLEEN.
   It's the worst sin.
   Without trust, there's no faith or hope or love.
QUINN.
   That kind of talk is like a penny cream puff,
   All wind and whey, and deadly when it sours.
   Trust no one. No one. Let no man too close.
   They are as quick to fury as to love.
   Once give them purchase, they will pull you down,
   And for a sigh let slip, for a ruptured smile.
   They're a pack of wicked mutts that go for shadows.
   There is no reason in their ugliness,
   No justice in their rage. Trust no one, missis.
KATHLEEN.
   Who are "they"? Is it my husband, Mayor,
   Or old John Haggerty or Mister Murphy?
   From what you say, you think the people devils
   Who've honored you as mayor of this city
   For thirty years. Do you really think them that?
QUINN.
   I do . . . And Stanton is the worst of all!—

KATHLEEN.

  Do you think I'll sit and listen to your slander!

QUINN.

  "Do you think this? Do you think this?" Or "Don't you?"
  "Faith and hope and love," and I mustn't slander—
  You're awful pious for a woman living
  With your husband in a state of Mortal Sin;
  And a Mortal Sin it is for a Catholic woman
  To marry a man outside the Catholic Church.
  I don't know much religion, but I know that,
   As, I might add, do all our holy voters. [*Pause*]

KATHLEEN.

  I suppose you must have got that from Miss Legg.

QUINN.

  No, my dear. From England. Where you did it.
  I've known it years. I hoped I'd not have to use it,
  But need is need. And it's not Miss. It's Mrs.

KATHLEEN.

  You rejoice when people go wrong, don't you, Mayor!

QUINN.

  We've no time now to talk morality.
  We'll wait for Stanton, then go get Father Coyne
  And the rest, and walk down to my stateroom
  And arrange what we will say. I've bought off those
   accountants,
  Paid back that little sum from the funds I borrowed,
  And the books are doctored. All that now remains is
  To find a way to break the joyous news
  That I will run again. I think Matt should do it!

KATHLEEN.

  If you're a man who'd ruin two reputations
  To gain your ends, what have you done with your life?

QUINN.

  What I have done with my life is my affair!
  Do you think I'll let that bastard have my office?
  I loved the woman that he took from me,
  And I let her go with him, but I kept my office.
  And I heard them here in Seagate making sport
  Of all I'd done for them, but I kept mum,
  And I kept my office. And I watched the poor bitch die

While he grew high and mighty, but I kept my office.
Keep my office I will to the day I die,
And God help those who try to take it.

KATHLEEN.

Make sense.
The scandal about the funds is a public fact;
But you and Mrs. Legg are the only ones
Who know about the marriage. Spare my husband.
Spare him, Mayor. God will bless you for it.

QUINN.

Sure, that's what Aggie said when she pleaded for him,
The first time that she met him, the poor slob,
Did God bless her, missis?

KATHLEEN.

They'll never let you run!
They'll gang up with the Party of Reform
And crucify you.

QUINN.

We'll see about that, missis.
Do you think I'll let them turn their backs on me
And turn their backs on me for the likes of him,
A narrow-back pimp, who rose to where he is
On the broken heart of the woman that I loved!

KATHLEEN.

Pour all the venom you want into my ears!
The Party will stand by us! They'll stand by us.
They'll cover us on the marriage. And they should!
For though we were not married in the Church,
May God forgive us, we are man and wife! [*Pause*]

QUINN.

I wouldn't be too sure of that now, missis.

KATHLEEN.

What do you mean by that, you lying devil?
     [QUINN *pulls a scorched paper out of his pocket, and
     throws it into* KATHLEEN's *lap*]

QUINN.

I'm a lying devil, am I! Look at that!
Look at it, why don't you. Are you blind!
How can you be his wife when he married Ag
In the Sacred Heart in Newark in '86!

[*Repeated sound of ship's bell. People are gathering, preparing to get off. Sound of winches, lowering gangplank.* KATHLEEN *sits as if shot, the paper in her hands*]

DECKHAND.

Seagate! Seagate! Everybody off.

KATHLEEN.

All gone. All gone.

[KATHLEEN *rises suddenly, the paper in her hand, swaying with shock, as if drunk. The disembarking passengers look curiously at her*]

God damn the day I met him.
God damn this mouth that spoke him fair, these eyes
That flooded my blood with his face. God damn this flesh
That kindled in his arms, and this heart that told me,
Say yes, say yes, to everything he asked.
It would have been better had I not been born.

[QUINN *grabs the paper out of* KATHLEEN's *hand and puts it back into his pocket fast*]

QUINN.

For God's sake, missis. Don't take on this way.
We have to keep this quiet. There's people watching.

[QUINN *runs to the table and fetches the half-finished glass of brandy.* KATHLEEN, *still swaying, her arms at her side, automatically accepts the glass from him and, as if by reflex, presses it to her breast. She does not see the people who are staring at her. Enter* STANTON *with* MURPHY *and* FATHER COYNE, *a group of voters around him*]

STANTON.

It isn't in the courts reform must work
But in each striving heart . . .

[STANTON *sees the people staring at* KATHLEEN *and* QUINN. *He breaks away from those around him and hurries over to her. He speaks in a steely whisper*]

Look at you. Look at you, for the love of Jesus.
In front of all these people. You're owl-eyed drunk,
With the bands about to fife us off the boat!
I'll get Maria to help you sober up.
Quinn and I will walk ashore together.
You are not fit for decent men to be seen with!

[KATHLEEN *smashes the glass to the floor. She speaks in a ringing voice*]

KATHLEEN.
Did you think that—
Did you think that when you lied to me in London,
And I let you marry me in the City Hall,
Because you said you couldn't wait for the banns,
You wanted me so much! Did you think that
When you had me in the bed in sacrilege
Above the corpse of your true-wedded wife,
Ag Hogan!

[*Hostile reaction from the crowd. The sound of the bands suddenly blares out*]

CURTAIN

## Act nine

*Very late the same night. The double set. There is a dim
light in the hall by the Haggertys' door; and the light in
Stanton's flat is on full. There are two trunks in the parlor,
one already locked, the other open.* KATHLEEN *moves in
and out of the bedroom, packing. Enter* FATHER COYNE
*and* MURPHY, *the* HAGGERTYS, BOYLE, *and* BESSIE. *The*
HAGGERTYS *and* BOYLE *are laden down with baskets and
pillows done up in steamer blankets, and have the tired,
apprehensive look of new immigrants.* HAGGERTY *sets down
his basket and unlocks the door.*

MARIA.
Open it, can't you! He may be right behind us.
And I'll not stand in the one hall with him!—
We'll be out of here before the week is done,
If I have to beg to do it—

FATHER COYNE.
Now, Maria—

MARIA.
Now Maria, Father? Are we saints!
If he got on his knees to me, I'd not forgive him!

MURPHY.
It's grand of you to let us wait here for him.
You must be tired.
[HAGGERTY *opens the door*]

MARIA.
I'll not close an eye
Until I'm out from underneath this roof!

HAGGERTY.
Come in the parlor, Father. I'll light the fire.

You're famished with the cold. May, bring the whiskey.
Come in now, Pete. Come in all.

> [MARIA, FATHER COYNE, MURPHY, BOYLE, *and* BESSIE
> *pass through the* portière, *followed by* HAGGERTY.
> *Pause.* KATHLEEN *moves in and out of the parlor, pack-
> ing. Enter* STANTON. *He runs lightly up the stairs and
> into the parlor. He looks at the trunks and falls into a
> chair. Enter* KATHLEEN, *with some clothes. She sees
> him, averts her gaze, and puts the clothes into the
> trunk*]

STANTON.
Where do you think you're going!

> [KATHLEEN *passes back into the bedroom for more
> clothes and returns with them*]

Answer me!

KATHLEEN.
I'm going home.

STANTON.
Your home is here with me.

KATHLEEN.
You haven't even the grace to beg my pardon!
How can you look me in the face again!

STANTON.
It's I should ask that question. It's all over.
They gave the nomination back to Quinn.
He brought me to the pitch of hope and betrayed me.
And you stood by and let him do it to me!

KATHLEEN.
It ill becomes you, man, to talk betrayals.
Can you tell me whom you've known you've not be-
trayed!—
You killed Ag Hogan. But you won't kill me!

STANTON.
I had the right to leave her. She played me false—

KATHLEEN.
Had you the right to marry me? The right
To cut me off from all that I hold holy?

STANTON.
Would "all that you hold holy," our precious Church,

Have granted me a divorce from Agnes Hogan,
An adulteress!—

KATHLEEN.

What kind of man are you!
That woman died without the Sacraments
Because in her last fever she was afraid
If she confessed her sins she might betray you.
She died cut off from God to spare you harm.
And you have the worst word in your mouth for her.
Do you know why? Because you're no good, man.
You waited for your chance to throw her over.
You saw that with her you'd be nothing. Nothing.
You had to be the mayor of this city
And she was in the way. You married me
To make yourself respectable again.
That's the only reason.

STANTON.

I loved . . . I loved you, Kate.
Kathleen, I've nothing left.
I need you.

KATHLEEN.

Yes. To patch your kick-down fences.
But I have my pride too!—

STANTON.

Go then, God damn you!
Do you think I'll kneel on the floor and beg your help!
I never begged for help from man or God,
And I won't now. You'll not drive me to my knees!

KATHLEEN.

To sit and tell me you have nothing left!
No more do I! You've taken it out of me
By demanding more than anyone can give.
That's what evil is,
The starvation of a heart with nothing in it
To make the world around it nothing too.
You never begged from man or God! You took!
You've taken all your life without return!
You never gave yourself to a single soul
For all your noble talk.—Even in bed
You stole me blind!—

STANTON.

    Get out of here! Get out!

    You're not a woman. You're a would-be nun!

    You were from the beginning.

KATHLEEN.

    God help you, Matt.

       [KATHLEEN *closes and locks the second trunk, and puts*
       *on her hat*]

    I'll book my passage quickly as I can.

    There's nothing in those trunks your money bought me.

    Leave May the key. The Express will call for them.

    I put the jewelry in the velvet box

    In the top drawer of the bureau by the window;

    And left the dresses and the sable coat

    Hanging in your wardrobe. And that perfume

    You bought me's on the vanity.

       [KATHLEEN *walks out the door to the head of the stairs*]

    Don't look so black.

    You're free now, Matt. That's what you always wanted.

    Marry if you like.

       [KATHLEEN *almost breaks down*]

    I'm not your wife. I never was.

STANTON.

    You mean to leave me here alone!

KATHLEEN.

    I'm sorry, man;

    But that's the way we all are, but for God.

       [STANTON *rushes out the door and grabs* KATHLEEN]

STANTON.

    You'll not leave me! I'll see to that!

       [*Blackout.* KATHLEEN *screams and hits the bottom of*
       *the stairs.* MARIA *rushes into the kitchen with a kero-*
       *sene lamp in her hand, followed by* HAGGERTY, FATHER
       COYNE, MURPHY, BOYLE, *and* BESSIE. BOYLE *is carrying*
       *a glass of whiskey.* HAGGERTY *flings open the door,*
       *revealing* KATHLEEN *at the foot of the stairs in a heap,*
       *and* STANTON *halfway down the flight in a near faint*]

HAGGERTY.

    Good Jesus, May! How did it happen, man?

    Give me your whiskey, Pete. Poor Mrs. Stanton.

KATHLEEN.

Ah, Jack. And May. And is that the Father there?
Amn't I a shame and a disgrace
To get so legless drunk I fall downstairs
Like an unwatched child—

STANTON.

Oh, Katie. Katie, Katie.
Are you hurt bad.

KATHLEEN.

Sh!

HAGGERTY.

Petey, go get Boylan on the beat,
And tell him to get a doctor that's still up,
There's been an accident—

KATHLEEN.

That's right. That's right.
I caught my heel on the baluster and fell.

BOYLE.

I see a man fall off a hoist through a hold
On Pier Sixteen down in the Erie Basin.
His head was bent that way. Her neck is broke—

HAGGERTY.

Don't stand there nattering. Go get the doctor.
　　[*Exit* BOYLE, *running*]

MURPHY.

I'd best go too. I've a thing to do, I must.
　　[STANTON *takes* KATHLEEN *from* HAGGERTY *and cradles
　　her in his arms*]

STANTON.

Will you get away from her so I can hold her!

HAGGERTY.

Be careful with her—

STANTON.

Katie, you were right.
I've taken without returning all my life.
And I'd the face to call Ned Quinn corrupt!
The harm I've done and called it good! The harm!
I saw that harm in Aggie Hogan's face,
And now I see it in yours. Can you forgive me?

KATHLEEN.

Hush now, Matt darling. Toc-sha-shin-inish:
Let others talk. We'll keep our own safe counsel.
There's been shame enough already without more—
Do you know what stopped my breath up on the landing?
I love you still. I thought of us on the boat from England.
There's few have been as happy as we were—
Is that the Father there? I want the Father.

[*Enter* BOYLE *with the policeman,* BOYLAN, *and a*
DOCTOR]

FATHER COYNE.

Here I am, child. Here I am right beside you.

[FATHER COYNE *leans over* KATHLEEN, *putting on his*
*stole as he does so*]

KATHLEEN.

Oh . . . my God . . . I am . . . heartily sorry
For . . . having . . . offended Thee—

[STANTON *pulls* KATHLEEN *away from the priest in a*
*tight embrace*]

STANTON.

You're not to die!

KATHLEEN.

The boat from England, Mattie . . .

[STANTON *kisses her on the mouth, and hugs her to*
*him, his hand on the back of her head*]

STANTON.

Yes, we'll have that again. I'll make it up to you.
I'll make it up. We'll go back home to Ireland.
I'll give the Court Café to Jack to run.
And we'll go home, and take a high-stooped house
In one of them good squares, I mean, those squares . . .

[STANTON *loosens his embrace to look in* KATHLEEN's
*face. Her head falls to the side*]

Why don't you answer me? Don't turn away!—
Where in the name of Jesus Christ's the doctor?

*The* DOCTOR *kneels and puts his ear to* KATHLEEN's
*chest. He rises with a negative shudder of his head to*
HAGGERTY. FATHER COYNE *motions* BOYLAN *and the*
DOCTOR *out with his head. Exit both. Pause*]

HAGGERTY.

She's dead, you know, Matt boy.

STANTON.

You're lying, man!

Do you think I have no feeling in my flesh!

She's warm as a newborn child. We're going home—

[STANTON *loosens his embrace again.* KATHLEEN's *hair comes down*]

I've sprung her hairpins on her—God in heaven,

I was making love to nothing. She is dead.

FATHER COYNE.

Get up please, son; let me finish giving her

Conditional absolution—

[STANTON *tightens his embrace on* KATHLEEN *again and glares at the priest like a cornered animal*]

STANTON.

Absolve *her,* Father!

Absolve your God, why don't you, He did this!

When she found out the marriage was no good,

She packed her trunks upstairs. She meant to leave me.

She never died in drink! She never fell!

I flung her down the stairs to keep her here.

I thought she'd sprain her ankle—Don't come near me.

I'll spit in your face if you come near me, Father—

FATHER COYNE.

Go easy, son. Go easy.

HAGGERTY.

Get up now, Matt.

FATHER COYNE.

Yes, Matt. You have to follow Boylan to the precinct.

When there's a question of murder, it's the law.

[STANTON *relinquishes* KATHLEEN *to* FATHER COYNE, *and rises.* STANTON *turns his back on his dead wife and the priest as if in mortal offense*]

STANTON.

Maria, lay my wife out on the bed

With some degree of decency, and spill

That bottle of the Worth perfume she loved

Over that bedspread that she was so proud of,

And sit with her until the coroner comes . . .

I will not have her stink, or lie alone—
[*With great difficulty,* STANTON *brings himself to turn
and look at his wife and the priest*]
With all her sins on my head, and the world a desert.
[STANTON *throws his arms out in a begging embrace
and falls on his knees. Enter* MURPHY *and* QUINN, *un-
noticed by* STANTON]
Maisie, Jack. And Petey. Bessie, Father,
Help me, for the love of Jesus, help me.
Dear God in Heaven, help me and forgive me.
[*The* HAGGERTYS *rush to him and grasp his hands.*
HAGGERTY *raises him, and relinquishes him to* FATHER
COYNE]

MURPHY.
God have mercy on her. Our election's lost.
[STANTON *wheels around. His eyes meet with* QUINN'S]

QUINN.
I never meant to do this to you, Matt.
I didn't know. I never meant to do it.
I only meant to look out for my good.
I'm nobody. I'm no one, if I'm not the mayor.
I'm nothing, Matt. I'm nobody. I'm nothing—
[STANTON *rakes* QUINN'S *face with a blind man's stare.*
*Exit* STANTON]

FATHER COYNE.
Why are you standing round like imbeciles!
Carry her up the stairs, and lay her out
As Mattie asked you to.
[HAGGERTY *and* BOYLE *lift* KATHLEEN, *and start up the
stairs with her.* MARIA *follows, her mouth in the crook
of her elbow, shaking with tears.* QUINN *and* MURPHY,
BESSIE, *and* FATHER COYNE *look on from below*]
Well you may cry!
Cry for us all while you're at it. Cry for us all!

CURTAIN

# WE BOMBED

# IN NEW HAVEN

by *Joseph Heller*

*To Joe Stein*
*who encouraged and helped me.*

## Act one

*The setting on stage is of an ordinary American Air Force briefing room in a bungalow in a war somewhere.*

*Even before the house lights have been fully dimmed, there is the noise of heavy objects being moved about on stage in back of the curtain. The curtain starts to rise; it jerks to a stop about halfway up, as though jamming by accident, or as though the person in control of the curtain has just realized it has been lifted a few minutes prematurely, for all of the stage scenery has not yet been put in place.*

*The premature lifting of the curtain has exposed about seven or eight airmen, dressed in flight suits and parachute harnesses, in the act of moving props and parts of the set out on stage into proper position. One by one they stop with looks of surprise and intense embarrassment at the realization that they are now in view of the audience. They stare helplessly, as though powerless to decide what to do next. A dull, even light falls over everything, for the correct illumination for the play has not yet been adjusted, either.*

*The briefing room is composed of three separate areas. One, on a slightly raised platform, is the main briefing section; it serves also as the Major's office and contains a long, large work-table, or desk, and several chairs. There is a blackboard on one wall and layers of maps, some on rollers, on another. There is a large globe in a floor stand near the corner of the desk. Written in chalk on the blackboard are columns of names that include those of most of the characters in the play, as well as the true surnames of many of the people connected with the actual production.*

*When the curtain rises,* THE MAJOR *is sitting at the desk with a sullen and preoccupied expression, working intently*

*over a manuscript that will eventually turn out to be the
script of the same play that is now being performed. He is
a somber, imposing man in his fifties, and his enigmatic
poise and self-confidence suggest a knowledge and authority that are ominous and inscrutable.*

*The second part of the briefing room is the general as-
sembly area, in which most of the indoor action by the men
will take place. It is almost a room apart from the area in
which* THE MAJOR *is working. It contains a window, some
benches, and a number of short sections of joined seats and
desks, similar to those found in children's schoolrooms, although these, rather than arranged in rows, stand around in
a haphazard lack of design, as though exactly as left by the
last people to use them. One section of two joined chairs
has actually been tipped over and left lying on the floor. On
one of the walls is a large sign that says "*NO SMOKING.*" A
few of the men were working in this area to create this dis-
orderly effect when the curtain started up and brought
them to a halt. And at least one of them is smoking.
Throughout the play, a few of the enlisted men will light
cigarettes whenever they are alone, extinguish them quickly
when one of the two officers appears.*

*The premature lifting of the curtain has also caught*
CAPTAIN STARKEY *in the process of entering and crossing
through this area toward* THE MAJOR. STARKEY *is a man in
his forties, and he is smoking a slim cigar with an air that is
placid and slightly jaunty. He carries a brown leather portfolio and a folded copy of* The New York Times (*or of the
local newspaper that would be most easily recognized by
the audience*), *and he is moving across the stage toward*
THE MAJOR *in much the same self-assured manner of any
well-placed civilian executive reporting for his day's or evening's work. He stops instantly with a look of sharp amazement when he discovers that he is already in view of the
audience, obviously a few minutes earlier than he had expected. His first reaction is to remove the cigar from his
mouth, as though to hide it, and he looks about in confusion.*

*The third section of the briefing room is the clear area
connecting the other two. It is bordered in the back by the*

*wall of the building, which contains the doorway, some
windows, some posters, and a bulletin board. A unit flag
stands here, bearing a garish cartoon symbol. It is mainly
this part of the stage set that has not yet been put in place.*

  *Flustered and awkward, all the men on stage stand gaz-
ing at* STARKEY, *as though awaiting instructions.* STARKEY
*surveys the mishap glumly; he looks at the men, the half-
raised curtain, the observing audience, and he frowns with
annoyance at the realization that something has gone wrong
with things from the very beginning. He mutters to himself
disconsolately and then calls out politely to* THE MAJOR.

STARKEY. Oh, Jesus. Major?
  [THE MAJOR *looks up from his work and studies the
  situation with a glower of severe displeasure. He
  glances at his watch, ponders a few seconds, and then
  nods curtly, giving a signal that* STARKEY *interprets
  immediately*]
Okay, men! Let's go to work! Finish it up—fast, fast!
  [*The men respond hurriedly and resume toiling with
  the flats and props that will constitute the completed
  set. As* STARKEY *watches, they slide the remaining sections of wall where they belong, make a few final ad-
  justments with the windows, posters, and chairs, and
  then vanish through the door or out into the wings by
  darting in front of the scenery.*

  *Satisfied,* STARKEY *resumes walking calmly across
  stage to* THE MAJOR'S *desk, still uncertain what to do
  with his cigar. With a sidelong glance at the audience,
  he crushes it out finally and lets it fall into a wastebas-
  ket. He takes a corner of the desk for his own use. He
  puts the newspaper down and starts to unzip his portfolio. The curtain starts moving again and opens fully,
  the lights adjust to throw the brightest illumination on*
  STARKEY *and* THE MAJOR, *and the play proper begins.*

  THE MAJOR *continues working in silence over the
  open manuscript before him, copying passages on the
  top page of a yellow pad. His desk is a litter of maps,
  documents, and ornamental objects that serve as toys
  or paperweights. These include miniatures of the Eif-*

*fel Tower, the leaning tower of Pisa, the Empire State
Building; there are three billiard balls on the desk,
some sets of colorful toy soldiers in the uniforms of
imperial fighters of another age, a few upright missiles
on their launching pads, and several pieces of conven-
tional cannon. There is a glossy souvenir Pan American jet airliner, a hand grenade, and a 37-millimeter
shell.*

*While* THE MAJOR *writes,* STARKEY *removes a clipboard from his portfolio and then a silver whistle attached to a cord that he slips around his neck. He
drifts casually to the wall containing the maps and
rolls one down. It is a map of the world.*

*A large clock in the briefing room keeps actual time
accurately throughout the play.* STARKEY *studies the
map of the world]*

Well, Major? Where are they bombing today?

MAJOR. Constantinople.

[STARKEY *takes a puzzled second glance at the wall
map]*

STARKEY. There is no Constantinople. It's Istanbul now.

MAJOR. I know that.

STARKEY. Then why are we going there?

MAJOR. We're not going there. They are.

STARKEY. Why are *they* going there?

MAJOR [*Tapping his manuscript*]. Because it says so. See?

STARKEY. So that's what we have to call it. Is it dangerous?

MAJOR. Not for those who survive. For those who don't—
well, I'd call that dangerous, wouldn't you?

STARKEY. Will anybody be killed there?

[THE MAJOR *nods*]

And we just go on working. If somebody's going to die
today, why must it be over something that doesn't even
exist, like Constantinople? Why don't we at least call it
*Istanbul?* Ha, ha—at least *that's* a name worth dying for.

MAJOR. It says Constantinople.

STARKEY. Can I ask a question?

MAJOR [*With a slight smile*]. You are.

STARKEY. I'm a pretty easygoing guy, Major. I think you

know that. I don't complain, and I do everything I'm told, and all in all I know I have a pretty soft time of it here. *And* I have the second prettiest girl on the base, who is also pretty soft. But every now and then I think I do want to ask a question. May I? Who's in charge here?

MAJOR. I am.

STARKEY. No. Who's the boss? Who's running the show?

MAJOR. I am.

STARKEY. The whole show. Who is the person who tells you to tell me to tell them that they've got to go today to—God help me!—*Constantinople?*

MAJOR. The colonel.

STARKEY. Which colonel?

MAJOR. Does that make any difference?

STARKEY. No. But who tells the colonel? The general. Who tells the general? I know—another general. Major, let me in on the biggest military secret of all. Who's really in charge and who's really responsible?

   [*Instead of replying,* THE MAJOR *smiles slightly again, looks at the clock on the wall, then at his wristwatch*]

MAJOR. What time is it?

STARKEY [*Sighs with disappointment*]. Do you want the men?

   [THE MAJOR *tears from the pad the sheet of paper on which he has been writing and hands it to* STARKEY, *who affixes it to his clipboard*]

MAJOR. Yes. There's work to be done.

STARKEY. I'll get them. [*Blows his whistle shrilly to summon the men*] There'll be time. Yes . . . I think . . .

   [*Carrying his clipboard,* STARKEY *walks leisurely into the assembly area, talking without pause, reciting formally the lines that follow. The door opens and the men begin filing in, carrying map cases and flight kits and wearing combat uniforms. They include the same men we saw earlier placing the scenery. They move toward the chairs and benches, some kidding with each other noisily, some very serious.*

   HENDERSON, *a young sergeant, seems the most confident and discerning, and there is a cocky self-assurance about him as he saunters forward that suggests a vain and mocking arrogance.* BAILEY, *a well-*

*built corporal, is a few years older than* HENDERSON; *he is something of a clown and athlete who is susceptible to sudden silences and sudden changes of temperament.* SINCLAIR, *another corporal, is surly and pulls away angrily when one of the others tries playfully to jostle with him.* FISHER, *a private, is the youngest and seems earnest, naïve, and polite. All of these men are young, about thirty or under.*

*The oldest of the others who enter is* PFC. JOE CARSON, *a career soldier almost ready for retirement, which puts his age near sixty. Service stripes indicating length of service form a long row up his arm and contrast with the single insignificant stripe designating his rank. He is, all in all, a soft, somewhat stupefied old man of a different era who seems to have neither affinity nor affection for any of the younger men in the group of soldiers of which he is a part. He is frequently puzzled by many of the things the others discuss, and he has the surprising habit of bursting pleasurably into song whenever a cue presents itself.*

*The five other men who comprise the group are as silent and slow as idiots; in fact, they are* IDIOTS. *With sparse exceptions, these* IDIOTS *will utter no sounds throughout the play, and there is something vaguely oafish and wooden about their movements as they join in with the others to obey the same orders and go through the same actions with the same willingness and competence.*

CAPTAIN STARKEY, *who is reciting his lines without interruption, and with considerable self-satisfaction, speaks first to the men as they enter and then directly to the audience.* THE MAJOR *continues studying his manuscript, turning a page every few seconds as though reading along with the spoken words, and glancing up from time to time to observe the others.*

HENDERSON, *instead of following the others to the benches and chairs, moves toward* STARKEY *with a contemptuous smirk and stands waiting beside him as Starkey concludes his recitation to the audience with a proud flourish]*

". . . . . . . . . . . there will be time
To prepare a face to meet the faces that you meet;
There will be time to murder and create,
And time for all the works and days of hands
That lift and drop a question on your plate;
Time for you and time for me,
And time yet for a hundred indecisions,
And for a hundred visions and revisions
Before the taking of a toast and tea."

HENDERSON [*Mimicking scornfully*]. "Before the taking of a toast and tea." [*Speaking with the same scorn*] Captain, that's T. S. Eliot you're doing, not Henry Wadsworth Longfellow. [*Reciting with a delicacy and irony more appropriate to the line*] "Before the taking of a toast and tea."

STARKEY [*Dryly*]. Thank you, Sergeant Henderson. It's a pleasure to be instructed by someone of your extensive training and education.

HENDERSON [*With equal sarcasm*]. Don't mention it, Captain Starkey. It's a pleasure to be of help, sir, to someone who needs it so badly.

[*The men laugh at* HENDERSON'*s rejoinder. Surprisingly,* STARKEY *frowns with only mild annoyance at this impertinence. He consults his clipboard, and his manner tightens and becomes more military*]

STARKEY. Okay, we'll begin now. Let's see who's here.

[*Comically,* BAILEY *takes a few giant goosesteps forward, clicks his heels, and delivers a massive salute, grossly exaggerating each movement*]

BAILEY. Corporal Rudolph Bailey, sir, reporting for duty as ordered, sir, and ready, willing, and able to go into action, sir.

[STARKEY *lets his clipboard drop and gives* BAILEY *a long look of displeasure.* BAILEY *finally wilts beneath* STARKEY'*s gaze and shifts uneasily*]

Don't you want me to do that?

STARKEY. No.

[BAILEY *shrugs and steps back toward the others, who taunt and ridicule him*]

BAILEY. If you don't try, buddy, you don't get.

STARKEY [*Calling the roll*]. Sergeant Henderson.

> [HENDERSON, *in contrast to his earlier manner of flip-pant disdain, snaps to attention and answers smartly*]

HENDERSON. Here, sir!

STARKEY. Corporal Bailey.

BAILEY. Here, sir!

STARKEY. Corporal Sinclair.

> [*There is silence, defiant silence, from* SINCLAIR. *He is directly in front of* STARKEY, *and the two men glare at each other, their faces only inches apart.* THE IDIOT *nearest* SINCLAIR *nudges him;* SINCLAIR *jabs back at him furiously*]

Sinclair!

> [SINCLAIR *still refuses to answer and* STARKEY *shouts still louder*]

Can't you hear me?

SINCLAIR [*Shouting back at him*]. Can't you see me?

STARKEY. Why don't you answer "present" when you hear me calling your name?

SINCLAIR. Why don't you *mark* me "present" if you see me standing here? [*Paces a step or two in anger*] You dumb son of a bitch!

STARKEY [*Defensively*]. I've got to call the roll, that's why! I've got this list to read! I've got my instructions to follow, too! Are you here or aren't you?

> [SINCLAIR *sighs wearily, as though unable to believe the question, or the situation, and maintains a silence for a few seconds, while* STARKEY *still stares at him, inches away, and glowers*]

SINCLAIR [*Finally*]. I am here, *sir.*

STARKEY. Thank *you.* Private First Class Joe Carson.

JOE. Here, sir.

STARKEY. Private Harry Fisher.

FISHER. Present, sir.

HENDERSON [*Mocking* FISHER]. Present, sir!

> [FISHER *throws* HENDERSON *a look of annoyance as he sits down*]

STARKEY. Good. All you men present and accounted for. And you five idiots? One, two, three, four, five. Fine. [*Moves to* THE MAJOR] Major, we're ready.

MAJOR. Good. Take this.

[THE MAJOR, *rising, licks the flap of an envelope, seals the envelope shut, and hands it to* STARKEY]

STARKEY. What is this, sir?

MAJOR. Those are sealed orders.

STARKEY. What should I do with them?

MAJOR. *Un*seal them and read them aloud to the men.

[*After a moment's surprise,* STARKEY *shrugs and walks back toward the men. He tears open the envelope and studies the sheet of paper inside with an expression that is first puzzled and then amused. He braces himself in a slightly dramatic pose and begins reading aloud, and there is a strong suggestion in much of the banter that follows that he is getting many of his lines from the sheet of paper*]

STARKEY. Greetings, boys. From the Major, from me, and from the President of the United States.

[*There is an impressed, suspenseful response from the men, exaggerated to the point of parody, as they bend forward intently to listen*]

BAILEY. Wow.

SINCLAIR. Gee.

HENDERSON. Glorioski.

STARKEY [*Still reading*]. You are all hereby ordered . . . to a war.

[*The men let out derisive comments and exclamations for a second or two and then seem to go completely out of control with various improvisational bits burlesquing the idea of military combat. One imitates a cavalry bugle call while another springs forward off his chair brandishing an invisible saber.* BAILEY *leaps toward* STARKEY *with a shout*]

BAILEY. Yankee pig! You make it with my sister!

HENDERSON [*To* BAILEY]. Yankee pig! *You* make it with my brother!

FISHER. Banzai!

BAILEY. Sukiyaki—Nagasaki!

HENDERSON [*To* BAILEY]. Rat-tat-tat-tat! Take that, you lousy Jap!

BAILEY. I'm not a Jap. I'm a Nazi.

SINCLAIR. Take that, you lousy Nazi!

BAILEY. I'm not a Nazi. I'm a Jew.

HENDERSON [*Comically*]. That's what they *all* say!

FISHER [*Affecting a heavy German accent*]. Halt! Yankee general, do you surrender?

JOE. Nuts!

HENDERSON. What did you just say?

JOE. Nuts!

HENDERSON. Write that down . . . for posterity.

FISHER. Yes, sir!

HENDERSON. And go raise that flag.

FISHER. Yes, sir!

OTHERS [*Singing*]. "From the halls of Montezuma."
[FISHER *brings the unit flag forward and, with the rest of the men, does an imitation of the Iwo Jima photograph*]

HENDERSON [*To the audience, holding the edge of the flag*]. Wouldn't that make a lovely picture?

BAILEY [*Assuming the dramatic pose of a man facing a firing squad*]. I only regret that I have but one life to give for my country.

OTHERS. Bang!

BAILEY [*Sinking backward against* HENDERSON]. I only regret that they took it!

OTHERS [*Singing*].
"Mine eyes have seen the Glory
   Of the comin' of the Lord."

STARKEY. Okay, fellas, that's enough.

HENDERSON [*Holding a "dying"* BAILEY]. So that's what it is, eh? A war.

STARKEY. Indeed it is.

SINCLAIR [*Bitterly*]. And Uncle Sam wants me.

STARKEY. Indeed he does. So now you know what we're doing here. All of us—all of *you*—are fighting a war. And the target for today is—[*Smiles and shakes his head in disbelief*]—somebody ask me what the target for today is.
[FISHER *rises to comply, while* HENDERSON *makes a contemptuous kissing noise to ridicule and embarrass him*]

FISHER. Sir? [*To* HENDERSON, *with annoyance*] Will you please stop that? [*Back to* STARKEY] Sir? What's the target for today?

STARKEY. Bailey, you wouldn't believe it.

FISHER. I'm Fisher, sir.

STARKEY. Fisher, *you* wouldn't believe it, either.

HENDERSON. Henderson would believe it. [*Pauses to build up suspense for his joke*] Bismarck, North Dakota.

STARKEY. No. Constantinople.

   [*The men are astonished*]

FISHER. Sir?

HENDERSON. I don't believe it!

BAILEY. Well, I'll be damned!

JOE [*Scratching his head*]. Where's that?

BAILEY. That's Byzantium.

ALL [*Kidding*]. Oh!

HENDERSON. Don't any of you bright people up on top know—

STARKEY. We know.

HENDERSON. It's Istanbul, now.

STARKEY. We know that, too.

HENDERSON. But you're sending us out to bomb—

STARKEY. Yeah!

HENDERSON. Why?

STARKEY. Because we're a peace-loving people, that's why. And because we're a peace-loving people, we're going to bomb Constantinople right off the map.

BAILEY. Why don't we just bomb the map?

HENDERSON. Constantinople isn't on the map, dummy. There just ain't no such place any more.

STARKEY [*With breezy good humor*]. Henderson, *ours* not to reason why. It's *yours* but to do as you're told . . . and die.

SINCLAIR. Yeah. And that's why all of *us* are already dead.

STARKEY [*Consulting the sheet on his clipboard*]. No, that isn't correct.

HENDERSON. Yes, it is. We're doomed, aren't we? So we're dead.

SINCLAIR. Yeah. And there's something very, very special about us being dead.

FISHER. Yes. As the poet A. E. Housman said . . .

"The lads in their hundreds to Ludlow come in for the fair.

There's men from the barn and the forge and the mill and the fold.

The lads for the girls and the lads for the liquor are there.

And there with the rest are the lads that will never be old."

STARKEY. Horseshit!

SINCLAIR. No. That's what's special about us. We die young.

BAILEY [*Kidding* FISHER]. That's right, young. We are "the lads that will die in our glory and never be old." As the good poet Housman said.

FISHER. Oh, all right!

STARKEY. How did all you kids get so smart?

FISHER. We went to college.

HENDERSON. And we learned a few things.

STARKEY. Well, you, Henderson, didn't learn nearly enough. Just remember that none of you are dead yet. Although you sure act it sometimes.

FISHER. Sir, the problem is, we don't know if we're dead or not.

BAILEY. Maybe we're only dead in spirit.

SINCLAIR. Like hell!

JOE. What's the problem anyway? There's no problem. We're here, we're alive and . . . [*Singing*] "We're in the army now." [*Speaking, as the others shout him down*] So what's the problem?

> [*To the surprise of the men, their discussion is interrupted suddenly by* RUTH, *who walks in rapidly from the side, simulating a trance, her posture and expression deliberately exaggerated.*
>
> RUTH *is a faintly attractive girl well into her thirties, dressed in the uniform of a Red Cross worker stationed at the base. In one of the hands outstretched before her, she carries a coffee maker; in the other, she carries a porcelain mug. She is talking loudly, emulating extravagantly an actress playing the role of someone in a trance.*
>
> *The men react to her entrance with sounds and ges-*

*tures of good-natured dismay and irritation.* STARKEY
*shows embarrassment and exasperation, denoting a re-
lationship between them, and tries vainly to shush her
with whispers and gestures.* RUTH *evades them all and
forges ahead persistently]*

RUTH. Nooooo! We're dead . . . dead . . . dead!

HENDERSON. Oh, Jesus! Look who's here.

STARKEY. Honey, cut it out now . . . please.

RUTH [*Ignoring* STARKEY]. I want to speak. I want to feel.
I want to touch.

BAILEY. Our angel of mercy!

RUTH. Why can't they hear me when I speak?

HENDERSON. Oh, get her out of here—someone?

RUTH. Why can't they feel me when I touch? I've been so
much a part of them.

SINCLAIR. Your mother and I have been very deeply concerned about you.

    [RUTH *abandons suddenly her pose of high, romantic
    melodrama and speaks complainingly in an abrupt
    change to realism]*

RUTH. Oh, knock it off, will you? You know, if we were
doing something beautiful here, something like—er—
*Our Town,* I could say beautiful, idealistic things like
that.

STARKEY. Oh, Ruth!

RUTH. Instead, I've got to carry this stinking coffee pot
back and forth. I don't want to carry a stinking coffee
pot. [*Resuming her trancelike state*] I carry messages from
the life ahead to generations of the life to come.

    [*As* RUTH *reverts to this earlier manner, the men go
    along with her kiddingly by singing the hymn "Bring-
    ing in the Sheaves" softly under her speech like a
    church choir]*

MEN [*Singing*].
  "Bringing in the sheaves,
    Bringing in the sheaves,
    We will go rejoicing,
    Bringing in the sheaves."

RUTH [*Continuing*]. I bring you poetic tidings of love and
tenderness and call out . . . [*Retreats from the fierce glare*

*of* THE MAJOR *and moves forward to the footlights to speak directly to the audience*] . . . and call out to all of you, "Welcome, folks. Glad to have you all aboard with me on the jolly ship of life." [RUTH *stands a moment, beaming out at the audience with vast self-satisfaction*]

MAJOR. Ruth?

RUTH [*Turning to him hopefully*]. Yes?

MAJOR. Get the hell out of here!

[THE MAJOR *jerks his thumb toward the wings. The men laugh and applaud and jeer*]

JOE [*Singing*].

"Good night, ladies."

HENDERSON. Give her the hook, the hook, the hook.

JOE [*Singing*].

"Good night, ladies. Good night, ladies."

ALL [*Singing*].

"We hate to see you go!"

[*As the men hoot and roar with laughter,* RUTH *sets the coffee pot and the mug on* THE MAJOR'S *desk and walks back across the stage in an indignant huff. She sticks her tongue out at the men, thumbs her nose, and hurries offstage, wiggling her backside deliberately*]

HENDERSON. Glory be, Captain! Where did *we* get *her*? [*Looks meaningfully at* STARKEY) As if I didn't know.

STARKEY [*A bit sheepishly*]. Well, she is the second prettiest girl on the base.

JOE. She makes stinking coffee.

BAILEY. She's got a stinking coffee pot, that's why.

STARKEY. Okay, cut the comedy. And let's go on.

[FISHER *rises and moves forward obediently toward* STARKEY]

FISHER. Captain Starkey?

[HENDERSON *makes the kissing noise again.* FISHER *whirls upon him angrily*]

Will you cut that out?

[*Back to* STARKEY, *politely*]

Captain Starkey? Are we really going to bomb Constantinople today?

STARKEY. Indeed we are, son.

FISHER. Is it very dangerous?

STARKEY. Yes, son. I'm afraid it is.

FISHER. Must we go there?

STARKEY. Someone has to.

FISHER. Is anybody going to be killed?

STARKEY. Yeah.

FISHER. Who? [STARKEY *stares at him without replying*]

MAJOR [*His voice booming out*]. Starkey!

STARKEY. Sir?

MAJOR. Come here now, please.

STARKEY. Yes, sir.

    [STARKEY *turns and strides away toward* THE MAJOR.
    FISHER *calls after him*]

FISHER. Who? [STARKEY *does not reply.* FISHER *is left gaping
after him, waiting in vain for an answer to his question.
He turns after another second or two and moves back
toward the others awkwardly, as though uncertain what
to say or do next*] What do we do now?

JOE. We wait, kid. That's what we do. And sooner or later,
someone will come along and tell us what to do next.

SINCLAIR. Yeah. That's just what I'm afraid of.

    [*There is a gloomy, worried lull in which they all
begin to shift in their seats or drift about restlessly*]

HENDERSON. Why don't we sing a song now? Yeah, that's
what *I* would do . . . if *I* was in charge.

BAILEY. Sure. We could try that. And I think I know just
the song we could—

HENDERSON [*Cutting* BAILEY *off before he can even begin*].
Nah, that's no good. We've got a better one, Joe . . . let's
have that old alma mater of yours.

JOE [*Opening his mouth wide suddenly and singing*].
"Beeeeee . . ."

    [HENDERSON, *then* FISHER, *then—after a moment of
pique at being interrupted—*BAILEY, *all join in on that
first note, and the words that follow are sung to the
tune of John Philip Sousa's* "Stars and Stripes Forever"]

ALL FOUR [*Singing*].
  "Beeeeeee . . . kind to your web-footed friends.
  For a duck may be somebody's mother.
  They live in a stream by a swamp,
  Where the weather is always damp.

Now you may think this is the end.
Well, it is!"

[SINCLAIR *sits in scowling silence. The others cluster around him, trying to cheer him up and urging him unsuccessfully to join in*]

SINCLAIR. Aw, cut it out, for Christ sakes! [SINCLAIR *springs up and shoves his way through them*] Cut it out! [*They break off singing*] What the hell are you all singing about? We've got this goddam mission to fly. Constantinople—gee whiz!

BAILEY. So . . . we won't sing a song.

FISHER [*To* SINCLAIR]. It's okay. I'm scared of this mission today too.

SINCLAIR. You? What are *you* scared about? I'm the one that has to be killed.

JOE. I'm a little scared also. I'm starting to get a little scared of all of them.

HENDERSON. I'm not.

BAILEY. Aren't you worried at all?

HENDERSON. Nah, not me. And should I tell you why?

[*The others press close with curiosity*]

FISHER. Why?

HENDERSON. Because I'm not really a soldier, that's why. I'm really something much different. I'm an *actor* . . . playing the part of a soldier. [*Indicating the audience*] They know that. [*Smiling, he addresses the audience directly*] Right? And I'm pretty good, too. [*To* SINCLAIR] It's just a little game we're having here now. It's only a play, a show, a little entertainment, so let's not get carried away too far and forget who we *really* are.

SINCLAIR [*Morosely*]. Yeah, sure.

HENDERSON. Sinclair—this soldier I'm pretending to be never even lived, so how could I get killed? He's fictitious, a figment of somebody's imagination. I never met him, and I don't care about him. So what do I give a damn how many guns they've got at Constantinople or what that dumb slob of a Major says. Huh?

BAILEY. So? How come you keep complaining all the time?

HENDERSON. Because my part is too small, that's why. [*To the audience*] I'm really the most important one here. And

I'll tell you all something else. I'm also the best one. Did any of you people see me last year in————? [*Names the best-known play or movie he was actually in recently. He turns to address the other men on stage*] Did any of you see me in ————? [*Names the same play or movie*]

BAILEY. I did. [*Pauses, while* HENDERSON *waits expectantly*] You stank.

HENDERSON. You're jealous, Bailey. You want to be the sergeant here, don't you, even though you wouldn't know how to handle it. [*Disconsolately, almost without realizing what he is doing, he takes hold of a piece of the wall and shakes it, providing a visible, unconscious reminder that it is only stage scenery*] Aah, what do any of us know about what's really going on here?

SINCLAIR. I put in two years of repertory with ————. [*He supplies a true fact from his actual experience as an actor*]

HENDERSON. A lot that will get you.

SINCLAIR. It got me a part in here.

HENDERSON. Some part. You'll be gone before anyone knows you're even here. [*To the others as well*] Hey, you know who's really killing things? Our famous Captain Starkey. I should be the captain.

FISHER. You're too young to be a captain.

JOE. I'm the oldest one here, and I'm only a Pfc.

HENDERSON. What does age mean? I could do everything in this war. He can't do anything.

FISHER. It's a hard role to play. He doesn't know whether he's on our side or theirs.

JOE. He's on their side. He's an officer, ain't he? And all he does is what the Major tells him. That's all he's supposed to do.

FISHER. That's what I mean. He's got nothing to hang on to. He's got no point of view of his own. That's a very difficult part to play.

HENDERSON. Not for me. I'd turn him into a hero. I'd put fire into his lines. [*Imitating* STARKEY] None of this "Greetings, boys. You are all hereby ordered . . . to a war." I'd give you . . . volume. I'd give you . . . [*Strides forward and recites to the audience loudly*]

"Once more unto the breach, dear friends, once more;

Or close the wall up with our English dead."

[*Speaking normally*] Oh boy! I'd stir this whole joint up. I'd give you . . . [*Calling out into the theater at the top of his voice*] "Cry God for Harry! England and Saint George!" [*To the men, speaking normally*] Well? How's that?

BAILEY. You still . . . [*Shouting, in humorous imitation*] . . . *stink!*

FISHER. Yeah. And this isn't Shakespeare, either. If this were *Henry the Fifth,* you could say that—if some lunatic gave you the part. But I'm not sure what it is. I think it's more like Pirandello.

HENDERSON. If it's Pirandello, it's lousy Pirandello.

BAILEY. Only the way you play it, baby.

JOE. It's a war, kid, that's what's going on. We're in a big, dangerous war, kid, so what's the problem?

FISHER. Okay, then it's a war. But what are we doing here? Who are we fighting, and who are we really supposed to be? I mean—are we really flying a mission to Constantinople today, or are we just making believe?

SINCLAIR. That's right. If we are going, *why* are we going? What's our motivation?

HENDERSON. Our motivation? Oh, I know our motivation.

SINCLAIR. Then tell us. What's making us go?

HENDERSON [*As the others press close*]. The Major! *That's* our motivation. *That's* what's making us go . . . that old hippopotamus of a—

[*The men laugh and begin kidding around noisily with each other*]

MAJOR [*To* STARKEY]. Sergeant Henderson.

STARKEY. Sergeant Henderson!

[HENDERSON *draws himself to attention*]

HENDERSON. Sir?

STARKEY. Front, please!

HENDERSON. Yes, sir!

[*As* HENDERSON *starts away toward the officers,* FISHER *is able to give back to him the contemptuous kissing noise*]

FISHER. Go get 'em, tiger. Ha, ha!

[*The men resume their boisterous horseplay as* HENDERSON *walks across the stage to the officers. They sing a fragment of the Sousa march and then begin mocking* HENDERSON'*s recitation from* Henry V]

HENDERSON [*To* THE MAJOR]. Sir?

MAJOR. Keep those men quiet. You're supposed to be in charge now.

HENDERSON. Yes, sir! [*To the men as he returns to them, loudly and officiously, for* THE MAJOR'*s benefit*] Okay, you guys, keep it down, keep it down. Hear? [*To* THE MAJOR, *fishing for approval*] Sir? Okay?

MAJOR [*To* STARKEY]. Bring them in now and let's go on.

STARKEY. All right, men. It's time to go to work. Move along. Let's go.

[*At* STARKEY'*s loud and peremptory tone, the men snap back into attitudes of military obedience and hurry across the stage into the area of* THE MAJOR'*s office. They start to line up at attention there in two rows,* THE IDIOTS *all in the rear one.* STARKEY *moves forward to speed them along*]

Hurry up, boys. It's time.

HENDERSON [*Correcting him derisively*]. Hurry up, *please* . . .

STARKEY [*Grimacing angrily*]. Hurry up, *please* . . .

FISHER [*Furtively, the last to follow*]. . . . . it's time.

[STARKEY *jerks around and reacts with another grimace to* FISHER'*s gibe.* THE MAJOR *waits until the men are all lined up in their two rows and then moves around in front of his desk to address them*]

MAJOR. Okay, men, you all know where you are going now and what we're supposed to do. Is everything absolutely clear?

HENDERSON. Are we really going to bomb Constantinople?

MAJOR. Yes.

HENDERSON. Why?

MAJOR [*Reflects a moment before he decides to answer*]. Because it says so.

HENDERSON. *It?* What is *it?*

MAJOR. *It? It* is *it. It* is the thing we have to do, and *it* is the thing that makes us do *it*. Now stop complaining, all of you. This mission to Constantinople today is a military man's dream. It's a sneak attack. Are there any other questions?

BAILEY. Why are we killing Turks?

MAJOR. That's none of our business. Are there any other questions?

[*The men remain silent*]

This is a good mission you people are flying today. If everything goes well, there shouldn't be a single thing in Constantinople left alive. This is a mission we can all be very proud of.

SINCLAIR. I don't like it. I don't like it at all.

MAJOR. Why not?

SINCLAIR. It should come at the end of the last act, that's why. I don't want to be killed so early.

[*The men laugh*]

Yeah, it's easy for all of *you* to laugh. But I'm the one that's going to be killed now. And I've only just got here.

[*To* THE MAJOR]

Why can't I get killed in the last act?

MAJOR. Somebody else gets killed in the last act.

SINCLAIR. Why can't I get killed then?

MAJOR. Because you get killed now.

SINCLAIR. I don't want to die so soon. I don't even want to be here any more.

MAJOR. You should have thought of that before you volunteered.

SINCLAIR. I didn't volunteer.

MAJOR. That doesn't matter. You *are* here, and there isn't a single thing you can do about it now. Stand up at attention the way you're supposed to and show some respect for my position. [SINCLAIR *hesitates, then yields and stands up at attention*] Now get back in line. [SINCLAIR *steps back in line, where the others are standing in relaxed positions, watching and murmuring with amusement*] All of you! From now on, all of you stand up at attention whenever I talk to you. [*The men come to at-*

*tention immediately, all but* HENDERSON, *who deliberates
a moment and then strolls forward out of line and stands
waiting before* THE MAJOR *in insolent defiance.* THE
MAJOR *studies him a moment*] All right. What's the
matter with you?

HENDERSON [*Looks toward the globe*]. I'd like to blow up
the whole fucking thing.

[*Everyone on stage starts with vivid surprise—even*
THE MAJOR—*and all turn to stare at* HENDERSON *with
amazement.* STARKEY, *as though he has finally had all
he can take, moves belligerently to the globe*]

MAJOR. What thing?

HENDERSON. That thing.

STARKEY [*Pointing to the globe*]. Do you mean this?

HENDERSON. Yes, I mean that. That's what I would do if I
were in charge, instead of picking it apart so slowly,
piece by piece and person by person by person. Why
don't we just smash the whole fucking thing to bits once
and for all and get it over with?

STARKEY. Is that right? You want to smash the whole thing
to bits right now?

HENDERSON. Yeah.

[STARKEY *and* HENDERSON *glare at each other.*
STARKEY *glances toward* THE MAJOR. THE MAJOR
*nods, giving a signal of consent*]

MAJOR. Let him.

STARKEY [*To* HENDERSON, *taunting*]. Okay. Go ahead. [*Then,
to* HENDERSON's *surprise,* STARKEY *lifts the globe out of
the stand and lobs it like a basketball to* HENDERSON,
*who reaches out instinctively to catch it*] Smash it. Go
on. Smash it to bits.

HENDERSON. Can I? Can I really?

STARKEY. Sure. Go ahead. Smash it. And after you've done
it . . . what will you have?

[HENDERSON *hesitates a moment, on the verge of
hurling the globe to the floor, then relaxes suddenly
and smiles*]

HENDERSON. Bits. [HENDERSON *yielding, tosses the globe
back to* STARKEY]

STARKEY. That's right, Henderson. Bits. [STARKEY *replaces the globe on the stand*]

MAJOR [*To* HENDERSON]. Are you ready to continue now?

HENDERSON. Yeah. Sure.

MAJOR. Then say *sir* when you talk to me!

HENDERSON [*Snapping to attention*]. Yes, sir!

MAJOR. And get back in line with the rest of them.

HENDERSON. Yes, sir!

> [HENDERSON *responds obediently and takes his place in the line with the rest.* SINCLAIR *suddenly takes an impulsive step forward*]

SINCLAIR. What about me? Shouldn't I raise a bigger stink now about getting killed?

MAJOR. It won't do you any good.

SINCLAIR. But I don't want—

MAJOR. Get back in line, where you belong.

> [SINCLAIR *hesitates a second, as though tempted to rebel, and then steps back into line, resentful for a moment, and then cooperative.* THE MAJOR *is satisfied*]

That's better. Straighten it a little in the middle there. Yes, you're all doing fine now. Let's get this mission to Constantinople over with as quickly as we can. You're all due back here for calisthenics in exactly six minutes. Any more questions?

FISHER. Sir?

MAJOR. Yes?

FISHER. Can I bring my kid brother?

MAJOR. Not yet. Any other? Then get going. [*As the men fall out of line*] And take all this junk with you.

> [*By "junk" he means the stage scenery, and the men divide up into carefully drilled groups to begin clearing the stage.* HENDERSON *exits with one of the props. The area containing* THE MAJOR *and* STARKEY *is saved for last.* THE MAJOR *takes up his manuscript and prepares to leave*]

How do you feel about Henderson?

STARKEY. I don't like him. He's a conceited, disobedient, unreliable little punk.

[THE MAJOR *erases* SINCLAIR's *name from the list on the blackboard*]

MAJOR. I'm glad you think so. I'm getting rid of him on the next mission.

STARKEY. I think that's good. Major?

MAJOR. Yes?

STARKEY. Who gets killed in the last act?

MAJOR. You'll never guess.

STARKEY. Me?

MAJOR. No, of course not. You're safe, Starkey. Trust me. You'll always be safe, because you do your job and you don't take chances. So relax and take it easy, have fun, marry your girl friend. Nothing bad happens to you. Nothing bad ever happens to you.

STARKEY. That's good. Major? One more question. What's it all about?

MAJOR [*Encompassing the script, the stage, the theater, and the audience in a single, sweeping gesture*]. This? It's about time.

STARKEY. No, it isn't. It's about war.

MAJOR [*Motioning toward the clock*]. You'll find out. [THE MAJOR *departs with a wave, carrying his script*]

STARKEY. Okay, men! Let's go! Let's get the Major's office out of here. On the double!

[*While lights flash and bells ring and horns and sirens blare, the men rush back on stage to remove* THE MAJOR's *office. While this is going on,* RUTH *enters from the other side, wheeling in a coffee cart of a kind commonly seen in office buildings; it bears a coffee urn, mugs, and brown donuts stacked on wooden sticks.* RUTH *realizes she has entered a bit too early; she starts back into the wings, stops, and decides to wait. She covers her ears with her hands to drown out the chaotic noise while she waits for the men to finish.*

*With the briefing room and office gone, there is just the stage of the theater itself, bare, dark, and ominous, its doors, if any, in view, the entire enclosure looking a little weird and mysterious, like a cage or a prison,*

*from which the men might find it a bit difficult to
escape.*

*With* STARKEY *urging them on cheerfully, the men
hasten to push the office and props offstage on one
side. Then they all come running back onstage in a single line, donning bulky white flying helmets as they
head across the stage toward the opposite exit.*
STARKEY *calls out after them*]

Good luck, men! And happy hunting on your big combat mission!

[*The men exit at a trot. The flashing lights stop, and
all the harsh noises diminish and end.* STARKEY *moves
toward* RUTH, *still chuckling*]

RUTH. Why do you make all that weird noise?

STARKEY. Because it drives the men crazy. Well, I got them
all off, didn't I? Bet you didn't think I could do it!

RUTH. I'll bet I didn't care.

STARKEY. You're not so impressed with what I'm doing
here, are you?

RUTH. I'm not even impressed with what *I'm* doing here.
Starkey, couldn't we do something different now?

STARKEY. Like what?

RUTH. Like something sweet and warm and pleasant, in
which all of us here really like each other, and in which
a talented girl like me could have a much bigger part.

STARKEY. Not a chance. Pour me a cup of coffee, will you?
Maybe it will wake me up for what happens next.

RUTH. What happens next?

STARKEY. I have to interrogate. I have to take all the men
off someplace secret where nobody can see me and ask
them some very important questions I'm not interested
in.

RUTH. When?

STARKEY. In a couple of minutes. We just got through with
that mission to Constantinople.

RUTH. How did it go?

STARKEY. I'll let you know when I interrogate. Say, Ruthie
girl. What are you doing when you're finished here?

RUTH. I might be busy.

STARKEY. Don't be busy. I think I might want a hunk.

RUTH [*Indignant*]. A hunk of what?

STARKEY. A hunk of you.

RUTH. Now isn't that too bad? You know, Starkey, just about the only time you want to see me is when *you* want to see me.

STARKEY. It's my unselfish nature. I do that only for *your* own good. I would be pretty bad company if I began hanging around you when I *didn't* want to see you.

RUTH. And what am I supposed to do in between? Grind coffee beans? Or should I start giving *hunks* away to somebody else?

STARKEY [*Teasing her*]. Oh, that reminds me, honey. Are you sort of—er—sleeping with Henderson?

RUTH. I'm sort of—er—not sure. Which one is he?

STARKEY. The sergeant.

RUTH. Not yet.

STARKEY. Are you sleeping with the Major?

RUTH. Not any more.

STARKEY. Oh, come on, Ruthie. Give me a straight answer. I'm jealous.

RUTH [*Skeptical*]. Really?

STARKEY. Maybe.

RUTH. Then you give me one. Will you marry me?

[STARKEY *gasps with surprise and spews out coffee*]

STARKEY. Jesus Christ, Ruthie! Where's your manners? That's a helluva goddam personal question to ask a gentleman you *are* sleeping with!

RUTH. Then let's try another. Do you love me?

STARKEY. That's even worse!

RUTH. Well, I've got to know, dammit! I don't know who I am here or what I mean to anybody. I don't know how I'm supposed to act with you or anybody else. Am I just a goddam Red Cross girl? Is that all I mean to you? If you get killed—

STARKEY. I don't get killed.

RUTH. If you did get killed, am I heartbroken?

STARKEY. I would expect the whole world to be heartbroken.

RUTH. Starkey, stop smiling *all* the time. Please? There's not that much to smile about.

STARKEY. Okay. What's bothering you?

RUTH. I don't know how to respond to you. I don't know what I'm supposed to say to you . . . or even how I ought to feel about you? That's why I have to know. Do you love me, or don't you?

STARKEY. Okay. I'll tell you. Do you want the truth, or do you want a lie?

RUTH. Which is better?

STARKEY. If I were you, I would go with the lie.

RUTH. No. I want the truth. Do you love me?

STARKEY. No.

RUTH. Let's have the lie.

STARKEY. Yes, I do love you, Ruth, more than words could ever say.

RUTH. Darling! [RUTH *flings herself dramatically into* STARKEY's *arms, and the two embrace passionately with an ardor that is definitely histrionic*]

STARKEY. And, my darling, do you know what I love best about you?

RUTH. My body?

STARKEY. Right.

[RUTH *pulls away from him with a smile and begins strutting proudly*]

RUTH. It is a great body, isn't it? The head's a little worn. But the thighs are good, and the boobs are still first-rate.

STARKEY. You're the second prettiest girl on the base.

RUTH. I used to be the first prettiest. Then they sent another girl here. How do you like my coffee today?

[STARKEY *gives her a long, meaningful look*]

I know—it stinks, doesn't it? So what? I'm an actress, not a cook. I can play anything.

STARKEY. Except a cook.

RUTH. I could play a debutante . . . a queen . . . a housewife . . . a virgin. I could play ———. [*She mentions the name of any very popular and glamorous movie actress and attempts an imitation*] I can even play Cordelia in *King Lear,* by William Shakespeare, of England.

STARKEY. The hell you could!

RUTH. I could.

STARKEY. You couldn't keep your mouth shut long enough to play Cordelia. When Lear turns to you finally and says: [*Reciting*]

"Now, our joy,
    Although our last, not least; to whose young love
    The vines of France and milk of Burgundy
    Strive to be interess'd; what can you say to draw
    A third more opulent than your sisters? Speak."

RUTH. Hey, that's good, that's good. And what do I say?

STARKEY. "Nothing."

RUTH. Nothing?

STARKEY. That's right, "Nothing."

RUTH. I don't want the part!

STARKEY. Good. Play the part you've got.

RUTH. I don't want *that* part, either. Starkey, really—there must be something better for me to do than just stand around watching while you blow your whistle like a big executive, and all the rest of them go running and jumping back and forth to blow things up.

STARKEY. There is, honey.

RUTH [*Eagerly*]. What?

STARKEY. Pour coffee!

RUTH. Oh—

STARKEY. I mean it. Pour coffee, because I think I hear my idiots now, all marching back so proudly from *Constantinople.*

[*As* RUTH *begins pouring coffee into a line of cups, there is heard from offstage the sound of a voice counting marching cadence.* STARKEY *takes over the cadence count as the first of the men enter*]

Hup, two, three, four! Hup, two, three, four! That's the way, we earn our pay! Move along, lift your feet. *Un, deux, trois, quatre, cinq, six, sept, huit!*

[*The five* IDIOTS *enter first,* FISHER, JOE, *and* BAILEY

*follow. Only* THE IDIOTS *march to the cadence count. The others straggle, looking tired and bored*]

RUTH. Come and get it, boys. Hot coffee. Fresh donuts. We've got milk and cream and sugar and saccharin. Who's first? Who's next? Who's last?

[*One by one the men march past* RUTH, *each shaking his head and recoiling from* RUTH's *offer of coffee and donuts with gestures of eloquent revulsion. Her enthusiasm flags as the last of them passes*]

Well, I don't like your marching, either!

STARKEY [*Laughing*]. Stick around, baby. I'll be back to claim you as soon as I'm through.

RUTH. I might not be here.

STARKEY. Oh, you'll be here.

RUTH. Is that so? And just what makes you so sure?

[STARKEY *laughs confidently and points—to* THE MA-JOR, *who comes onstage then, carrying his manuscript.* STARKEY *leaves, thumbing his nose at* RUTH.

THE MAJOR *looks rather pleased with things as he heads for the coffee wagon. His relaxed and amiable manner suggests that he is taking a break.* RUTH *pours a cup of coffee for him, then preens herself a bit*]

MAJOR. Let's have a donut please, Ruth. Two.

RUTH. Sure. How is it going?

MAJOR [*Cheerfully*]. Very, very well, I would say. That mission to Constantinople was the hardest part. And all the men came back hale and hearty—except one.

RUTH. What happened to him?

MAJOR. Oh, he was killed. And now, where's Henderson? *Henderson!* [*Tapping his manuscript irritably*] He's supposed to be coming on and walking through here right now. *Henderson!*

[*After another few seconds,* HENDERSON *enters, walking wearily and despondently, his head down. He seems unaware of* THE MAJOR *or* RUTH *and moves as though he has not come on in response to* THE MAJOR's *call. His clothes are covered with matted blood. He walks as though in a daze, acting—and acting very well— the role of a soldier exhausted by combat.*

*HENDERSON does not head for the coffee wagon but moves directly across the stage.* THE MAJOR *watches him with an angry frown for a few moments; then* THE MAJOR *falls into a role of his own and begins walking across the stage in a direction that brings him toward* HENDERSON. *Only when they are almost abreast of each other does* HENDERSON *appear to see him. He straightens immediately and salutes.* THE MAJOR *returns the salute, and they both stop. Both are playing roles now—but playing them very seriously*]

Rough over Constantinople, wasn't it?

HENDERSON. Yes, sir. It was . . . rough.

MAJOR. I know. And I'm sorry. I'm proud of you today, Henderson. Very proud.

HENDERSON. Thank you, sir. I did my best.

[*They exchange salutes again as* THE MAJOR *resumes walking and exits.* HENDERSON *walks a few steps and then takes a furtive peek over his shoulder. When he sees that* THE MAJOR *has gone, his whole manner changes instantly, as though he is dropping out of the role he has been performing once there is nobody to supervise him. He stops, lets out an exclamation of condescending contempt, and saunters casually toward the coffee wagon*]

Oh, boy—what I have to go through with that old guy. I'm glad you're here. Gimme some coffee, sweetie, will you? I'm beat.

RUTH [*Pours a cup*]. Say please.

HENDERSON. Oh, come on!

RUTH. I love *you*, too.

HENDERSON. I don't blame you.

RUTH. How do you like my coffee?

HENDERSON. It really stinks. [HENDERSON *moves to the sugar bowl and keeps dropping spoonful after spoonful of sugar into his cup as they continue talking*]

RUTH. How do you like me?

HENDERSON. Quiet.

RUTH. You know who's jealous of you?

HENDERSON. Everybody.

RUTH. Captain Starkey. Did you tell him you were sleeping with me?

HENDERSON. Why would I do that?

RUTH. He thinks you are.

HENDERSON. He's crazy.

[RUTH *reacts with a look of indignant surprise*]

RUTH. What's so crazy about it? I could be your mistress.

HENDERSON. You're too old. You could be my mother.

RUTH. I could play Juliet to your Romeo—if *you* could play a Romeo. Say, I've got a hot idea. [*Suggestively*] Let's play *Oedipus Rex* together.

HENDERSON. Jesus—you've got a filthy mind!

RUTH. I've got talent, that's what I've got. But they won't let me use it. I don't even have any good lines. I've got to *make* them funny if I want to make people laugh.

HENDERSON. You're not supposed to make people laugh. You're supposed to make people coffee.

RUTH. See? *You* get that line, not me. Hey, what's that stuff you've got all over you?

HENDERSON [*With scarcely any concern*]. This? It's blood.

RUTH. You've got an awful lot there.

HENDERSON. I used all he had.

RUTH. Where'd you get it?

HENDERSON. From Sinclair.

RUTH. Which one is he?

HENDERSON. He's that kid who ————. [*Inserts fact used earlier from* SINCLAIR'*s previous acting experience*] He was killed just now on the mission to Constantinople.

RUTH. Really?

HENDERSON. Yeah. He died in my arms just a little while ago. Hey, what's the matter with you?

[RUTH *is distraught and virtually in tears*]

RUTH. Oh, that's terrible! He's really dead? I get so broken up when I hear something like that. Oh, that poor, poor little kid!

HENDERSON. Okay. You don't have to make such a big scene out of it.

RUTH. No? How am I supposed to act? Brave? "It's all right, folks, he died for his country, so let's not make any fuss about it." No thanks! That's one part I *don't* want. *You* can have that speech. I'd rather make a big scene out of it. I'd rather scream.

HENDERSON. He wasn't really killed, you know. He isn't really dead.

RUTH. Where is he, then? Show him to me.

[JOE *and* BAILEY *enter from the side and move across the stage toward an exit*]

JOE. Come on, Bailey. We've got to hurry up and change.

HENDERSON. Okay, I'll show him to you. Hey Bailey . . . Joe! Sinclair? Is he out over there?

JOE. Sinclair?

BAILEY. No. Of course not.

RUTH. You see?

JOE. Henderson, you better come along and change too. You've got to bring us out here for calisthenics soon.

[JOE *and* BAILEY *exit.* HENDERSON *starts away in a different direction, speaking to* RUTH *as he goes*]

HENDERSON. You just wait here. I'll get him.

RUTH. Okay. Get him.

HENDERSON. I'll get him. I'll bring him right back here.

RUTH. Go ahead—get him. [HENDERSON *exits with annoyance, leaving* RUTH *alone onstage.* RUTH *gazes after him with a look of intense grief and speaks softly at first*] Oh, God! God . . . God . . . God! [RUTH *turns and drifts forward. She speaks directly to the audience with a deep sincerity of emotion*] He *was* killed, wasn't he? And all of you just sat there. It happened right now. Didn't you care? Doesn't it mean anything to you?

[STARKEY *strolls in while* RUTH *is speaking and halts, as though taken aback to see her so deeply moved. He carries his newspaper and his businessman's portfolio*]

STARKEY. Hey, Ruthie! *Ruthie!* Take it easy, will you? What do you want from *them?* This is only a show . . . a comedy. They never heard of this character Sinclair before. He's a stranger to them. He's like a name in this newspaper.

RUTH [*To* STARKEY]. What difference does *that* make? He's dead, isn't he? [*Throws her hands up disgustedly*] Aaaah, what do I care? I don't even know anybody in ————. [*Names the city in which the play is being performed. She moves to the coffee wagon and pours a cup of coffee for herself, addressing the audience, rather than* STARKEY, *as she continues*] Why should I be the one to worry and cry over other people, when nobody else does? I can cry over myself—God knows I've got enough to cry about, and God knows I want to cry often enough. I'm a girl, and I'm thirty-six years old. [*She makes a face, realizing what she has just said*] He thinks I'm only thirty-one and a half. Don't you? [*Looks at* STARKEY, *who shrugs and shakes his head noncommittally*] I've never been married, and if I had been, I'd probably be divorced. My face isn't too good, and my skin isn't so soft any more, in spite of all those rejuvenating facial oils I've been packing on. And, if the truth must be told, my body is not quite as good as it may look; it's kind of—er—propped up a little here and there. All in all, I have to admit I'm getting a little long in the tooth. I never really knew what I wanted to be—except a pretty girl, a happy sweetheart, a blushing bride, and a good wife. And a wonderful mother. Oh, what a wonderful mother I used to think I would make! Since it didn't look like I could become any of those, I had a crack at acting. For a while I wanted to be a nurse . . . but I couldn't type. For the time being, I'm a Red Cross worker— [*Sips the coffee and reacts to its bad taste*]—and I've got a stinking coffee pot. I don't want to sound conceited, but I think I would be an awfully good thing for somebody who wanted me. But nobody wants me, not for very long.

STARKEY. I want you.

RUTH. For very long?

[STARKEY *shrugs evasively again, murmuring something almost inaudibly*]

STARKEY. Well . . . I mean . . . nobody . . . any girl . . . for very long.

[RUTH *turns from him to address the audience again*]

RUTH. So tell me, all you people, who sit here in a theater while I grow old and pour my heart out, and while a nice young man who never did us any harm is ordered to fly to Constantinople and be killed—what do I do now?

STARKEY. Let's go to bed.

RUTH. And what do I say to that?

[THE MAJOR *enters, carrying his manuscript. He is accompanied by* THE GOLFER *and* THE HUNTER, *two gentlemen of middle age who are dressed in a way appropriate to their respective hobbies. Both Sportsmen radiate an affluence and geniality that are suggestive of middle-class business executives out on a harmless spree. They grin, as though with delight to find themselves on a stage in a crowded theater, and stare about with happy shyness and uncertainty.* THE GOLFER *carries a golf club;* THE HUNTER *carries a shotgun.* THE MAJOR *speaks to* RUTH *as though prompting her, supplying the answer to her question*]

MAJOR. Say "yes."

RUTH [*Makes a face at* THE MAJOR *and then says, soulfully, to* STARKEY]. Ye-e-e-e-s.

[*In trite, theatrical tradition* RUTH *and* STARKEY *fall into each other's arms*]

GOLFER. Who is she?

MAJOR. She's our Red Cross girl.

[THE GOLFER *chortles knowingly*]

GOLFER. What does she do, roll bandages?

[*Both* SPORTSMEN *laugh loudly*]

MAJOR. Shhhh!

RUTH. Starkey, it's really important, so tell me the truth. Please. Do you love me or don't you?

STARKEY. Just *why* is that suddenly so important?

RUTH. I'm going to have a baby.

[STARKEY *gawks and lets out a low whistle of surprise*]

STARKEY. And what do *I* say to *that?*

RUTH. You might ask me if it's yours.

STARKEY. We know it's *yours*. Is it mine?

RUTH. Do you want the truth, or do you want a lie?

STARKEY. Which is better?

RUTH. It's yours.

STARKEY. Yes, Ruth. I do love you.

RUTH. Will you marry me? Right now?

> [STARKEY *looks over his shoulder at* THE MAJOR. THE MAJOR *nods, giving permission*]

STARKEY. Sure. [*They embrace tenderly*] Can I smile a little now?

RUTH. Yes.

STARKEY. Can I sing?

RUTH. No. [*He does anyway*]

STARKEY [*Singing*]. "Just Molly and me."

RUTH [*Singing*]. "And baby makes three."

BOTH [*Singing*]. "We're happy in our blue heaven."

> [*Together, while singing, they take the handle of the coffee wagon and wheel it offstage as though it were a baby carriage.* THE MAJOR *claps his hands in applause and watches them go with an approving smile*]

MAJOR. It's going pretty well, I'd say. Right?

GOLFER. I love it.

HUNTER. I think it's great. I'm real proud to be one of the backers.

MAJOR. That's fine, then. Now this is the stage—that's all there is to it. This is the proscenium, up there are the flies, and out there in the theater is the audience.

GOLFER. How many seats are there?

MAJOR. Here? ———. [*He gives the exact number of seats in the theater in which the play is being performed*] It's a small (big) theater, but it's a good place for us to work from now.

GOLFER. Suppose we bomb here?

HUNTER. Yeah. Suppose they don't like us?

MAJOR. I'll blast them off the map.

HUNTER. You mean that?

MAJOR. Why not? We just killed them in Constantinople, didn't we? I can kill these people here just as well.

GOLFER. I think that's marvelous. What happens next?

MAJOR. We bomb in Minnesota.

HUNTER. *That* sounds like fun. Right now?

MAJOR. Oh, no, a little later. First Henderson brings the
men out for some calisthenics. Then I have Starkey
come out with some brand-new war equipment that will
really stop the show.

GOLFER. That captain's pretty good, isn't he?

MAJOR. He's all right.

HUNTER [*Surprised*]. Don't you like him?

MAJOR [*Without emotion*]. No.

HUNTER. Why don't you get rid of him?

MAJOR. I won't have to. He does everything I want him to
do, and he does it very well. Wait till you see how beau-
tifully he handles Henderson, and what he does with all
that new equipment he brings out.

GOLFER. I can *hardly* wait.

HUNTER. Me neither. [*He lights a cigar*] Say, why don't
you let the men smoke?

MAJOR. Because they want to.

GOLFER. That sounds funny too. Listen, I'd like to have a
part in this, sort of. Could you kind of—er—arrange
that?

MAJOR. Are you sure you want to?

GOLFER. And how!

HUNTER. Me too. I've never really been in one before.

MAJOR. Okay, both of you. Keep your gun and your club.
I'll scrape up some uniforms for you later. [*Looks at his
watch*] Stand together there now, and I'll teach you a
few things. Good. Now . . . 'tention! [*Grinning with delight to find themselves playing soldier,* THE GOLFER *and*
THE HUNTER *snap clumsily to attention; they are not
quite sure what to do with the golf club and the shotgun.*
THE MAJOR *watches them pleasantly*] Present . . . arms!
[THE SPORTSMEN *are at a complete loss. Using his manuscript as a weapon,* THE MAJOR *counts them through the
stages of what they are intended to do. On the second
attempt they get it right, and the three go through the
maneuver together, one using a golf club, one a shotgun,*

*and* THE MAJOR *his script*] Port . . . arms! Right shoulder . . . arms! [*One of the two gets the wrong shoulder,
and the other laughs at him good-naturedly*] No, right
shoulder. Very good. You've both got a knack for this.
[*Looks toward the wing impatiently and waits a few seconds more before speaking*] And now, where is Henderson? *Henderson!* He's always late. He's supposed to be
bringing those men out here for calisthenics right now!

HUNTER. Why don't you get rid of him?

MAJOR. I'm going to, very soon. *Henderson!* I'm going to
kill him on that mission to Minnesota. *Henderson!*
[*From offstage, in the distance, there suddenly sounds
the voice of someone counting out double-time cadence.
Gradually, together with the noise of running feet
pounding in step, the voice draws closer*] Here he
comes. Okay . . . let's go. Fall in. Left face. [*One faces
left, the other right*] No—left. [*This time they both respond correctly, so that they end up facing in opposite
directions. There is another moment or two of confusion
before* THE MAJOR *is able to point them in the direction
he wants*] No—this way, both of you. Good. Now forward march. Left, right, left, right. [*Smirking self-con-
sciously,* THE SPORTSMEN *begin marching away awkwardly in the same direction from which the men are coming.
The first of the men appear, jogging onstage in single file.
They are dressed in sweatshirts and athletic shorts, and
they wear sneakers. The first in line are the five* IDIOTS;
*then come* FISHER *and* JOE. *The man in charge is running
alongside; when he enters, he turns out to be not* HEN-
DERSON, *but* BAILEY! THE MAJOR *is amazed and barks
his first words at the two* SPORTSMEN] Halt—hold it!
Bailey! Bailey!

BAILEY. Yes, sir. [BAILEY *pulls away from the line of trotting men and stops at attention in front of* THE MAJOR.
*Unnoticed by either, the other men keep trotting across
the stage and go out of sight on the other side*]

MAJOR. Where's Henderson?

BAILEY. I don't know, sir. He wasn't there when you began

calling, so I thought I'd better bring the men out here. Did I do right, sir?

MAJOR. I'll find him. You keep them busy until Captain Starkey gets here.

BAILEY. Yes, sir. Okay, you men——men? Where are you? [BAILEY *turns to issue an order and perceives with astonishment that the men have trotted out of sight. With alarm he starts after them, running offstage as he shouts at the top of his voice*] Hey, come back! Come back, men. About . . . face! To the rear . . . run! [*In response to the order the men reappear, trotting back onstage like expressionless automatons in reverse order and almost trampling* BAILEY *underfoot.* BAILEY *untangles himself from them and turns to* THE MAJOR *to apologize*] I'm sorry, sir. I——[*Again with alarm,* BAILEY *notices that the men are about to trot out of sight now on the other side of the stage*] Men! Group! Squadron! Army! [*He looks at* THE MAJOR *in total confusion*]

MAJOR. Company!

BAILEY. Thank you, sir. [*Running after them*] Hey, company—to the rear . . . run! [*The men trot back onstage again, heading in their original direction in their original order*] Sir. I——company . . . company . . . company . . . [BAILEY *grows flustered with the realization that the men are heading offstage away from him again.* THE MAJOR *steps away from* BAILEY *to take charge*]

MAJOR. Company, halt! [*The men stop*]

BAILEY. Oh, *that's* the word!

MAJOR. Right face! Parade rest! At ease!

BAILEY. I'm sorry, sir. I guess I'm not used to taking Henderson's place—*yet.*

MAJOR. I can see that. Do you know what you're supposed to do next?

BAILEY. I think so. Straddle jumps and pushups.

MAJOR. Then do it. [*To* THE SPORTSMEN] We'll go. 'Tention! Forward march. Hut, two, three, four, hut, two, three . . . [THE MAJOR *counts* THE SPORTSMEN *off the stage, then stops to watch* BAILEY *who springs into action*]

BAILEY. Okay, men. Straddle jumps. Hands high overhead when you clap them, legs wide apart when you jump. Touch the sky, touch the sky. All together now. One, two, three, four, one, two, three, four, one . . . [*The men begin the straddle jumps, all completely out of time.* THE MAJOR *goes, and* BAILEY *stops almost immediately, in mid-sentence*] . . . two, three—you lousy sons of bitches! [*The men break formation and sprawl out indolently, a few of them lighting cigarettes, while* BAILEY *prowls about among them in resentful frustration*] Why'd you make me look so stupid in front of the Major?

JOE. You are stupid. You don't even know how to give good commands for close-order drill.

BAILEY. What a chance I had! What a golden opportunity! There we were, just me and the Major . . .

FISHER. And us.

BAILEY. Yeah . . . and *you*. How could you all be so dumb? Why'd you keep running back and forth like that? Where the hell did you think you were running to?

JOE. We were only doing what you told us to do.

BAILEY. Why'd you have to *listen* to me? Look—I could be a better sergeant than he is, if you guys would only pitch in next time and cooperate. Wouldn't you rather have me? I would work hand and glove with you guys all the way down the line.

FISHER. You can stop dreaming now and relax. Here he comes.

JOE. And I'm only a Pfc.
[HENDERSON *enters slowly from a direction opposite the one in which he left, moving as though in a perplexed and brooding daze. He looks behind him, nibbling his lip, and studies the people onstage. He is still wearing his blood-spattered combat uniform*]

HENDERSON. Who's got a cigarette? [*He pulls a cigarette from* JOE's *hand as he passes him and moves about restlessly in a kind of aimless search*] Thanks.

JOE. Hey!

BAILEY. Where the hell have you been? [BAILEY's *question does not register on* HENDERSON] Henderson!

HENDERSON. What?

BAILEY. I said where the hell have you been?

HENDERSON. What the hell is that your business?

BAILEY. You're supposed to bring these men the hell out here. Not me. The Major was looking for you.

HENDERSON. The hell with him, too. Where the hell is Sinclair?

[*The others exchange a puzzled look*]

JOE. Who?

[HENDERSON *meditates gloomily a moment and then comes forward to take the others into his confidence*]

HENDERSON. Listen. I've been looking for Sinclair. I can't find him.

BAILEY. He's dead.

FISHER. He was just killed on the mission to Constantinople.

BAILEY. Maybe that's why you can't find him.

HENDERSON. I know all that. But where is he really? Right now.

BAILEY. In Heaven?

JOE. In Hell.

BAILEY. I'll betcha nickel.

[HENDERSON *pulls away from them angrily, rebuffed by their unwillingness to take him seriously*]

HENDERSON. Stop clowning, will you? I've looked all over for him. [*With a gesture of his arm he takes in the entire stage and the backstage area*] I can't find him.

BAILEY. Did you look in the men's room?

FISHER. Maybe he's in the hospital.

BAILEY. Or in the morgue.

JOE. He's dead, that's where he is. Maybe he's in the cemetery already. That's where dead people are.

HENDERSON. Oh, you idiots!

JOE [*Pointing*]. They're the idiots. Not us.

HENDERSON. You're no better, any of you. You guys are kidding, aren't you? You don't think Sinclair was really killed, do you? You don't think he's really dead, do—

[*From offstage, there comes all at once the clear sound of a bugle playing "Taps." For a few seconds, the men are all stricken with surprise. Then, as the melancholy music continues,* BAILEY, JOE, *and* FISHER *burst out together into raucous laughter, taunting* HENDERSON, *who whirls away in furious disgust*]

How corny can you get!

BAILEY. We were right! Bigshot, hotshot, wiseguy!

FISHER. *That's* where he is! In the cemetery!

JOE. I told you. They're burying him! That's what they're doing—they're burying him!

HENDERSON. Will you listen to that bugle? I'm almost ashamed to be here.

[STARKEY *enters while the bugle still plays, pushing onstage a square green bin that rides on wheels. On the side of the bin are lettered the words:* "WEAPONS DIVISION. TOP SECRET." STARKEY's *manner is brisk and joyful: he is eager to put on the flashy performance with* HENDERSON *and the equipment about which* THE MAJOR *boasted to the two* SPORTSMEN *earlier. He wears his whistle around his neck and perhaps smokes one of his cigars*]

Starkey! Hey, Starkey! Whose idea is *that,* for Christ sake! Taps!

[STARKEY *comes to a stop, removes his hat, and stands in respectful silence until the bugler finishes*]

STARKEY. That was for Sinclair. They're burying him now. [*Stares with surprise at the men resting on the ground*] What are you people doing?

[*The men are embarrassed*]

BAILEY [*Moving up and down a bit on one arm*]. Pushups.

STARKEY [*Dryly*]. You'll get a hernia on your elbow. [*To* HENDERSON] And what are you doing in that uniform?

HENDERSON. I've been trying to find Sinclair. I'm a little confused about a few things.

STARKEY. You're supposed to be dressed for calisthenics. There's nothing confusing. Sinclair is dead and buried now, and we just go ahead without him.

HENDERSON. But where is he really?

STARKEY. Are you serious?

HENDERSON. I want to know.

STARKEY. There was no Sinclair.

HENDERSON. Then how can he be dead and buried?

STARKEY. He wasn't real. I'm not real. I'm pretending, and
I'm sure that all of you— [*To the audience, altering the
details of his speech to correspond to his actual experience as an actor*]—and all of you out there, have seen
me act many, many times before in many different roles.
As you know, I've been doing very, very well lately. I've
had much bigger parts than this one. I've also made lots
more money. But I do like to be involved in serious, important things, when I can find some time between my
movies. And that's why I consented to play this part of a
captain, for a little while. [*To the men*] Do you understand?

> [BAILEY *and* FISHER *applaud deadpan.* STARKEY, *miss-
> ing their sarcasm, is pleased*]

BAILEY. That's the hardest part you ever played.

STARKEY. A captain?

BAILEY. No. An actor.

> [*The men guffaw*]

HENDERSON. Starkey—

STARKEY. *Captain* Starkey.

HENDERSON. About Sinclair.

STARKEY [*Enjoying this baiting of* HENDERSON]. There *was*
no Sinclair. He never lived. He didn't die.

HENDERSON. Then who did we just bury?

STARKEY. Sinclair. But he wasn't real. It didn't happen.

HENDERSON. Why did we bury him?

STARKEY. Because he was killed.

HENDERSON. Where is the boy who was playing the soldier
who was killed by accident just now—

STARKEY. Not by accident. There are no accidents.

HENDERSON. By accident! He was killed in my plane when
one of his own bombs exploded, wasn't he? That's an
accident. He used to be an actor about my own age.
He was here a little while ago. He isn't here now.

STARKEY. He isn't supposed to be here. That's why we
killed him.

HENDERSON. I'm going to look for him.

STARKEY. No, you're not!

HENDERSON. I am.

STARKEY. Not now, you aren't! I need you here to help me distribute this new equipment. That's your job. You stand right there with those idiots. Go ahead! I'm in charge now. And I'm getting sick and tired of arguing with you over every little thing that has to be done.

HENDERSON. Then can I go?

STARKEY. Then you can go get into a clean uniform for the mission to Minnesota—like you're supposed to.

HENDERSON. Minnesota?

STARKEY. Yes, Minnesota. That's your next target, men.

BAILEY. What's in Minnesota?

STARKEY [*Rumpling* BAILEY's *hair*]. Your next target. Any questions?

FISHER. Sir? Captain Starkey, sir? Is this mission to Minnesota going to be dangerous?

STARKEY. Not for those who survive, as I once heard the Major say. Any other questions?

HENDERSON. Where's Sinclair?

STARKEY. I've already answered that one. And now, everybody up and on your toes! Hear ye, hear ye! Step right up and gather 'round. I've got something good for each and every one of you. It's time for the wonderful new equipment that will put you all in just the perfect frame of mind for the big mission to Minnesota.

BAILEY. What new equipment?

STARKEY. You'll all love every piece of it.

JOE. Girls?

STARKEY. Oh, shut up, Joe, you silly old degenerate. This is serious. [*Opens the bin*] Gather close and listen carefully. Henderson, you'll come first . . . because *you're a sergeant*. Now, men, war isn't just bullets and bombs. Oh, no. There's such a thing as the battle for men's minds and souls, including yours, and we've got in here the secret weapons that are going to win it. There's no doubt about it. Are you ready, Henderson—my protégé, friend, colleague, and good soldier? One . . . two . . . three!
[STARKEY *reaches inside the bin and pulls out, holds up,*

*and then flips to* HENDERSON *a miniature baseball bat.*
HENDERSON *is puzzled*]

HENDERSON. It's a little baseball bat.

STARKEY [*Grinning*]. That's right.

[HENDERSON *flings the bat away furiously*]

HENDERSON. We've got a real baseball bat! [*He starts away*]

STARKEY. Then how about this? [*With sly amusement, as though relishing what he knows is to come,* STARKEY *pulls out a basketball and lobs it to* HENDERSON. HENDERSON *catches the ball and looks at it with surprise*]

HENDERSON. A basketball!

[STARKEY *nods. Angrily,* HENDERSON *flips the ball away. One of* THE IDIOTS *jumps forward and catches it. He gazes at the ball in dumb puzzlement for a few seconds and then flips it to a second* IDIOT; *and suddenly about four of the men are playing with the basketball intently*]

STARKEY. Here, Henderson! How's this? [STARKEY *pulls out another basketball and lobs it to* HENDERSON, *who with slightly hypnotic bewilderment, catches it*]

HENDERSON. It's another basketball!

STARKEY. A replacement. The Major wants us to have lots of replacement parts. Come on, Henderson, play. Play.

[HENDERSON *shakes his head determinedly and flings the ball away.* FISHER *lunges for it. He tries to dribble around* BAILEY, *then passes off instead to* JOE, *who dribbles toward the rear a few steps and passes back to* FISHER. *Now there are two basketballs being passed around. As* HENDERSON *stares and* STARKEY *grins, an orgy of ball playing develops that grows in noise and accelerates in action, with the five* IDIOTS *playing most vigorously of all.* HENDERSON *starts away as though he is going to leave the stage.* STARKEY *next takes out a football and shoots a pass to him*]

Yo! Henderson! Nice catch. Play, Henderson, play. Join the team.

[HENDERSON *continues shaking his head and flings the ball angrily toward the center.* BAILEY *scoots out and catches it*]

BAILEY. Hey, a football! A football!

[*The men let out exclamations of delight when they
see the football and set up a cry for* HENDERSON *to
play football with them.* HENDERSON *starts away offstage, but they surge after him and pull him back, urging him to play. Finally,* HENDERSON *yields*]

HENDERSON. Okay, then, you guys! Line up into two
teams. Let's go.

[*The men divide into opposing teams, and* HENDER-
SON *begins calling signals. He executes a football play, taking the ball from the center and throwing
a pass to a man on his own team. At the end of the
play, a few of the men are shoving each other angrily and blaming each other for playing dirty and being
unnecessarily rough*]

Hey, take it easy, will you? Take it easy! It's only a game.
Let's go. Let's play.

[*The men divide again into opposing teams and exe-
cute two more football plays, each successively more
violent, each provoking reactions that are more hostile
and aggressive, while* HENDERSON *tries to calm them
down, shouting at them to stop their quarreling and
continue the game. By the end of the third play,
tempers go completely out of control: most of the
men are bellowing at each other wildly, and a brutal
free-for-all begins to erupt in different places all over
the stage. Just when it seems a group of men in the
foreground is about to smash one of the others and
tear him completely apart,* STARKEY *appears above
them with a large carton from his toy bin. He turns it
upside down, and a large number of children's colored
building blocks spill out. The men leave off their fighting to stare with amazement.* HENDERSON *is the first to
speak*]

What's that?

STARKEY. Building blocks! Build, men, build.

HENDERSON. You must be kidding.

STARKEY. Play, men, play.

[*Giggling like children, the men crawl across the floor*

*for the blocks and join together to begin building walls
and towers*]

HENDERSON. Fellas, don't do it. Don't play with those
things. Please. Fellas—goddammit!

[HENDERSON *charges into the center of the men, kick-
ing over the blocks. A few of them spring up furiously
to swing at him and drive him away.* STARKEY *returns
from the toy bin with another box. He tosses a few
baby rattles among the men*]

Rattles!

[STARKEY *moves among the men handing out other
rattles individually. The men take them eagerly.
When, with something of a sneer, he holds one out to*
HENDERSON, HENDERSON *pulls back with a look of
fear and revulsion.* STARKEY *laughs*]

Harmonicas. Does anybody here play a harmonica?

[*One of* THE IDIOTS *puts his hand up, and* STARKEY
*tosses a harmonica to him. Falteringly, he begins play-
ing "Old Folks at Home."* STARKEY *hums along, and
the men, like babies, try to keep time with their rattles
and listen to the noise intently.* STARKEY *puts his hand
in the box and draws out a rubber baby nipple attached to a long colored ribbon*]

Pacifiers!

[STARKEY *begins passing out the baby pacifiers to each
of the men. The men put the nipples in their mouths
and begin slowly to relax and lie down in positions
that suggest a complete reversion to infancy.* STARKEY
*regards with pleasure the results he is producing.*
HENDERSON *stands to the side and watches in utter
horror until he can bear it no longer*]

HENDERSON. Starkey! *Starkey!* What the hell are you doing
to these men? We're not babies! We're not kids. We're
grown-up men!

STARKEY. Men? Are you men? That's good, then. For I've
got just the game for all you grown-up men. All right, on
your knees now and form a circle. [*Coaxing, as though
to children*] On your knees. Form a circle.

[*The men, all but* HENDERSON, *rise to their knees and
form a circle, watching with curiosity and anticipation*

as STARKEY *returns to the toy bin.* STARKEY *takes out a
large replica of a round, black toy that is called "Time
Bomb." He begins winding it up. Immediately, a loud,
ominous ticking is heard from center stage.* STARKEY
*hands the bomb to the man nearest him*]

Okay, pass it around. Fast! Keep it moving.

[*Uncertainly, the man with the bomb tosses it to
someone else, and the men begin passing it from one
to the other*]

JOE. What is it? Captain, what is it?

STARKEY. It's a toy. It's called "Time Bomb." It's a game,
just like musical chairs. Keep it moving—fast, faster!
Whoever's got it when the bell rings, loses.

[*The men fall readily into the spirit of the game once
they understand, and they toss the bomb back and
forth like a hot potato. After a few seconds, a bell inside the bomb goes off loudly. The man holding the
bomb grins sheepishly; the others laugh and taunt him
good-naturedly as the bell rings for about five seconds
and runs down*]

JOE. Hey, this is pretty good. Let's play some more.

STARKEY. I'm glad you like it. Because I've got another one
for you. The Major wants us to have lots of replace-
ments. Put that one down now, and all stand up.

[STARKEY *takes out a second bomb, winds it, listens to
the ticking begin, and tosses the bomb out to start the
game again. The men play with freer enjoyment and
zeal, tossing the bomb from one to the other with
shouts and laughter. In a little while, the bell goes off.
The men begin to laugh again. But this time, as soon
as the bell rings,* STARKEY *speaks sharply to the man
holding the bomb*]

Throw it! Quick! Get rid of it! Throw it away! *Throw it!*

[*The man freezes with terror for an instant, then finally reacts. He turns, pulls his arm back, and hurls
the bomb away into the wings. Immediately, there is a
tremendous explosion from where the bomb has van-
ished. Fire flashes and smoke billows out onto the
stage around a shower of debris that spills from the
side and floats from above; and the men, all but*

STARKEY, *hit the floor and freeze, lying there as though dead for a few seconds. They are utterly without motion, all but* STARKEY, *who, wearing a smile, drifts back toward the toy bin.* BAILEY *lifts his head, and* HENDERSON *springs up in rage*]

BAILEY. Hey, what's the idea?

HENDERSON. Starkey—you bastard! You son of a bitch! Do you want to kill us? What—

STARKEY. Hold it! The Major wants me to give you one more. Everybody up. Up.

[*The men stir.* STARKEY *takes another bomb from the bin and begins to wind it*]

HENDERSON. Fellas, don't do it. Don't take it. You don't have to.

STARKEY. Yes, Henderson. They do. They do have to. See? On your feet now. Let's go. [*The men stand up slowly, as though lacking the power to disobey, and draw apart from each other in a wider circle than before*] Okay? One more time. Everybody ready and willing? Good. Keep it moving, boys. Remember—keep it moving.

[STARKEY *listens to the ticking for a second or two and tosses the bomb out, and the game begins again. This time, though, the men are rigid with fear and fling the bomb away as quickly as they can. An air of panic grows steadily*]

FISHER. Captain Starkey, sir. Please— [*The bomb is tossed to* FISHER *and he has to break off to catch it and throw it to somebody else*]

JOE. Sir? Sir? Which one is this? Is it the toy or is it the bomb?

STARKEY [*Laughing*]. Boys, that's where the real fun comes in. *I don't know!*

[*The men go almost wild with fear now as they pass the bomb around from one to the other rapidly. Finally the bell sounds. The man holding the bomb lets out a wailing gasp. In vivid horror, he tosses the bomb to* HENDERSON. *Startled,* HENDERSON *utters a loud cry and throws the bomb to* STARKEY. STARKEY *catches it and is thunderstruck to find himself holding it. He seems paralyzed. After an instant more of shocked be-*

*wilderment, he rushes toward the front of the stage, and, letting out a terrified, ear-splitting scream, draws his arm back to hurl the ringing time bomb out into the audience.*

*Suddenly, in mid-motion, STARKEY stops, chuckles pleasantly, and relaxes entirely. Holding the bomb up harmlessly, STARKEY continues moving toward the front of the stage with a comfortable, reassuring smile and addresses the audience, obviously enjoying the joke he has just played]*

It's okay, folks. This is not a real bomb, and nobody here is going to get hurt. Not yet. We're not really going to blow you up. So we can all relax now, because it's only a toy, isn't it?

*[Grinning and chuckling in the friendliest fashion, he stands there a moment. Then suddenly, with a brief, ferocious, hate-filled snarl, he again makes a motion to throw the bomb at the audience. The men on stage gasp and cringe reflexively]*

Isn't it?

*[The men on stage wait tensely until STARKEY smiles and begins chuckling heartily at this new prank. With an air of careless geniality, STARKEY tosses the bomb gently off the stage onto the floor in front of the first row of spectators. He turns back to the men]*

Okay, boys—that's it for now. Henderson, you get into a clean uniform. We're going to need you for an important assignment on that mission to Minnesota. The rest of you men can get this junk out of here now and take a ten-minute break. *[To the audience]* You too.

*[STARKEY takes his portfolio and his newspaper from inside the toy bin and starts away with a jaunty wave. The men stare after him speechlessly for a moment and then sink down to begin picking up the balls and baby toys as the curtain closes for a ten-minute intermission]*

## Act two

*The curtain opens on a silent and empty stage. The balls and toys have been removed.*

*FISHER and FISHER's KID BROTHER enter slowly. FISHER is dressed in his uniform. FISHER's KID BROTHER wears civilian clothes appropriate to his age and the current local fashion. He is very young, in his early teens. He looks about the stage with great amusement and curiosity, obviously pleased to be there.*

YOUNG FISHER. Is this where it all happens? [FISHER *nods*] Where are the planes and the bombs and the targets?

FISHER. Oh, that's all out there someplace. All the fighting takes place far away.

YOUNG FISHER [*Referring to the audience*]. They don't see it?

FISHER. No, they wouldn't like that. There's no violence out here, and no blood. Nobody gets killed here, so you don't have to worry. There's no violence in public.

YOUNG FISHER. There's lots of violence in Shakespeare.

FISHER. Shakespeare had a low audience. We've got a high audience. We're all here for a good time. That's why we've got all those guns and planes and toys.

YOUNG FISHER. Can I make a speech? To them?

FISHER. Sure. If you do it before anyone comes. Go ahead.
    [YOUNG FISHER *steps forward hesitantly toward the audience*]

YOUNG FISHER [*To FISHER*]. What should I say?

FISHER. Say "thanks."

YOUNG FISHER. For what?

FISHER. For letting you come here. You can thank them all for letting you come here and be a soldier.

YOUNG FISHER [*Stricken with shyness*]. No.

FISHER. Say hello. Go ahead. It's just like talking into a telephone. [YOUNG FISHER *shakes his head bashfully and starts to drift back*] I'll show you. [*Steps forward to address the audience*] Hello? [*Listens a moment and turns back to his brother*] See? It's just like talking into a telephone.

YOUNG FISHER. Maybe later. Where's everyone else?

FISHER. They'll be here soon. Wait till you see the way we all get going. Look . . . look!

[*Two men burst suddenly onstage, struggling earnestly and violently for possession of a basketball*]

That's an idiot!

YOUNG FISHER. Which one?

FISHER. I can't tell.

[*The two men pull apart angrily. One of them, an* IDIOT, *has the ball and guards it defiantly. The other man is* JOE. JOE *snarls at* THE IDIOT]

JOE. Aah, to hell with you. [*To* FISHER] Where's Bailey? Where's Henderson? [*Calling across the stage into the wings*] Hey, Bailey! Hey, Henderson! Who's got a goddam ball?

[*Another* IDIOT *comes on with a basketball.* JOE *grabs it away from him and holds it up triumphantly.* BAILEY *and the other* IDIOTS *stream back onstage slowly, returning from their dressing rooms after the intermission. The mood of most of them is still somewhat subdued, as at the end of Act I.* JOE *walks toward* YOUNG FISHER]

Hey, who's this?

FISHER. My kid brother. He's with the company now.

JOE. Welcome aboard, kid. How old are you?

YOUNG FISHER. Fifteen.

JOE. You're lucky. You're gonna have a good time here.

BAILEY [*Bitterly*]. Yeah, a great time. That bastard almost blew us up just now.

JOE. Aaah, he was only fooling.

[RUTH *enters from the side, balancing a stack of donuts on a wooden stick. Seeing that no one is noticing her, she steps forward hurriedly toward the footlights to address the audience, brandishing her stack of donuts like a sword*]

RUTH [*Kidding*]. "Once more, unto the breach, dear friends, once more."

BAILEY. Hey, get out of here, goddammit! That's my speech!

[RUTH *retreats and exits on the other side*]

FISHER. No, it isn't. It's Sergeant Henderson's.

BAILEY. Well, it will be mine when I take Henderson's place. "Once more, unto the——"

[HENDERSON *enters, looking resentful, chewing on a pacifier for ironic effect. Under his arm, he conceals and grips something the same way he might hold a football. He has changed his bloodstained uniform for a clean one*]

HENDERSON. Well, listen to that greedy corporal!

BAILEY. Yeah? Well, look at the great big sergeant with the baby nipple in his mouth. Hey, is that our football?

HENDERSON. Do you want it? Then run out for a pass.

[BAILEY *darts away eagerly, and the others respond also*]

BAILEY. Throw it, throw it!

[HENDERSON *fades back like an experienced ball-player and cocks his arm to throw; what he is holding is now seen to be some rolled-up garments.* HENDERSON *lofts the garments toward* BAILEY *as he would pass a football. They come apart in midair and fall to the floor.* BAILEY *holds them up in surprise, a pair of trousers, a sports shirt, and an old pair of shoes*]

What's this?

HENDERSON [*Sardonically*]. Don't you recognize him?

BAILEY. Who?

HENDERSON. Sinclair. Don't you remember Sinclair? Our friend? Our contemporary? The one that didn't want to go on the mission to Constantinople. Those are his remains.

BAILEY. These?

HENDERSON. Two rags and an old pair of shoes. That's all
that's left of him. That's all I could find.

JOE. You mean he left with his uniform?

HENDERSON. I mean he left with his boots on, if he left at
all. [*Cups his hands around his mouth and calls out into
the theater at the top of his voice*] Sinclair!

    [*There is no answer.* HENDERSON *turns back to the
others with a shrug. Before he can speak, there is heard
suddenly from offstage the voices of the two* SPORTS-
MEN *counting a strange, droning military cadence,
coming closer*]

SPORTSMEN [*Offstage*]. Glup ... glup ... glup, gloop, glup.
Glup ... glup ... glup, gloop, glup.

BAILEY. Well, I'll be damned! Make way for the army.

    [*While the others all stare with amusement, the
two* SPORTSMEN *march happily out onstage, still carrying the golf club and shotgun. They wear military
pants now and military shirts, open at the collar, and
on their arms are loose MP bands. On their heads,
they still wear respectively the golfing and hunting
caps in which they were seen earlier, and the total effect of their marching and costume is to give them an
incongruous and totally ridiculous appearance. A few
of the men let out taunting shouts and follow in jeer-
ing emulation, while* BAILEY *moves up to take over the
cadence count*]

Left ... left ... left, right, left! You had a good home
when you left!

SPORTSMEN. You're right!

    [*The men are impressed by the smart, accurate re-
sponses of* THE SPORTSMEN]

BAILEY. Your mother was sad when you left!

SPORTSMEN. You're right!

BAILEY. Sound off!

SPORTSMEN. One, two!

BAILEY. Hit it again!

SPORTSMEN. Three, four!

BAILEY. Change count!

    [*Others, all but* HENDERSON, *join in*]

ALL. One, two, three, four, one, two ... three, four!

[THE SPORTSMEN *halt at attention. Before the men can resume making fun,* THE MAJOR *enters, carrying his script and wearing a smile, as though he has been observing the stage action with approval*]

MAJOR. That was good. Right? [*The men nod and* THE MAJOR *adjusts the MP band on the arm of one*] Let's show them what else you've learned. Attention! Right face! Left face! Present arms! Shoulder arms! Port arms! Ready!

[THE SPORTSMEN *respond efficiently to each order. At this last command, issued in a louder voice, each assumes a position appropriate to the implement he is carrying.* THE GOLFER *turns to the side and takes the stance of a man about to tee off.* THE HUNTER *extends his shotgun in the manner of a skeet shooter waiting for the target to appear.* THE MAJOR *observes them for a second or two*]

Aim!

[*At this command,* THE GOLFER *swings his club back and up and holds his position.* THE HUNTER *aims his shotgun and waits alertly for* THE MAJOR *to issue his next command*]

Fire!

[THE GOLFER *swings;* THE HUNTER *pulls the trigger and there is a click from his unloaded gun*]

HUNTER [*Speaking*]. Bang!

MAJOR. Very, very good. [*To the others*] Right? [*The others nod in perfunctory agreement*] Now . . . double-time . . . march! Hut . . . two . . . three . . . four . . .

[THE SPORTSMEN *begin trotting offstage. A second or so before* THE SPORTSMEN *disappear,* THE MAJOR *begins clapping his hands, applauding their performance. He signals to the other men, and they begin clapping too. After* THE SPORTSMEN *go,* THE MAJOR *turns, still clapping, to include the men in his approval also. He stops. The men continue clapping their hands for a few more seconds before they take notice of the glowering look on* THE MAJOR's *face and realize that he wants them to stop applauding too*]

Very good. Now we're all doing fine. Where's Starkey?

BAILEY [*Before* HENDERSON *can reply*]. I think he's with his wife now, sir. [*Points after* RUTH] She just went out that way with her stack of donuts.

MAJOR. Henderson?

HENDERSON. Sir?

MAJOR. You take charge of them till Starkey gets here.

HENDERSON. *Yes, sir!*

MAJOR. Do you know what to do?

HENDERSON. Oh, yes indeed, sir. I certainly do. I can handle it all. I could do everything the captain does. I could take over for him right now if you wanted me to.

MAJOR [*Sharply*]. I *don't* want you to. I only want you to keep them going until the captain gets here, and that's all I want you to do. Do you understand?

HENDERSON [*Backing away in humiliation*]. Yes, sir.

MAJOR. Carry on, then.

HENDERSON. Yes, sir.

> [THE MAJOR *glares at him a moment longer and begins walking away.* HENDERSON, *sulking with disappointment, puts the pacifier back in his mouth.* THE MAJOR *turns slowly back toward him with a look of contempt*]

MAJOR. And by the way, Henderson. Take that silly thing out of your mouth and start acting your age. There's nothing really funny about this, you know.

> [HENDERSON *removes the pacifier from his mouth and looks meekly for some place to dispose of it. Finally, he shoves it into his pocket*]

HENDERSON [*Sheepishly*]. Yes, sir.

> [THE MAJOR *exits. The men are motionless until* THE MAJOR *has gone. Then they separate and sprawl out on the ground. A few light cigarettes.* YOUNG FISHER *seats himself on a basketball.* HENDERSON *gazes after* THE MAJOR *furiously*]

God, I hate that bastard! I really do. When I stop to think about him, I hate him!

YOUNG FISHER. What's wrong with him?

> [HENDERSON *whirls angrily and kicks the ball from under him*]

HENDERSON. Who the hell are *you?*

FISHER. He's my kid brother. He's replacing Sinclair.

HENDERSON. Him? [*Relenting immediately, he helps the frightened boy to his feet and tries apologetically to calm him*] I'm sorry. I'm really sorry. Are you all right? He's so young. You're just a little kid, aren't you?

YOUNG FISHER [*Seriously*]. They said that the younger they took me into the service, the better it would be for me. They said it would disrupt my life less if I got killed sooner.

HENDERSON. Well, I'll be damned. They want a kid, so they get a kid. They want some idiots, so they get some real ones. [*Scanning* THE IDIOTS] That's something I'm still not sure of. Are you idiots really idiots, or aren't you? [THE IDIOTS *regard him in expressionless silence, giving no clue at all*] No help. [*To the audience*] They're pretty good, aren't they—for a bunch of idiots! [*Speaking to* THE IDIOTS] You know, I'm starting to figure something out. You five idiots are either very smart or very dumb. If you're very smart, you wouldn't be here with us. But you are here with us, so that means you're very dumb. But we're not very dumb, are we, and we're here with you. We're pretty bright, in fact. We're much smarter than you, but here we are *with* you. So that means we may be much dumber than you after all, doesn't it? Doesn't it? [*One of* THE IDIOTS *giggles*] Hey, listen to *him!* Next thing you know they'll all begin talking. *Then* what a time we'll have trying to figure out who's in charge. Everybody's got big ambitions around here. Especially Rudolph, who wants to be a sergeant and take my place. Right, Bailey, boy?

BAILEY. Yeah, what about you just now when you thought you had a chance to be captain? [*Jumps up and does a derisive imitation of* HENDERSON *earlier*] Oh, yes, sir, Major, sir. I can handle it all, sir. I can do everything the captain does if you wanted me to, sir. Yes, sir, no, sir, no, sir, yes, sir.

> [BAILEY *bends over to deliver an imitation of* HENDERSON *kissing the* MAJOR's *rear end.* HENDERSON *advances upon him in anger and embarrassment*]

HENDERSON. How would you like a punch in the face?

[BAILEY *is not intimidated and faces him aggressively*]

BAILEY. You just try it buddy. You just try it and I'll throw you the hell out into the eighth row center.

[HENDERSON *is startled by* BAILEY'S *response and already sorry for his own truculence*]

HENDERSON. Okay. Okay.

BAILEY. Don't get carried away by those sergeant's stripes. They're only decorations, you know.

HENDERSON. Okay, I said. I said okay, didn't I? Everybody's turning very mean around here suddenly, aren't we?

JOE. It's a war, kid. I told you that.

FISHER. Hey, Henderson. You're supposed to get busy now. The Major said you should keep things going until Captain Starkey gets here.

HENDERSON. Let Starkey do his own God damned work. He's getting all the credit.

[HENDERSON *and the others settle down comfortably on the floor*]

YOUNG FISHER. Is this all we do?

FISHER. Just for a little while. Then we've got some real good things coming up.

HENDERSON [*Sarcastically*]. Sure, some wonderful things. War can be a pretty beautiful experience . . . if you're on the winning side and you don't get hurt. I was killed once, a long time ago, in a play called *Journey's End*.

BAILEY. Hey, I saw you in that.

HENDERSON. Yeah, I know—I stank.

BAILEY [*Enjoying his own malice*]. No—you had one good moment.

HENDERSON. But I didn't mind getting killed then, because it was all in fun, although I forget which war that was. I've been in lots of wars. I was in World War II three times, once in a movie. But this war beats them all. There's no enemy in this one. There are just things, and we go out and destroy them, just because they're things. It's a war against things, and I'm not sure I like it any more.

FISHER [*To* YOUNG FISHER]. Aah, don't mind him. You

joined up with us at a very good time. We go on leave soon.

HENDERSON [*Caustically*]. And get more medals and more money.

BAILEY. And I get promoted.

JOE. We have lots of dames and lots of booze.

FISHER. We visit the best cities in the world.

HENDERSON. Before we destroy them.

BAILEY. And I get promoted.

FISHER. In Rome, we see the Colosseum.

BAILEY. Just once.

JOE. And then we go dancing and loving with those beautiful Italian girls.

FISHER. We visit St. Peter's.

BAILEY. Just once.

JOE. And then it's back to those beautiful girls. Hey, Henderson, remember the fun we used to have—you, me, and those beautiful girls? [JOE *laughs, draws a deep breath, and begins singing softly*]

"Roll me over,
 In the clover,
 Roll me over, lay me down, and do it again."

HENDERSON [*Remembering with enthusiasm*]. Yeah, yeah, yeah—I've got to admit that. Kid, they've got these big things built in Naples that will knock your eyes out. They're called . . . *hookers*.

BAILEY. In Paris—

FISHER. We visit the Louvre.

BAILEY. Just once! And then I flop into bed with one of those beautiful French cuties and really make love—

HENDERSON. Just once!

[BAILEY *and the others laugh*]

BAILEY. Hey, I make the jokes here. You make the speeches.

HENDERSON. Yeah. And you get promoted.

JOE [*Enumerating on his fingers*]. We have sex orgies in New York, New Haven, Los Angeles—

BAILEY. No—we bombed in New Haven three weeks ago.

FISHER. Before that, it was Philadelphia.

BAILEY. Boston.

JOE. Amsterdam. And Stockholm, Sweden.

FISHER. Denver, Colorado.

HENDERSON. *That's* what we do! You want to know who
we are? You want to know what we really do?

> [YOUNG FISHER *nods enthusiastically, and* HENDERSON
> *begins singing. The others join in, and they romp
> boisterously through a song for* YOUNG FISHER's *amusement*]

SONG.
> "With my feet on the glass.
> And my head up my ass,
> I just go bomb, bomb, bombing along.
> It's easy to rate,
> When you're dropping 'em straight,
> And just keep bomb, bomb, bombing along.
> With plenty of hits,
> And a low C.E.
> Oh, what Saint Peter
> Will do to me!
> We've got our feet on the glass,
> And our head up our ass,
> As we go bomb, bomb, bombing along."

BAILEY [*Singing*]. "Let's kill New Haven."

ALL [*Singing*]. "As we go bomb, bomb, bombing along."

> [*The song ends with laughter and with exaggerated
> bows and other gestures of self-congratulation. Then
> a sudden letdown seems to seize them all, as though
> the consequences of what they've been saying and
> singing about are really not so funny after all*]

HENDERSON. Oh, yes. I've got to admit it. We are going to
have a hell of a good time.

BAILEY [*Relishing the reminder*]. But first we've got to fly
that mission to Minnesota.

FISHER [*To* HENDERSON]. And you get killed.

> [*The grin on* HENDERSON's *face freezes, then turns
> slowly into a frown*]

HENDERSON. I do?

JOE. Sure.

BAILEY. That's why *I* get promoted.

HENDERSON. That's right, I do.

BAILEY. Sure. You and you—Fisher—and one of the idiots, that big one with the blond hair. Right?

[*At this,* FISHER *looks confused.* JOE *begins moving stealthily away to the side*]

HENDERSON. I'm gonna be dead—so soon? Just like that?

FISHER [*Rousing himself*]. Hey, wait a minute! Wait a minute! I'm not the one who gets killed now! [*To* JOE] *You're* the one who gets killed now. Aren't you?

JOE [*Somberly*]. Yeah. I was kind of hoping you wouldn't notice the difference. I'd like to be around a little longer too, even though I'm getting old.

HENDERSON. You mean I'm really supposed to go out now and get killed? Just like Sinclair?

BAILEY. Oh, no. He got wounded and bled to death. You blow up . . . in a big explosion . . . right over the field, where *everybody* can hear you.

HENDERSON. And then you're all gonna go out and have a good time? After I'm dead?

BAILEY. Why not? You're not the only person who ever got killed in a war.

HENDERSON. Well, Jesus Christ. I'd like to have something happen after I'm gone—something to show that I'd been here once. I'd like to be remembered. Really, I would.

BAILEY. You'll be remembered. We'll even talk about you once in a while. Just like we talk about Sinclair.

JOE. Will you talk about me, too?

BAILEY. Sure, Joe. Why not?

HENDERSON [*Bitterly*]. Yeah. I know how we miss Sinclair. I'm the only one that even looks for him. Aren't you ever gonna be sad?

FISHER. I'll be sad.

BAILEY. Just once.

HENDERSON. And then?

BAILEY. We have fun.

HENDERSON. Oh, great. While I'm lying out there dead.

BAILEY. What do you want us to do? Hold services?

HENDERSON [*Indicates audience*]. What about them? Are they gonna care if I get killed?

BAILEY. Why should they? That's what they came to see.

HENDERSON. Did they? Well, it's too bad about them. Look what happened to Sinclair?

BAILEY. What happened to Sinclair?

HENDERSON. I don't know what happened to Sinclair! [*Fumbles through* SINCLAIR's *shirt and trousers and shoes as though searching for him there and then calls out again*] Sinclair! [*Listens a moment, hears no response, and then tosses the clothes away*] You see?

BAILEY. Goddammit—I want my promotion! You've got to fly to Minnesota now, and you've got to be killed.

HENDERSON. Who says so?

BAILEY. I say so. And the Major says so.

HENDERSON. Well, I'll tell you something. [*To the audience*] I'll tell you all something. [*To the audience and the men on stage*] I'm not going to go out now and get killed just because I'm expected to. I don't like the Major. And I suddenly don't like any part of this, either. Because after I get killed, you get killed, and after you get killed, you get killed, and after—

YOUNG FISHER. Me? I just got here.

HENDERSON. So what? Why the hell do you think they got you here? And after you get killed—

BAILEY. I get promoted.

HENDERSON. You get promoted! Big deal! You get promoted! And after you get promoted, then what do you get?

BAILEY [*Puzzled*]. Killed?

HENDERSON. How should I know? By that time I'm already dead and gone . . . and forgotten, too!

BAILEY. I don't care! I want my promotion, anyway. I don't know what I want! But I know I want my promotion!

HENDERSON. Well, that's just too bad. Because I have a small announcement to make to you, to the Major . . . [*Facing the audience*] . . . and to everyone else concerned with the progress of this enterprise. I'm not going. [HENDERSON *sits down.* JOE *and one of* THE IDIOTS *begin applauding*]

BAILEY. What are you applauding for?

JOE [*Glumly*]. If he don't go, I can't go. I don't want to die yet, either.

BAILEY [*To* IDIOT]. What are you applauding for?

  [THE IDIOT *sits down*]

HENDERSON. He's learning, that's why! He's not such an idiot after all!

BAILEY. Okay, I don't care. It's not my worry. Let everything stop. Just sit here and do nothing and see what happens when Starkey comes.

JOE. What happens when Starkey comes?

BAILEY. I straighten up and I holler—

FISHER. Attention!

BAILEY [*Pushes* FISHER *roughly and angrily*]. Hey, I'm supposed to say that! What the hell are you stealing my line for? Attention!

  [BAILEY *and a few of the others stand up at attention.* HENDERSON, JOE, *and* THE IDIOT *remain seated.* STARKEY *strolls in, smiling pleasantly, chewing on a piece from a donut he holds in one hand. In his other hand, he carries his portfolio and his newspaper*]

STARKEY. Hey, up, up. You're all supposed to be at attention when I walk in. [*Senses something amiss*] What's wrong?

BAILEY. There's a slight rebellion in progress. A kind of insurrection.

STARKEY. What kind of rebellion?

BAILEY. Ask him.

STARKEY [*To* HENDERSON]. What kind of rebellion?

HENDERSON. Ask him.

STARKEY. Come on, fellas, we've got work to do. There's no more time for games.

BAILEY. It's him, sir. He doesn't want to go to Minnesota and get killed.

STARKEY. Why not?

HENDERSON. Why not?

STARKEY. Yeah, why not? Why don't you want to get killed?

HENDERSON. What are you eating?

STARKEY. A donut.

HENDERSON. That's why not. How come you have a donut now and I don't?

STARKEY. Oh, Jesus, is that all? If I give you the donut, will
   you go get killed?

HENDERSON. You've *got* the donut. So *you* get killed.

STARKEY. It isn't even a good donut. Listen, Henderson—
   I'm sorry if I've been picking on you and criticizing you,
   and I'm sorry if the two of us don't like each other and
   don't get along. But you haven't exactly been making
   things easy for me either, you know. Let's try to keep
   personal feelings out of this. We've both got a job to do.
   You've got yours, and I've got mine.

HENDERSON. Your job is better than mine.

STARKEY. Well, we all can't have everything.

HENDERSON. Say, that's a swell line. We oughta bomb that
   line instead of Minnesota.

STARKEY. Now you're getting rotten again.

HENDERSON. Let's change jobs now, you and me.

STARKEY. Oh, no. Not a chance. I like my job. I kind of
   like my job here an awful lot, Henderson. And that's
   why I'm just not going to let you jeopardize it. I'm going
   to keep giving you orders. And you're going to keep
   right on obeying them. Because I kind of like things here
   just the way they are.

HENDERSON. Is that right? Why should I have to go out
   and die now while you and the Major live? Is that fair?

STARKEY. Who cares whether it's "fair" or not? You've got
   to go out now and destroy Minnesota before it's too late.

HENDERSON. Too late for what?

STARKEY. Well . . . too late to destroy it, I guess. Henderson, my friend—[*slips an arm around* HENDERSON's
   *shoulders*]—let me advise you, once more just—[*Almost without realizing it*, STARKEY *begins to recite, turning into an actor consciously playing a cherished role*]
   "Once more unto the breach, dear friend, once more."

HENDERSON. Are you queer?

STARKEY [*Surprised*]. No, of course not. [*Reciting*] "Or
   close the wall up with our English dead." [*Speaking normally*] Why do you ask?

HENDERSON. Why do you have your arm around me?

STARKEY. Huh? Just to be kind of friendly to you . . . you
   know, fatherly . . . to speak to you like a father to a son.

HENDERSON [*Coldly*]. I don't want you to.

　　[STARKEY *removes his arm and shrugs*]

STARKEY. Okay. Why not?

HENDERSON. I've already had a father. I don't trust *you*, either.

STARKEY. You *can* trust me. I'm not a liar. And I'm not a phony or a hypocrite. Henderson, let me tell you something as an older and wiser man, something sincere that comes right from the heart. [*Carried away again by the opportunity to perform,* STARKEY *begins reciting*]

"In peace there's nothing so becomes a man
As modest stillness and humility;
But when the blast of war blows in our ears,
Then imitate the action of the tiger!"

　　[STARKEY *breaks off abruptly when he notices that the men are listening with expressions that are impassive and scornful*]

What's the matter? Don't you like what I'm saying?

HENDERSON. I do it better.

BAILEY [*He sits down*]. Even your wife does it better.

STARKEY. I'm not doing this for effect, you know. [*There is a shade too much of the histrionic in* STARKEY's *denial; and the men react with catcalls and jeers.* STARKEY *continues heatedly, but soon reverts to his manner of pompous and pedantic recitation*] Do you know what the Roman emperor Augustus Caesar said just before he died? He called it "The Comedy of Life." "Remember," said the Emperor Augustus, as he lay on his deathbed, "that you are an actor in a play, the character of which is determined by the Playwright."

BAILEY. That great playwright in the sky.

　　[STARKEY *frowns, but goes on*]

STARKEY. "If He wishes the play to be short, it is short; if long, it is long; if He wishes you to play the part of a beggar, remember to act even this role adroitly; and so if your role be that of a cripple, an official, or a layman. For this is your business, to play admirably the role assigned you—"

HENDERSON. Especially if it's the role of an emperor.

BAILEY. Or a major.

JOE. Or even a captain.

STARKEY. "—but the selection of that role is another's."
And then Augustus asked those around him if he had
played well the comedy of life. And when they nodded—

HENDERSON. Of course they nodded. He was the emperor.

STARKEY. —and when they nodded, Augustus added:
"Since well I've played my part, all clap your hands. And
from the stage dismiss me with applause."

> [FISHER *and a few of the standing* IDIOTS *applaud, and*
> STARKEY *starts to bow.* HENDERSON's *sharp question
> stops him*]

HENDERSON. How old was the Emperor Augustus when he
died?

STARKEY. Seventy-seven.

HENDERSON. Let *me* live till seventy-seven, and *I'll* play
well the comedy of life.

> [STARKEY *is stopped a moment by the request. He an-
> swers earnestly*]

STARKEY. I can't . . . do that.

HENDERSON. Let me live ten more years. Can you promise
me that?

STARKEY. I can't promise.

HENDERSON. One more year.

STARKEY. It can't be done.

HENDERSON. One more hour?

STARKEY. It's too late.

HENDERSON. Will you let me live until ———? [*He names
the exact time at which the play might be expected to
end*] Until the curtain finally comes down?

STARKEY. It's too late.

HENDERSON. And you're advising me to go?

STARKEY. You have to go.

HENDERSON. Are you telling me that now as a father? Or
as a captain? Or as an actor? Or as a friend?

STARKEY. I'm telling it to you as a man.

HENDERSON. That's a crooked answer.

STARKEY. I have no other.

HENDERSON. Then I'll quit.

STARKEY. You can't quit. It's against the rules.

HENDERSON. Change the rules!

STARKEY. It's too late! And it's too late for any more of this argument, too. Come on, before the Major gets here. [*Claps his hands to rouse the men*] Let's go, all of you! We've got work to do. We've got one more city to bomb and a million more men to kill. [*To* HENDERSON] You, too. When you've been in this business as long as I have, you'll learn that the moving finger writes, and having writ—

HENDERSON. Pokes you in the eye.

STARKEY. —moves on! On! On your toes, men! On your feet! On with the scenery. Let's get cracking! Where's that wall? Where's that door? Where's the Major's office? Bring them all on! On with the show!

BAILEY [*Rises to obey*]. Okay—let's go!

[*The others follow after* BAILEY *to begin working, all but* HENDERSON]

STARKEY [*To* HENDERSON]. There's the rub, my lad. The play's the thing, and the play must go on. So pitch in now with the others—get going—and give us our maps and our planes and our benches and our bombs.

[HENDERSON *moves reluctantly to join the others. Slowly at first, but with increasing zeal, the men get busy bringing out the props and scenery that create the briefing room of* ACT ONE. STARKEY *observes with pleasure as they respond. He begins to hum. They are engaged in doing exactly what they were doing when the curtain rose prematurely to begin the play. Even* HENDERSON *joins in.* YOUNG FISHER *stands around awkwardly a moment and then approaches* STARKEY]

YOUNG FISHER. Sir?

STARKEY. Who are you?

FISHER [*Calling out*]. He's my baby brother. I brought him here to replace Sinclair.

STARKEY. Good.

YOUNG FISHER. Are you going to kill me, too?

STARKEY [*Arrested by the question*]. What?

YOUNG FISHER. Are you going to kill me, too?

STARKEY. Who?

YOUNG FISHER. You, sir.

STARKEY. When?

YOUNG FISHER. Now,

STARKEY. Me? No, of course not. I don't kill anybody. Go get into a flight suit like the others. Ha, ha—we won't kill you until we have to.

YOUNG FISHER. Thank you, sir.

[YOUNG FISHER *exits eagerly.* STARKEY *turns from him with relief, only to have his attention beckoned by* RUTH, *who steps out on stage timidly.* STARKEY *reacts to her with frantic alarm*]

RUTH. Starkey! Hey, Starkey!

STARKEY. Ruthie, honey! What the hell are *you* doing out here?

RUTH. Can I come out again and say something?

STARKEY. No, darling, you can't! You're all finished now.

RUTH. Can't I even bring a cup of coffee to the Major?

STARKEY. You did that before!

RUTH. I thought of something new.

STARKEY. There isn't time. Go away now.

RUTH [*Looking around*]. What's going on?

STARKEY. We're getting ready to bomb Minnesota.

RUTH. This is better. Listen— [*She dodges past* STARKEY *as he tries to restrain her*] Let me try it out! That's the least you can do.

STARKEY. Okay, okay. But hurry it up, will you?

RUTH. I will. I promise. [*She braces herself regally to deliver a speech of immense dramatic import, draws a deep breath, and finally begins*] "Babylon once had two million people in it, and all we know—"

STARKEY [*Amazed*]. Oh, come on!

RUTH. Shhhh—shhhh! [*Resuming*] "—and all we know about them is the names of their kings and we have some copies of wheat contracts and contracts for the sale of slaves."

STARKEY. Ruth!

RUTH. Listen. I want to say something beautiful now so that people a thousand years from now will know: "This is the way we were. This is the way we were: in our growing up and in our marrying and in our living and in our dying." *That's* what I want to say.

STARKEY. You do, do you?

RUTH. Yes, That's pretty important.

STARKEY. I know it is. That's the stage manager's speech from *Our Town!* And *you* can't say it.

RUTH. But you can.

STARKEY. I'm a captain here, remember?

RUTH. That's better than being a captain and doing what you're doing now. Ten minutes after you bomb Minnesota everyone will forget you even did it.

STARKEY. So what?

RUTH. But they might remember you, they might care more about us, they might understand us all a lot better if you came down to the front of the stage—right now—and said something simple and beautiful and true about the kind of people we are and the way we live.

STARKEY [*Shakes his head sadly*]. This is the way we live. This is the kind of people we are. And I am a captain here. That's my role now, and this is my business, to help get this mission to Minnesota over with. So go away now, darling, and let me do my job—before I lose it.

   [RUTH *gives up. She comes into his arms and they kiss quickly*]

RUTH. Okay—at least I tried. When'll I see you?

STARKEY. Home. No—back in your dressing room. But get out of here now—before the Major comes.

   [RUTH *frowns as* STARKEY *begins leading her offstage. In haste, she pulls away from* STARKEY *to make a final address to the audience*]

RUTH. Thank you. Thank you all for everything. And goodbye. You've been a wonderful audience. And this has been a wonderful occasion for me. I want to thank every one of you for making it possible for me to be here to receive this wonderful honor, and I want to give credit to everyone connected with this for—I could not have done it without them!

   [RUTH'*s last words rise to a scream, for* STARKEY *manages to seize her while she curtsies, and he pulls her out of sight with him into the wings as she is speaking.*

STARKEY *returns a few seconds later, shaking his head indulgently. He starts back toward the center to continue supervising the setting of the scene. The last elements of the set are being pushed into place.*

THE MAJOR, *back in his military uniform, strides out from the other side, carrying his script again. He seems in a great hurry.*

*In other parts of the stage, the other men are rushing about putting the final touches on the set they have assembled, working in a way that becomes almost an exact repetition of the opening moments of the first scene*]

MAJOR. Starkey?

STARKEY. Yes, sir.

MAJOR. Have them stay right here when they're finished. I don't want to lose any more time.

STARKEY. Yes, sir! [*To the men*] Stay right here when you're finished. We don't want to lose any more time. And snap it up! Snap it up! We don't want to lose any more time.

[*The men move more quickly*]

MAJOR. Starkey!

STARKEY. Yes, sir!

MAJOR. This time we'll call the roll immediately. I want to blow Minnesota off the map before someone else does.

STARKEY. Yes, sir! [*To the men*] Okay, finish up, finish up! And then everybody line right up for the roll call. Let's go, men. Let's go. [*The men speed up their activities still further, putting the last things in place, then come together in the assembly area and mill about uncertainly in an attempt to form a line. Starkey approaches with his clipboard*] All set? Then let's begin. [*Bends toward his clipboard*] Henderson! [*There is no answer.* STARKEY *calls out again, still with his head down*] Sergeant Henderson! [*Again there is no answer. This time, a few of the men begin looking around among themselves, searching for* HENDERSON. STARKEY *speaks again, more loudly than before and with growing irritation*] Henderson, goddammit—why the hell don't you . . . answer . . . when . . . [STARKEY *advances in anger toward the men,*

[Shouts toward ... about this!
on!

... kets and military boots to their MP uni- ... quickly, one carrying his golf ... ying his shotgun. They have added ole , and there is about them now an air of inexora- ble competence, as though they have learned very quickly all the things they are supposed to be doing]

BOTH SPORTSMEN. Yes, sir!

MAJOR. That sergeant is missing. Henderson. Have you seen him?

BOTH SPORTSMEN. No, sir!

... ot see
... e each
... g them] when they

... ently]

... ee isn't. [As he gets no answer] He's sup-

... I go get him. What do you mean he isn't here? He's sup-
and JOE. Fast. You, you. [THE MAJOR points to FISHER calling HENDERSON's name] He has to be here. We can't go
ahead without him. He's got to die now on the takeoff
for Minnesota.
  [FISHER returns, then JOE]
FISHER. He didn't answer me.
JOE. I don't see him.
MAJOR. Dammit, I'll kill him! Where is he?
JOE [Serious]. Maybe he went A.W.O.L.
  [BAILEY starts to laugh]
MAJOR. There's nothing funny ...
the wings] Hey, Bill! Hey, R... son.
  [THE SPORTSMEN enter ...
club, the other car ...
ties and helm ...
forms ...

... ailey! My favo...
... aven't you?

[*The men receive the question in stubborn silence. They would just as soon stop*]

We can't just stand here, can we?

FISHER. Can we go home then?

MAJOR. No, you can't go home!

JOE. Can I go on furlough? I've got lots of leave coming to me.

MAJOR. No, you can't go on furlough, not now.

JOE. When then?

MAJOR. After the mission.

JOE. I get killed on the mission.

MAJOR. Then you won't need the furlough.

JOE. I want my furlough.

MAJOR [*Shouting out into the theater in exasperation*]. Where's Henderson? [*There is no response*] I'll blast him apart!

BAILEY. Can we go to our dressing rooms and wait?

MAJOR. No! You can wait right here! [*To* STARKEY] We have to do *something!*

STARKEY. We could close the curtains now and take another break.

MAJOR [*Shouts*]. Yes, close the curtains. But no break. [*To the men as the curtains start to close and the lights dim*] Just move all that junk out here. Wait till I find Henderson. Then I'll really show you all something. Starkey, you can come with me.

[*As the curtain is closing, the men go to the side and begin moving a set and props onstage.* THE MAJOR *and* STARKEY *walk downstage in front of the curtain, and the curtain closes completely behind them.* THE MAJOR, *alone with* STARKEY *in front of the curtain, shows a trace of anxiety, weariness, and despair*]

They've got to be watched. I never really trust them. I bet they're horsing around and complaining right now. I'll bet they're even smoking. They've always got to be watched.

STARKEY. Should I go back and watch them?

MAJOR. I want you to find Henderson.

STARKEY. Suppose he's already gone?

MAJOR [*Tiredly, and with a touch of sadness*]. He has to

be somewhere. Find Henderson and bring him back. I'm
tired. I work hard, too.

STARKEY. I never heard you talk like *that* before.

MAJOR. That's because you never listen. You're always so
busy with your wife and your donuts.

STARKEY. I do my job, don't I?

MAJOR. You do it very well. Go find Henderson.

STARKEY. What will you do with him?

MAJOR. I'm gonna kill him.

STARKEY. No, I mean it.

MAJOR. So do I. I'm going to kill him.

STARKEY. You can't *kill* him, really.

MAJOR. Why not?

STARKEY. Are you kidding?

MAJOR. Are you?

STARKEY. You can't just kill people.

MAJOR. Why not?

STARKEY. Because you just—well, can't.

MAJOR. And just what do you think we've been doing?

STARKEY. Are you serious?

MAJOR [*Turning away*]. Go find Henderson and bring him
back so I can kill him and get it over with.

STARKEY. You really think you're going to kill him?

MAJOR. If I have to.

STARKEY. Right here? Right out in front of all these people?
In front of all these witnesses?

MAJOR. If I have to.

STARKEY. Oh, no. They won't let you. They won't just sit
there and let you kill him.

MAJOR. Yes, they will.

STARKEY. Listen. Do you mean it when you say that?

MAJOR. Do *you* mean it when you ask that?

STARKEY. Oh, God! Why won't you ever answer a question?

MAJOR [*Taunting him*]. Why won't you?

STARKEY. Goddammit, are you trying to make a fool out of
me now . . . out here . . . with everyone watching?

MAJOR. Don't shout at me.

STARKEY. I'm sorry.

MAJOR. Don't swear at me.

STARKEY. I'm sorry.

MAJOR. Don't contradict me.

STARKEY. I'm sorry.

MAJOR. And don't challenge my authority.

STARKEY. I'm sorry. I am sorry, but . . . are you acting now? Or do you really mean everything you're saying?

MAJOR. It doesn't matter. Can't you see that? All that does matter is what happens. That's the thing you don't realize. And that's the reason you're always so aimless and wishy-washy in just about everything you do.

STARKEY. Hey, wait a minute! You start talking that way to me and I'll quit, too.

MAJOR. No, you won't quit. You haven't got the character to quit. Popping off in front of a lot of people like this is just about as far as you'll ever go.

STARKEY. Don't you be so sure.

MAJOR. I am sure. Quit, if you think you can. Go ahead, quit.

STARKEY. I quit! [STARKEY *starts away, while* THE MAJOR *watches confidently.* STARKEY *slows after a few steps, hesitates, and comes to a stop, hanging his head with shame*]

MAJOR. No, you won't quit. You're a captain, and captains don't quit. Captains obey. You're conditioned to agree and you're trained to do as you're told. You like the pay and the prestige, and you do enjoy your job here, remember? So you'll stay right where you are, do just what you're supposed to, and continue reciting your lines exactly on cue—just as you're doing right now.

STARKEY. No, I'm not! I am not! Goddammit, I'm not!

MAJOR. Yes, you are. Should I show you? [*He holds open the script and points to a page*] You can shout it out to them even louder one more time, if it makes you feel so free, and honest, and independent. You can even go on pretending to yourself that you have convictions—but only for another few seconds. And after that you will have to go on saying and doing exactly what you're supposed to, because *that's* what you are—let's face it— that's *all* you are, a captain. And also, because you're

afraid of this. [*Holds up his hand, his fingers outstretched*]
Do you know what this is?

STARKEY. A hand.

MAJOR. No. [*Bending his fingers to clench them*] It's a
fist. You're afraid it can smash you to bits, and it can.
And you also know that I can summon a whole army of
people with guns and clubs just by blowing on this marvelous little military whistle of mine. [THE MAJOR *reaches
into his pocket, pulls out his baby pacifier, and begins
munching on it.* STARKEY *laughs*]

STARKEY. That's not a whistle. It's a baby's pacifier.

MAJOR. It's a whistle, if I say it is. And if I do say it is, do
you know what you'd better say?

STARKEY [*Capitulating, after a moment*]. Yes, sir.

MAJOR. What do you say?

STARKEY [*With alacrity*]. Yes, sir!

MAJOR. It's a whistle.

STARKEY [*Saluting*]. Yes, sir!

MAJOR. Good. Find Henderson and bring him to me.

STARKEY. Yes, sir!
  [THE MAJOR *has won and is satisfied, and his air of
  antagonism leaves him. He speaks in a tone that is
  suddenly soft and almost apologetic, appealing to*
  STARKEY *for understanding and forgiveness*]

MAJOR. My friend—I really don't want to talk to you this
way.

STARKEY [*Surprised*]. No?

MAJOR. But I must. Do you understand?

STARKEY. Yes, sir.

MAJOR. Thank you. [THE MAJOR *leaves, carrying his script.*
STARKEY *stares after him with resentment*]

STARKEY [*Sardonically*]. Yes, sir. [*He turns and shuffles
forward a step or two to address the audience*]
I am a man.
I'm not a thing.
I'm a modern, contemporary, adult human be-
    ing.
I'm a very decent and respectable and sensi-
    tive human being.
I'm married now and have children, and I

work for a living, just like you—you all
know that.
I've got pride and character and dignity, and
I have a wish and a determination to main-
tain my self-respect.
I do have convictions.
I have very deep convictions and very gen-
uine and powerful feelings that I want to
give voice to in loud, rolling sentences like:
"Was this the face that launched a thousand
ships and burnt the topless towers of Ilium?
Sweet Helen, make me immortal with a kiss."
    [*With a wishful smile*]
I want to make long speeches like that.
    [*With even greater longing*]
I want to play tragedy.
    [*Turning grave again*]
That's why I'm really not so happy here right
now.
The part I have is too . . . limited.
I'm not sure I like it here any more,
Squeezed in between the curtain
And the edge of the stage,
Squeezed into this small narrow role,
Pressed into a tight uniform,
Between the curtain
And edge of the stage,
And forced to say,
"Yes, sir."
    [STARKEY *turns bitterly and starts to walk offstage. He
    comes to a stop at a sharp, frightening sound from be-
    hind the curtain—three raps on a door as loud and
    sharp as gunshots, then three more. From behind the
    curtain* RUTH'S *voice is heard, shrill and quavering
    with terror, answered by the voices of the two*
    SPORTSMEN, *who alternate in their responses*]
RUTH. Go away!
GOLFER'S VOICE. Is he in there?
RUTH. Go away!
HUNTER'S VOICE. Is he in there?

[STARKEY *looks through the curtain, then hurries off-stage in fright, while the curtain opens slowly and the conversation in back of it continues.*

*The curtain opens on* RUTH *in her dressing room, which has been set inside the briefing room. There is a closet, a mirror, a stool, and a makeup table.* RUTH *is in a state of panic as she tries frantically to slip a jacket on over her blouse and pack some of her things in a small traveling case. She is shouting toward the door, and the voices of the two* SPORTSMEN *are replying from outside*]

RUTH. What do you want?

GOLFER'S VOICE. Have you seen him?

RUTH. Leave me alone!

HUNTER'S VOICE. We want to find him.

RUTH. He isn't here!

GOLFER'S VOICE. Have you seen him?

RUTH. Leave me alone!

HUNTER'S VOICE. We'll be back.

RUTH. He isn't here!

GOLFER'S VOICE. We'll be back.

RUTH. No—leave me alone! Oh God! God, keep them away! [RUTH *shakes so violently that she can scarcely fasten the buttons of her suit. As she moves to the traveling case, three knocks sound softly on the door.* RUTH *shudders with alarm and cries out hysterically*] Go away! Go away!

[*The door opens and* STARKEY *looks in with surprise and enters*]

STARKEY. Hey, let me in. What's the matter, honey?

[RUTH *collapses against him, hugging and kissing him with relief*]

RUTH. Oh, Jesus, darling, it's you! I'm so glad! I'm so scared!

STARKEY. Easy, honey. What are you scared of?

RUTH. Them.

STARKEY. Who?

RUTH. I don't know. They're after someone. Every few seconds they come here and—[*The three knocks thunder at the door again, then the second three*] You see?

HUNTER'S VOICE. Where is he?

RUTH. I don't know! I tell you, I don't know!

STARKEY [*To* RUTH]. Who?

RUTH [*To* STARKEY]. I don't know.

GOLFER'S VOICE. Have you seen him yet?

RUTH. Go away.

HUNTER'S VOICE. Is he in there yet?

RUTH. Go away!

GOLFER'S VOICE. We'll be back.

RUTH. Go to hell!

STARKEY. Calm down, baby. Don't fall apart.

RUTH. Let's get out of this place . . . *please!* Something terrible is happening—I just know it is.

STARKEY. Nothing's happening. They're just looking around—

RUTH. They're waiting outside, to knock again. They're not looking anywhere.

STARKEY. You're a little crazy, darling. Do you know that?

RUTH. Oh, God—I know who they're really after! They're really after *us*.

STARKEY. Oh, come on. You *are* a little crazy, aren't you? [STARKEY *tries to comfort her with an embrace, but* RUTH *pulls away*]

RUTH. It's true. That's why they keep coming here. They're after *us!* Every few seconds—[*The three knocks sound on the door again, a bit softer and slower than before, then the second three*] You see?

HUNTER'S VOICE. Where is he?

STARKEY [*Calling out*]. Who?

GOLFER'S VOICE. Is that a man in there?

STARKEY. Yeah. What the hell do you want?

[STARKEY *moves to the door and pulls it open. The two* SPORTSMEN *are there, as amiable and inquisitive as ever. But now they are dressed completely and formidably in MP uniforms, with belts, clubs, and pistol holsters added, and at least one of them carries the bullhorn through which they have been shouting through the door. They are menacing as they enter, although they greet* STARKEY *with frank and easy cordiality*]

GOLFER. Oh, hi!

HUNTER. Hiyah, Captain. Good to see you.

STARKEY. What's going on?

GOLFER. We're trying to find that sergeant.

HUNTER. Henderson. The one that's missing.

STARKEY. Why do you keep coming here?

GOLFER. We don't keep coming here.

HUNTER. We've got to look everywhere.

GOLFER. Until we find him.

HUNTER. He's not in here, is he?

STARKEY. *I'm* in here.

HUNTER. Oh, sure. I forgot. Sorry to disturb you.

GOLFER. We're just looking around now. [*Glances at his wristwatch*] You'll let us know when you see him, won't you?

HUNTER [*With confidence*]. Sure, don't worry. He'll let us know. So long, Captain.

GOLFER. See you later.

[*Both wave good-bye, smiling genially, and close the door*]

STARKEY. See? It's just those two characters the Major worked in.

RUTH. They'll be back. Didn't you hear them? They said they'll see you later.

STARKEY. So what? There's nothing to be afraid of.

RUTH. That's what you say. Darling, let's get out of here. *Now!* Something's gone wrong—I just know it has. I want to get out of here while we still can.

STARKEY. Nothing's gone wrong.

RUTH. Then what are you doing in here now? Why do they keep knocking at my door? Why aren't you out there somewhere, flying that stupid mission to Minnesota like you're supposed to?

STARKEY. Henderson copped out. He's disappeared.

RUTH. Good for him. I'm quitting too.

STARKEY. What do you mean, *you're* quitting? You're all through, anyway.

RUTH. I'm quitting for good. I mean it. Let's get out of ———— [*name of the city in which performance is taking place*] before you blow this up, too.

STARKEY. You're silly. [*He kisses her and holds her close*] Where's that great sense of humor of yours? In the old days, you'd have had something funny to say about that crazy knocking on the door.

RUTH. There's nothing funny about it. [*The three knocks sound again, then the second three, softer and slower than before.* RUTH *jerks away at the first sound and speaks in a small scream*] You see?

HUNTER'S VOICE. Where is he?

    [STARKEY *strides angrily to the door*]

RUTH. What do you want from me?

GOLFER'S VOICE. Is he in there yet?

    [STARKEY *pulls open the door and confronts the two* SPORTSMEN *again. They enter calmly, still smiling, but their manner is more purposeful and deliberate now than earlier*]

STARKEY. What the hell are you two doing?

HUNTER. Oh, hi.

GOLFER. Have you got him yet?

STARKEY. No, I haven't got him.

HUNTER. We're still looking for him.

GOLFER. That's what we're doing.

    [STARKEY *and the two* SPORTSMEN *converse now as though understanding each other perfectly, without urgency or alarm*]

STARKEY. Well, don't come back here. I'll be here. I'm in charge here.

HUNTER. If you see him—

STARKEY. I'll take care of things here.

GOLFER. Oh, that's fine then. [*To* THE HUNTER] He'll take care of things.

    [THE HUNTER *looks at his watch*]

HUNTER. See you soon.

    [THE SPORTSMEN *leave, closing the door.* STARKEY *heaves a sigh*]

STARKEY. You see? There's nothing to worry about now. Is there? [*Despondently, with resignation,* STARKEY *looks at his own watch. Then, with a stretch of great, agonized reluctance, he speaks from in back of* RUTH] Where is he?

RUTH [*Startled*]. Who?

258 *Joseph Heller*

STARKEY. Is he in here?

RUTH. Who? What are *you* talking about? What do *you* want from me?

STARKEY. You know who. Henderson. The one we're looking for.

RUTH. Oh, no! Not *you*, too! I don't know.

STARKEY Yes, you do.

RUTH. Well, I can't remember.

STARKEY. Ruth, Ruth—*where is he?* Don't you understand? [*He takes her by the shoulders*]. I've got to find him!

[RUTH *ponders heavily a moment, and finally yields*]

RUTH. In my closet.

[STARKEY *turns from her with relief and moves to the open door of the closet*]

STARKEY [*In dry singsong, facing the closet*]. Come out, come out, wherever you are.

[*The garments hanging in the closet stir, and slowly, almost one limb at a time,* HENDERSON *emerges from inside. He is dressed in the casual clothes that a young professional actor of the time and the place would be likely to wear on his way to the theater. He waits in silence, a bit defiantly.* STARKEY *regards him with a look of wry hostility*]

Where'd you get the funny costume?

HENDERSON. They're civilian clothes. They used to be very popular.

RUTH. Darling, help him.

STARKEY. *Help* him?

RUTH. Help him get away.

STARKEY. Help *him*? [*To* HENDERSON] Do you know the kind of trouble you've—[*The three knocks sound suddenly on the door again, then the second three.* STARKEY *shouts*] What do you want?

GOLFER'S VOICE. Is he in there yet?

STARKEY. Go away.

HUNTER'S VOICE. Who's that?

STARKEY. You know who it is.

GOLFER'S VOICE. Have you got him yet?

STARKEY. Go away. [*There is a second or two of silence*

*during which the three wait tensely*] Do you realize the trouble you're causing? Everything is stopped. Nobody can do anything. Nobody can go home and eat their supper and drink their coffee and go to bed, all because of you. What are you doing here now in those silly civilian clothes when you're supposed to be out there bombing Minnesota?

HENDERSON. I'm quitting.

STARKEY. What do you mean you're quitting? Right now? Right in the middle? Right—

HENDERSON. Right before I have to fly to Minnesota and be killed! Why should I if I don't want to?

STARKEY. Why shouldn't you if we want you to? It's only make-believe.

HENDERSON. I don't *want* to make believe any more. I'm tired of playing soldier—like those two jokers out there. I don't want to make believe I'm going to be killed. I don't want to make believe I'm *not* going to be killed. I don't want to make believe I'm killing other people, and then have to make believe I'm not killing them. I don't even want to be an actor any more. [*With a touch of genuine sorrow*] I just wanna go home. [*Pauses humbly*] I want to see my mother again.

STARKEY [*kindly, but with a trace of scorn*]. Do you want your nipple back?

HENDERSON. I just wanna go home.

STARKEY. If we give you medals and more money and promote you to lieutenant? [HENDERSON *shakes his head*] To a captain? [HENDERSON *shakes his head again*] You really mean it, don't you?

> [HENDERSON *nods.* STARKEY *gazes at him soberly a moment and then sits down helplessly on the stool in front of the dressing-room mirror. In wonderment, he studies his reflection for a few seconds, as though trying to figure out who he really is. At last, he speaks to* RUTH]

What am I supposed to do?

RUTH. Honey, you have to help him—

STARKEY. I'm supposed to find him and bring him back.

RUTH. —you have to help him get away.

STARKEY. The doors are locked.

RUTH. You and I can get out, can't we? Maybe we can sneak him out with us.

STARKEY. I can't do that. That's not why I'm here.

RUTH. Yes, you can, darling. That's *just* why you're here.

STARKEY. Goddammit—I'm not the villain around here! Am I? I'm not the one who's running things! Am I? *Am I?* I just do what I'm told to do, along with everyone else.

> [RUTH *and* HENDERSON *remain silent, watching him.* STARKEY *averts his eyes, hesitates a few moments longer, and then gives in*]

All right, I'll help him. I'll do what I can. It's not that hard. [*To* HENDERSON] Just go to the Major and tell him you're quitting so he can get someone to take your place. That's all you have to do. [*As* HENDERSON *shakes his head*] Why not?

HENDERSON. You'll laugh.

STARKEY. I'm not doing any more laughing tonight.

HENDERSON. I'm afraid.

STARKEY. Of what?

HENDERSON. The Major.

STARKEY. The Major? The Major is almost out of his mind with hysteria. He doesn't know what to do next.

HENDERSON. You tell him for me. I don't want to see him again.

STARKEY. What are you afraid of? He can't make you go if you don't want to.

RUTH. What *can* he do?

STARKEY. Nothing. It's a free country, isn't it? [*To* HENDERSON] He can get angry and call you a few names. Maybe he can hold back your pay awhile. But that's about all.

HENDERSON. Are you lying now? Or are you telling me the truth? Buddy, I just can't tell any more.

STARKEY. I haven't got time to lie. I just want to get things going smoothly again, without any inconvenience to anybody. Come on back, will you, and make it easier for all of us.

HENDERSON. Will you come with me?

STARKEY. Sure, I will.

# We Bombed In New Haven 261

RUTH. Will you explain for him?

STARKEY. Sure, I'll explain. I promise I will. I'll take care of you. I'll take care of everything, if you'll just come back now.

[STARKEY *puts his arm around* HENDERSON's *shoulders as he attempts to persuade him. This time,* HENDERSON *makes no move to recoil, but stands in silence, deliberating.*

*The three knocks sound on the door again, softer and slower still.* STARKEY *looks at* HENDERSON, *awaiting permission to reply*]

What do you say?

HENDERSON. You promise? You promise you'll protect me?

STARKEY. I give you my word. [STARKEY *puts his hand out by way of emphasizing his promise, and* HENDERSON *shakes it.* HENDERSON *nods, giving assent*] Good. [STARKEY *sighs with relief, glad that it's over, and calls out toward the door*] Come in. Come on in.

[THE SPORTSMEN *enter. They react with grins of affable delight when they see* HENDERSON *standing there*]

GOLFER. Oh, hi. There you are.

HUNTER. We've been looking all over for you. [*They move to* HENDERSON's *side to take his arms and lead him out*]

STARKEY. You haven't been looking all over—take your hands off him! You've been looking right here. Take him to the Major and stop dragging things out.

GOLFER. Sure, Captain. Thanks.

[HENDERSON *moves toward the door. He pauses as he comes in front of* STARKEY]

HENDERSON. Remember—you promised.

STARKEY. I'll be right there.

[HENDERSON *passes close to* RUTH. *He reaches out and touches her arm gratefully*]

HENDERSON. Thanks . . . thank you. You know—[*Attempts an affectionate joke*]—I always even liked your coffee.

[RUTH *offers a forced smile of encouragement as* HENDERSON *exits between the two* SPORTSMEN. *They slap* HENDERSON's *shoulder in friendly fashion and leave with cordial waves to* STARKEY, *closing the door*]

RUTH [*Sadly, when she and* STARKEY *are alone*]. What's going to happen to him?

STARKEY. Nothing.

RUTH. You're lying, aren't you?

STARKEY. No, I'm not.

RUTH [*Sitting down*]. I'm going to wait and see.

STARKEY. Go home, Ruth. They've got to take this junk away.

> [*By "junk,"* STARKEY *is referring to the flats and props that constitute the dressing room.* RUTH *rises and picks up her traveling case to take it with her.* STARKEY *reaches for it and puts it back down*]

Leave that here. Honey, nothing bad happens to us. The Major promised me that.

> [*Doubtfully,* RUTH *relinquishes the traveling case.* STARKEY *guides her toward the door*]

RUTH. If this is a trick—

STARKEY. It's not a trick.

RUTH. If you lied to him—

STARKEY. I didn't lie to him.

RUTH. He's just a boy.

STARKEY. I know that.

RUTH. If anything happens to him—

STARKEY. Nothing will happen to him.

RUTH. If anything does happen to him—

STARKEY [*Indulging her*]. Yeah?

RUTH [*Quietly, for emphasis*]. Don't come home.

> [STARKEY *looks at her with sober surprise*]

STARKEY. Hey . . . darling. You really mean that, don't you?

RUTH. I just . . . won't want you there.

STARKEY. Trust me, will you? I'll be home in half an—[*He bends to kiss her. She puts her hand to his face and stops him, then exits grimly.* STARKEY *turns away with a shrug and calls out into the darkness surrounding the dressing-room set*] Okay, boys! Let's get this junk out of here.

> [*The men hurry onstage to remove the dressing-room set into the wings.* BAILEY *takes charge of them*]

BAILEY. Okay, men. Move it! On the double. Let's go. Line up now—let's go.

[*After the set is removed, the men fall into formation under* BAILEY's *instructions*]

STARKEY. Very good, Bailey. Okay, boys, get ready, and douse those cigarettes.

[*As they all stand waiting, the door to the briefing room opens and* HENDERSON *enters with the two* SPORTSMEN. THE SPORTSMEN *are still smiling, and for a moment the three of them seem to form a close, congenial group. But suddenly,* THE SPORTSMEN *seize* HENDERSON *by the arms and fling him into the room roughly, taking him completely by surprise and sending him toppling to the floor. The men react with looks and exclamations of interest and alarm*]

HENDERSON. Ow! Hey, what the hell's the idea? [*As* HENDERSON *tries to get up,* THE SPORTSMEN *slam him down again*]

STARKEY [*Angrily*]. Hey! I told you guys to keep your hands off him!

[THE SPORTSMEN *ignore* STARKEY. *Before* STARKEY *can speak again,* THE MAJOR *strides onstage with a clenched fist, moving toward* HENDERSON *in a threatening fury*]

MAJOR. I oughta knock your God damned head off!

[HENDERSON *scrambles to his feet and retreats a step or two with fear and bewilderment*]

HENDERSON. Hey, take it easy, will you? Take it easy.

MAJOR. What the hell are you doing here out of uniform?

HENDERSON. I'm quitting. That's what. [*Motioning toward* STARKEY] He'll tell you.

[STARKEY *takes a doubtful step forward to intervene and musters a very firm voice*]

STARKEY. Yes, Major, I told him he—

[THE MAJOR *pays no attention to* STARKEY *but speaks sternly again to* HENDERSON]

MAJOR. Get back into uniform.

[HENDERSON *motions imploringly toward* STARKEY *and waits expectantly*]

STARKEY. Major! I gave him my word that if he came back, he wouldn't have to—

MAJOR. And *I* just ordered him to get back into uniform. Are you going to interfere?

STARKEY. Couldn't we get someone else?

MAJOR. *Are you?*

> [STARKEY *hesitates defiantly a moment longer and then
> wilts beneath the menacing gaze of* THE MAJOR. *He
> looks away, dropping his eyes in weakness and shame*]

STARKEY. No, sir.

> [THE MAJOR *turns back to* HENDERSON. *A moan of
> disappointment and despair escapes* HENDERSON *when
> he sees that* STARKEY *will not help him and that he now
> must brave* THE MAJOR *alone*]

HENDERSON. I'm not going to.

MAJOR. Henderson, I'm ordering you to get back into your
uniform.

HENDERSON. Ordering me? Are you crazy? *Ordering me?*
Who do you think you are?

MAJOR. Henderson, I am giving you a direct order. And I
am giving you that direct order for the last time.

HENDERSON. I think you're nuts. I'm getting out of here.

MAJOR. Stop him.

HENDERSON. You just try!

> [HENDERSON *starts away toward one side.* THE GOLFER
> *bars his way and draws his golf club back threaten-
> ingly.* HENDERSON *stops in disbelief*]

Hey! What do you think you're gonna—

> [*Suddenly,* THE GOLFER *swings the club at* HENDERSON
> *murderously.* HENDERSON *jumps back and just does
> elude the head of the club in time. Now* THE GOLFER
> *brandishes the golf club as a weapon and blocks* HEN-
> DERSON's *path. Incredulous,* HENDERSON *starts away in
> the other direction, approaching* THE HUNTER, *who
> readies his shotgun.* HENDERSON, *exclaiming indignant-
> ly about* THE GOLFER, *is unaware of* THE HUNTER *and
> his gun for the first few seconds*]

Are you crazy? Did you see what that guy just did? He
tried to kill me with that club. He—

> [HENDERSON *is speaking directly now to* THE HUNTER.
> *He breaks off with increased amazement when he real-
> izes that* THE HUNTER *has leveled his shotgun right up
> against his stomach. He points a childlike finger, as
> though to ask an innocent question*]

Hey, mister, what are you doing with that? Mister—
Mister, cut it out, will you?

[THE HUNTER *fires, and the gun goes off with a deafen-
ing roar.* HENDERSON *is knocked across the stage by the
blast, emitting a loud, agonized, howling cry. He slams
into* STARKEY *and clings to him for a few seconds,
screaming again and shuddering violently. His hold
weakens and he slides to the floor slowly, leaving a
large, bright smear of fresh blood on* STARKEY's *shirt-
front.* THE GOLFER *watches* HENDERSON *alertly, as
though ready to bludgeon him should he attempt to
rise.*

THE MAJOR *and* THE SPORTSMEN *form a silent group
as* HENDERSON, *on the floor, goes through a protract-
ed death agony, moaning and gasping, shrieking, muttering, shivering, babbling, reaching upward toward
nothing once or twice for help, turning, writhing,
struggling, giving up at last, sinking flat, and finally,
after a waning gasp, lying absolutely still.*

*For a few seconds, there is complete silence as*
HENDERSON *lies there, and the men stare down at him
mutely in utter horror. Then* THE MAJOR *speaks quietly*]

MAJOR. Starkey?

STARKEY. Sir?

MAJOR [*Pointing to* HENDERSON]. Get that junk out of here.

STARKEY. Yes, sir.

[THE SPORTSMEN *withdraw, and* THE MAJOR *walks off
into the wings. As soon as* THE MAJOR *is gone,* STARKEY
*relaxes a bit, chuckles, and begins clapping his hands
softly over the motionless body*]

Very good, kid, I've really got to hand it to you. Oh,
boy! That was really very good.

[*The others relax also and come forward slowly with
sighs and chuckles of relief. There is no response from*
HENDERSON. STARKEY *seems surprised for a few moments, then annoyed*]

Okay, okay. Don't overdo it. You can get up now. Come
on. Hey!

[*Perplexed by the absence of any response from* HEN-

DERSON, STARKEY *kneels to shake him and then turns him over onto his back*]

Hey! Move, will you? Let's go now, let's—oh!

[STARKEY *pulls his hand back from* HENDERSON'S *body and stares at his fingers with alarm. They are covered with blood*]

My God!

[STARKEY *looks closely at* HENDERSON'S *face. He touches his hand and his cheek and then goes rigid with amazement*]

Oh, my God! He's really dead!

[*The men are stunned.* STARKEY *remains kneeling beside* HENDERSON'S *body, as though unable to move.* THE MAJOR *reenters from the side*]

MAJOR. Starkey?

STARKEY. Sir?

MAJOR. Don't you know?

STARKEY. Yes, sir. [*To the men, pointing toward* HENDERSON] He wants us to get this junk out of here.

[*The men stand without moving, still astounded*]

Come on. We have to. Bailey . . . Joe. Bailey!

[BAILEY *remains motionless a second longer, deliberating, and then comes to a decision and barks out a command*]

BAILEY. Okay, men—move it! [*As the others are slow to respond*] I said, move it!

JOE. I guess we gotta. [*The men follow* JOE *to* HENDERSON'S *body*] Who would have thought—look at that blood. Gee—look at all that blood.

BAILEY. All right, let's go!

[THE IDIOTS *and* JOE *lift* HENDERSON'S *body at* BAILEY'S *command and carry it off.* FISHER *starts to follow. His* KID BROTHER *stops him*]

YOUNG FISHER. Hey! I thought you told me nobody got killed here.

FISHER [*With cold, cruel, contemptuous pleasure*]. I was lying to you.

[FISHER *saunters out indifferently.* YOUNG FISHER *halts a moment, shaken by the reply, and then follows him offstage, slowly, almost crying.* STARKEY *and* THE

MAJOR *are left alone.* THE MAJOR *watches* STARKEY
*with composure, waiting for him to speak, confident
already that he knows what's to come*]

STARKEY. You really killed him, didn't you?

MAJOR [*Quietly, almost regretfully*]. Do you want the truth?
Or do you want a lie?

STARKEY. I didn't know you were going to kill him.

MAJOR. Why should *you* care?

STARKEY. I just didn't know it, that's all.

MAJOR. But what difference does it make, really? Were you
so fond of him? Did you know him so well, or even at
all? Was he anything more to you than just a name? You
didn't even *care* for him, did you? So what difference does
it make to you really if he lives or if he dies?

STARKEY. No difference. [THE MAJOR *smiles slightly at this
admission from* STARKEY *and is now ready to proceed*]

MAJOR. Of course not. So get me a replacement for him
now, will you? That's your job.

STARKEY. Okay. Send him in.

MAJOR [*With amused surprise*]. I should?

STARKEY. I'm sorry, sir.

MAJOR. I'll get some help. [*Calls offstage*] Hey, Ronnie!
Billy!
      [*The door at the rear of the briefing room opens and
      the two* SPORTSMEN *enter, still in their MP uniforms*]

BOTH SPORTSMEN. Sir?

MAJOR. Help the Captain find a replacement, will you? [*To*
STARKEY] I'll get the planes ready. All right?

STARKEY. Yes, sir.

MAJOR [*Mildly*]. Don't I even get a salute?

STARKEY [*Managing a tired smile*]. Sure. Sorry, sir. [*He
salutes politely*]

MAJOR. That's better. Ten minutes, then?

STARKEY. Yes, sir.
      [THE MAJOR *exits into the wings, carrying his manu-
script.*
      STARKEY *sags a bit after* THE MAJOR *has gone. He
shakes his head, as though to rouse himself, and pinches
his eyes as though to alleviate an inner pain*]

GOLFER. Which one would you like, sir? Have you got a preference?

STARKEY. How many have we got?

HUNTER. We have three hundred names on the list.

STARKEY [*Shrugs*]. Send in the first one. Give me half a minute, though.

GOLFER. Yes, sir.

[THE SPORTSMEN *exit through the door, closing it after them.* STARKEY *pokes aimlessly around at his newspaper, portfolio, and clipboard for a few seconds. Abstractedly, he tries to wipe the bloodstain from his chest with a crumpled sheet of paper. From far away, and very faintly, there is heard the eerie, whistling sound of jet engines starting up; the noise fades after a few seconds. A quiet knock sounds on the door.* STARKEY *speaks without looking up*]

STARKEY. Come in. Come on in.

[*The door to the briefing room opens, and a young man we have not seen before enters timidly, dressed in the same combat attire worn by the others, except for flight boots. He is* STARKEY'S SON. *He is about nineteen, but so slight and so sad and uncertain that he seems scarcely older or sturdier than* FISHER'S KID BROTHER. *He hesitates a few moments, waiting for* STARKEY *to look up and take notice of him. Finally, the boy breaks the silence and speaks, in a tone of soft melancholy*]

STARKEY'S SON. Hello.

[STARKEY *stares up in astonishment. He rises and comes forward slowly in fearful amazement, as though unable to believe what his eyes and ears have told him is true*]

STARKEY. What are you doing here?

STARKEY'S SON. I'm in the army now.

STARKEY [*With a pained, unnatural smile*]. Oh, no. *You?* Not you. You can't be. You were only born—[*Looks toward the clock*]—just a little while ago. It seems like— just a little while ago.

STARKEY'S SON. I'm nineteen years old now.

STARKEY. It doesn't seem possible.

STARKEY'S SON. What's going to happen to me?

STARKEY. You're going to be killed, son. You're going to go away in an airplane and be killed in an explosion.

STARKEY'S SON. Pop—I don't want to go.

STARKEY [*Musing*]. You know, I can't believe it. You were just a little kid the last time I saw you.

STARKEY'S SON. I'm just a little kid now.

STARKEY. It's not my fault.

STARKEY'S SON. What were you doing when all this was happening?

STARKEY. What?

STARKEY'S SON. What were you doing when all this was happening?

STARKEY. I was working. I was doing my job, I guess.

STARKEY'S SON. Pop, you had nineteen years to save me from this. When I was born, why didn't you—

STARKEY. It didn't seem possible.

STARKEY'S SON. When I was a little boy, of five, or ten, or fifteen, when I was growing up—you loved me then, didn't you? You must have loved me then! Didn't you know they would take me into the army someday if I just kept growing?

STARKEY. It didn't seem possible.

STARKEY'S SON. And now?

STARKEY. It still doesn't seem possible.

STARKEY'S SON. Pop . . . don't you understand?

STARKEY [*Ruminating aloud, as though in a wistful daze*]. You know, it's very funny . . .

STARKEY'S SON. Don't you see? Don't you know?

STARKEY. . . . a little while ago . . . just a little while ago . . .

STARKEY'S SON. I don't want to die yet!

STARKEY. . . . I wasn't even married . . .

STARKEY'S SON. I don't want to go!

STARKEY. . . . so it's not my fault.

STARKEY'S SON. It is your fault! You were doing your *job,* weren't you?

STARKEY. Shut up! You're my son!

STARKEY'S SON. *You* shut up! You're my father! [*Pleading with him*] Pop . . . dad . . . father . . . stranger . . . won't you help me? [*As* STARKEY *remains silent*] If I were still a baby in a baby carriage, and someone wanted to take

me away and kill me, you wouldn't let them, would you?
Are you really going to let them take me away to be killed?
[STARKEY *hesitates a moment longer with a look of intense misery, then he shakes his head emphatically and hugs the boy to his chest with great emotion*]

STARKEY. No! I'm not going to!

STARKEY'S SON. Pop!

STARKEY. I'm going to get you out of here! I'm going to let you escape! You get away now. Hurry, hurry! [*As the boy starts toward the door*] No, not that way! [STARKEY *looks about frantically in all directions, even out into the theater for an instant, and then points offstage to the side opposite the one taken by* THE MAJOR] This way! Run, run! [STARKEY'S SON *exits hurriedly.* STARKEY *waits until he is well out of sight. The noise of jet engines starts up again, closer than before.* STARKEY *looks at his watch, then hurries back to the desk, calling out*] Corporals! Sergeants! Ronnie! Billy! Whoever the hell you are!
[*The door opens and* THE SPORTSMEN *look in.* THE HUNTER *carries a clipboard*]
Send in the next one.

GOLFER. What happened to the first one?

STARKEY. He wasn't good enough. Who's next?

HUNTER [*Reading from list*]. Brandwine.

STARKEY. Send in Brandwine.

HUNTER. Yes, sir.

GOLFER [*Calls to someone outside the door*]. Hey, you! Yes, you. You're the one. Get in here.
[THE SPORTSMEN *stand aside to make room for a young soldier to enter. It is* STARKEY'S SON. *He is grave and sad; he looks almost completely resigned.* THE SPORTSMEN *exit, shutting the door*]

STARKEY. What are *you* doing here?

STARKEY'S SON. They were waiting for me. They caught me. They told me I had to come back in here and be killed.

STARKEY. It's a mistake. You don't have to.

STARKEY'S SON. It's not a mistake. It's just too late now.

STARKEY. It's not too late! *I* can save you! I can help you get away. Go out the window this time. Don't let anyone catch you. If they try to stop you, tell them you're my son. Tell them you're *my* son and I said it's okay. [STARKEY *hurries with the boy to the window, and the boy climbs out.* STARKEY *calls out toward the door*] Billy! Ronnie! Hurry! [*The door opens and* THE SPORTSMEN *return*] Who's next on the list?

HUNTER. Mendoza.

STARKEY. Mendoza! Yes, that's the one I want! Ha, ha— send in Mendoza!

BOTH SPORTSMEN. [*Calling to someone outside the door*]. Mendoza! Mendoza! Come on, Mendoza! Come inside.
  [*As* STARKEY *stares at the open door and waits,* THE MAJOR *enters slowly from the side, materializing from the wings with his manuscript. He wears a knowing, solemn look; his voice is soft and almost compassionate*]

MAJOR. Starkey? [*As* STARKEY *turns*] Hurry up, please.

STARKEY. I've got him coming in right now. [*Calling toward the open door*] Mendoza! Where is—
  [THE SPORTSMEN *stand aside to admit another young soldier. It is* STARKEY'S SON *again. He stands it attention in despondent silence as the door closes behind him and gives not the slightest sign of recognition.* STARKEY *reacts with shock and dismay when he sees him. Finally,* STARKEY *turns slowly toward* THE MAJOR *with a look of mournful comprehension*]
  It's just no use, is it?

MAJOR. No.

STARKEY. Major! They've got three hundred names on that list.

MAJOR. They all belong to him.
  [STARKEY *turns from* THE MAJOR *and looks at the boy closely*]

STARKEY. Do you know who I am?

STARKEY'S SON. Yes, sir. You're the captain.

STARKEY. Do you know why you're here?

STARKEY'S SON. They want me to go into an airplane and be killed. You're the one that's going to send me.

STARKEY. And you'll go?

STARKEY'S SON. If I have to.

STARKEY. What's your name, son?

STARKEY'S SON [*With a trace of bitterness*]. Son.

[STARKEY *pulls back from him, wincing with grief, and turns to appeal to* THE MAJOR]

STARKEY. Does he have to go?

[THE MAJOR *nods and glances at the clock on the wall*]

MAJOR. It's about time. I told you that once.

STARKEY [*To the boy*]. You see? You have to go.

STARKEY'S SON [*His voice rising in disbelief*]. Then will you get angry now? Will you at least raise your voice? Won't you do anything to show you even care?

STARKEY. Like what?

STARKEY'S SON. Like what? [*Indicating* THE MAJOR] Like—smash his face!

[STARKEY *is surprised by the suggestion. He turns to stare at* THE MAJOR, *as though weighing the possibility.* THE MAJOR *waits without flinching, daring him to do something. For a few seconds the two men look at each other in tense silence, while the boy watches hopefully. The boy cries out again*]

Smash it . . . *please!*

[STARKEY *stares at* THE MAJOR *a few moments longer . . . and does nothing. Finally, he turns away. He lowers his eyes in shame and shakes his head, and his fingers find their way feebly to the whistle around his neck*]

STARKEY. No.

STARKEY'S SON [*With a sneer*]. Then will you gnash your teeth?

STARKEY. What?

STARKEY'S SON. Will you rend your clothes? Will you beat your chest with both fists and tear your hair? [*Seriously, wanting to know*] Will you weep for me?

STARKEY. I will weep for you. I promise you that.

STARKEY'S SON. When King David was told his son had been killed, and that was in a rebellion against him, he cried: "O my son Absalom! My son Absalom! Would God I had died for thee!"

STARKEY. I will weep for you. I will cry: "My son . . . my son! Would God I had died for thee!"

STARKEY'S SON. But will you mean it?

STARKEY [*Slowly, truthfully*]. I won't know. I won't ever really know.

MAJOR. It's time now.

STARKEY'S SON. I'll go.

[*STARKEY reaches out toward his son as though to embrace him. His son watches him coldly, and STARKEY comes to a stop and lets his hands drop awkwardly*]

STARKEY. Good-bye . . . son.

STARKEY'S SON. Bastard.

[*STARKEY'S SON turns and follows THE MAJOR out. The door closes behind them. Left by himself, STARKEY gazes after him sorrowfully for a few seconds. The noise of the jet planes picks up again; they are taking off. Suddenly STARKEY seems to grow aware of the audience watching him. He fidgets uncomfortably, as though realizing he has been observed committing some dreadful act, and he comes forward guiltily in an effort to explain*]

STARKEY [*To the audience*]. Now, none of this, of course, is really happening. It's a show, a play in a theater, and I'm not really a captain. I'm an actor. [*His voice rises with emotion, as though to drown out the noise of a plane that passes very close and recedes steadily into the distance*] I'm ————. [*He mentions his real name*] You all know that. Do you think that I ————, [*Repeats his real name*] would actually let my son go off to a war and be killed . . . and just stand here talking to you and do nothing? [*An edge of hysteria and grief comes into his voice, as though he knows what is to follow*] Of course not! There is no war taking place. [*In the distance, there is the sound of a single, great explosion, and STARKEY whimpers and seems on the verge of weeping as he shouts out insistently*] There is no war taking place here now! [*He sags a moment, then continues desperately*] There has never been a war. There never will be a war. Nobody has been killed here tonight. It's only . . . make-believe . . . it's a story . . . a charade . . . a show [*Bitterly, sarcastically, as though giving up the attempt to persuade the audience—and himself—that what he is saying is true*] Nobody has ever been killed. [*He shrugs and*

*looks about and then speaks ruefully, as though remem-
bering* RUTH's *last words to him*] I'm going home now.
[*He takes up his portfolio and his folded newspaper and
prepares to leave*] In a few minutes, ushers will pass
among you collecting money for the Will Rogers Tuber-
culosis Sanitarium in Lake Saranac, New York. [*With
irony, a broken man*] Give generously.

[*He starts away slowly, departing in the direction from
which he first entered, carrying his portfolio and his
folded copy of* The New York Times, *a solitary working man on the way home, his job, for this occasion,
done*]

**CURTAIN**

# THE INDIAN

## WANTS THE BRONX

*by Israel Horovitz*

*To my children and their friends, with love*

From *First Season* by Israel Horovitz.
Copyright © as an unpublished work 1967, 1968
by Israel Horovitz.
Copyright © 1968 by Israel Horovitz.

Reprinted by permission of Random House, Inc.

## AUTHOR'S NOTE

In rereading the text for this new edition, I was greatly tempted to alter the play; to shape it to my more recent discoveries about stage prose.

I resisted however and have only altered the text to comply with the edition used by actors and directors. Otherwise the play is as it was originally published by Random House in 1968.

Finally, I should note that on rereading this early play, I do find it very much representative of my attitudes during the 1960s. Curiously, in a period of instant vogue, the 1960s signaled the end, really, of American Naturalism: the formal factor which seemed to make this play popular in its first decade. Inversely, as its naturalistic form died, its theme of irrational violence zoomed with new life into the 1970s.

The occasion also rises.

ISRAEL HOROVITZ

*New York*
*April 15, 1971*

THE INDIAN WANTS THE BRONX *opened for the press*
*on January 17, 1968,*
*at the Astor Place Theater, New York City,*
*with the following cast:*

*(In order of appearance)*

GUPTA, AN EAST INDIAN, *John Cazale*
MURPH, *Al Pacino*
JOEY, *Matthew Cowles*

DIRECTED BY *James Hammerstein*

*Prior to its New York opening,* THE INDIAN WANTS THE
BRONX *was presented as a work-in-progress at The Loft
Workshop, New York; The Eugene O'Neill Memorial
Theatre Foundation, Connecticut; Canoe Place Caba-
ret Theatre, New York; and The Act IV Café Theatre,
Massachusetts. During its New York run,* THE INDIAN
WANTS THE BRONX, *along with its companion play,* IT'S
CALLED THE SUGAR PLUM *and a new Horovitz play,*
CHIAROSCURO (OR MORNING), *was performed by invita-
tion at the 1968 Festival of Two Worlds, Spoleto, Italy.
The plays were directed by the author.*

Place: A bus stop on upper Fifth
Avenue in New York City.
Time: A chilly September's night.

*The lights fade up.* GUPTA, *an East Indian, is standing alone, right of center stage, near a bus-stop sign. An outdoor telephone booth is to his left; several city-owned litter baskets are to his right.*

GUPTA *is in his early fifties. He is anything but sinister. He is, in fact, meek and visibly frightened by the city.*

*He is dressed in traditional East Indian garb, appropriately for mid-September.*

*As* GUPTA *strains to look for a bus on the horizon, the voices of two boys can be heard in the distance, singing, flatly, trying to harmonize.*

FIRST BOY.
  I walk the lonely streets at night,
    A-lookin' for your door,
  I look and look and look and look,
    But, baby, you don't care.
  Baby, you don't care
  Baby, no one cares.
SECOND BOY [*Interrupting*]. Wait a minute, Joey. I'll take
  the harmony. Listen. [*Singing*]
  But, baby, you don't care.
  Baby, you don't care.
  Baby, no one cares.
  [*Confident that he has fully captured the correct harmony, boasting*] See? I've got a knack for harmony. You take
  the low part.
BOYS [*Singing together*].
  But, baby, you don't care.
  Baby, you don't care.

Baby, no one cares.

[*They appear on stage.* FIRST BOY *is* JOEY. SECOND BOY
*is* MURPH. JOEY *is slight, baby-faced, in his early twenties.* MURPH *is stronger, long-haired, the same age*]

MURPH [*Singing*].

The lonely, lonely streets, called out for lovin',
But there was no one to love . . .
'Cause, baby, you don't care . . .

JOEY [*Joins in the singing*].

Baby, you don't care . . .

JOEY AND MURPH [*Singing together*].

Baby, you don't care.
Baby, you don't care.
Baby, no one cares.
Baby, no one cares.

MURPH [*Calls out into the audience, to the back rows across
to the row of apartment houses opposite the park*]. Hey,
Pussyface! Can you hear your babies singing? Pussyface.
We're calling you.

JOEY [*Joins in*]. Pussyface. Your babies are serenading
your loveliness.

[*They laugh*]

MURPH. Baby, no one cares.

MURPH AND JOEY [*Singing together*].

Baby, no one cares.
Baby, no one cares.

MURPH [*Screams*]. Pussyface, you don't care, you Goddamned idiot! [*Notices* THE INDIAN] Hey. Look at the
Turk.

[JOEY *stares at* THE INDIAN *for a moment, then replies*]

JOEY. Just another pretty face. Besides. That's no Turk. It's
an Indian.

MURPH [*Continues to sing*].

Baby, no one cares.

[*Dances to his song, strutting in* THE INDIAN's *direction.
He then turns back to* JOEY *during the completion of
his stanza and feigns a boxing match*]

Baby, you don't care.
Baby, you don't care.
Baby, no one cares.

[*Pretends to swing a punch at* JOEY, *who backs off laughing*] You're nuts. It's a Turk!

JOEY. Bet you a ten spot. It's an Indian.

MURPH. It's a Turk, schmuck. Look at his fancy hat. Indians don't wear fancy hats. [*Calls across the street, again*] Hey, Pussyface. Joey thinks we got an Indian. [*Back to* JOEY] Give me a cigarette.

JOEY. You owe me a pack already.

MURPH. So I owe you a pack. Give me a cigarette.

JOEY. Say "please," maybe?

MURPH. Say "I'll bust your squash if you don't give me a cigarette!"

JOEY. One butt, one noogie.

MURPH. First the butt.

JOEY. You're a Jap, Murphy.

[*As* JOEY *extends the pack,* MURPH *grabs it*]

MURPH. You lost your chance, baby. [*To the apartment block*] Pussyface! Joey lost his chance!

JOEY. We made a deal. A deal's a deal. You're a Jap, Murphy. A rotten Jap. [*To the apartment*] Pussyface, listen to me! Murphy's a rotten Jap and just Japped my whole pack. That's unethical, Pussyface. He owes me noogies, too!

MURPH. Now I'll give you twenty noogies, so we'll be even. [*He raps* JOEY *on the arm.* THE INDIAN *looks up as* JOEY *squeals*]

JOEY. Hey. The Indian's watching.

MURPH [*Raps* JOEY *sharply again on the arm*]. Indian's a Turkie.

JOEY [*Grabs* MURPH's *arm and twists it behind his back*]. Gimme my pack and it's an Indian, right?

MURPH. I'll give you your head in a minute, jerkoff.

JOEY. Indian? Indian? Say, Indian!

MURPH. Turkie? Turkie?

JOEY. Turkie. Okay. Let go. [MURPH *lets him up and laughs.* JOEY *jumps up and screams*] Indian! [*Runs a few steps*] Indian!

MURPH [*Laughing*]. If your old lady would have you on Thanksgiving you'd know what a turkey was, ya' jerk.

[*Hits him on the arm again*] Here's another noogie, Turkie head!

[THE INDIAN *coughs*]

JOEY. Hey, look. He likes us. Shall I wink?

MURPH. You sexy beast, you'd wink at anything in pants.

JOEY. Come on. Do I look like a Murphy?

MURPH [*Grabs* JOEY *and twists both of his arms*]. Take that back.

JOEY. Aw! ya' bastard. I take it back.

MURPH. You're a Turkie-lover, right?

JOEY. Right.

MURPH. Say it.

JOEY. I'm a Turkie-lover.

MURPH. You're a Turkie-humper, right?

JOEY. *You're* a Turkie-humper.

MURPH. Say, *I'm* a Turkie-humper.

JOEY. That's what I said. You're a Turkie-humper. [MURPH *twists his arms a bit further*] Oww, ya' dirty bastard! All right, I'm a Turkie-humper! Now, leggo! [JOEY *pretends to laugh*]

MURPH. You gonna hug him and kiss him and love him up like a mother?

JOEY. Whose mother?

MURPH. Your mother. She humps Turkies, right?

JOEY. Owww! All right. Yeah. She humps Turkies. Now leggo!

MURPH [*Lets go*]. You're free.

JOEY [*Breaks. Changes the game*]. Where's the bus?

MURPH. Up your mother.

JOEY. My old lady's gonna' kill me. It must be late as hell.

MURPH. So why don't you move out?

JOEY. Where to?

MURPH. Maybe we'll get our own place. Yeah. How about that, Joey?

JOEY. Yeah, sure. I move out on her and she starves. You know that.

MURPH. Let her starve, the Turkie-humper.

JOEY [*Hits* MURPH *on the arm and laughs*]. That's my mother you're desecrating, you nasty bastard.

MURPH [*Hits* JOEY *on the arm*]. Big words, huh?

JOEY. Hey! Why don't you pick on som'body your own size, like Turkie, there.

MURPH. Leave Turkie out of this. He's got six elephants in his pocket, probably.

JOEY [*Laughs at the possibility*]. Hey, Turkie, you got six elephants in your pocket?

MURPH. Hey, shut up, Joey. [*Glances in* THE INDIAN's *direction and* THE INDIAN *glances back*] Shut up.

JOEY. Ask him for a match.

MURPH. You ask him.

JOEY. You got the butts.

MURPH. Naw.

JOEY. Chicken. Want some seeds to chew on?

MURPH. I'll give you somethin' to chew on.

JOEY. Go on, ask him. I ain't never heard an Indian talk Turkie-talk.

MURPH. He's a Turkie, I told ya'. Any jerk can see that he's a definite Turk!

JOEY. You're a definite jerk, then. 'Cause I see a definite Indian!

MURPH. I'll show you. [*Walks toward* THE INDIAN *slowly, taking the full time to cross the stage. He slithers from side to side and goes through pantomime of looking for matches*]

JOEY. Hey, Murph. You comin' for dinner? We're havin' turkey tonight! Hey! Tell your Turkie to bring his elephants.

MURPH. Schmuck! How's he going to fit six elephants in a rickshaw?

JOEY [*Flatly*]. Four in front. Three in back. [*He reaches* THE INDIAN]

MURPH. Excuse me. May I borrow a match?

INDIAN [*Speaking in Hindi*]. Mai toom-haree bo-lee nrh-hee bol sak-tah. Mai tum-hah-ree bah-sha nah-hee sah-maj-tah. (*I cannot speak your language. I don't understand.*)

MURPH [*To* JOEY, *does a terrific "take," then speaks, incredulously*]. He's got to be kidding.
    [JOEY *and* MURPH *laugh*]

INDIAN. Moo-jhay mahaf kar-nah mai toom-hah-ree bah-art nah-hee sah-maj sak-tah. (*I'm sorry. I don't under-stand you.*)

MURPH. No speak English, huh? [THE INDIAN *looks at him blankly. Louder*] You can't speak English, huh?

[THE INDIAN *stares at him, confused by the increase in volume*]

JOEY [*Flatly*]. Son of a bitch. Hey, Murph. Guess what? Your Turkie only speaks Indian.

MURPH [*Moves in closer, examining the Indian*]. Say some-thing in Indian, big mouth.

JOEY [*Holds up his hand*]. How's your teepee? [THE INDIAN *stares at him. He laughs*] See.

[THE INDIAN *welcomes* JOEY's *laugh and smiles. He takes their hands and "shakes" them*]

MURPH [*Catches on as to why* THE INDIAN *has joined the smile and feigns a stronger smile until they all laugh aloud.* MURPH *cuts off the laughter as he shakes the* INDIAN's *hand and says*]: You're a fairy, right?

INDIAN [*Smiles harder than before*]. Mai toom-haree bah-at nah-hee sah-maj-tah. Mai ap-nay lah-kay kah gha-r dhoo-nd rah-haw hooh. Mai oos-kah mah-kan dhoo-nd rah-hah hoon. (*I don't understand you. I'm looking for my son's home. We were supposed to meet, but I could not find him. This is his address.*) [THE INDIAN *produces a slip of paper with an address typed on it. And a photo-graph*]

MURPH. Gupta. In the Bronx. Big deal. [*To* THE INDIAN] Indian, right? You an Indian, Indian? [*Shakes his head up and down, smiling.* THE INDIAN *smiles, confused*] He don't know. [*Pauses, studies the picture, smiles*] This picture must be his kid. Looks like you, Joe.

JOEY [*Looks at the picture*]. Looks Irish to me. [*He hands the picture to* MURPH]

BOTH. Ohhh.

MURPH. Yeah. Why'd you rape all those innocent children? [*Pause*] I think he's the wrong kind of Indian. [*To* THE INDIAN] You work in a restaurant? [*Pauses. Speaks with a homosexual's sibilant "s"*] It's such a shame to kill these Indians. They do such superb beaded work. [MURPH *shakes his head up and down again, smiling*]

INDIAN [*Follows* MURPH's *cue*]. Toom-hara shah-har bah-hoot hee barah hai. (*Your city is so big and so busy.*)

JOEY. Ask him to show you his elephants.

MURPH. You ask. You're the one who speaks Turkie-Indian.

JOEY. White man fork with tongue. Right? [THE INDIAN *stares at him blankly*] Naw, he don't understand me. You ask. You got the right kind of accent. All you foreigners understand each other good.

MURPH. You want another noogie?

JOEY. Maybe Turkie wants a noogie or six?

MURPH [*Shaking his head*]. You want a noogie, friend?

INDIAN [*Agrees*]. Moo-jhay mahaf kar-nah. Moo-jay. Yah-han aye zyah-da sah-may na-hee hoo-ah. (*I'm sorry. I haven't been here long.*)

MURPH. Give him his noogie.

JOEY. Naw. He's your friend. You give it to him. That's what friends are for.

MURPH [*Looks at the paper and photograph, gives them back*]. Jesus, look at that for a face.

JOEY. Don't make it.

MURPH. Don't make it. Prem Gupta. In the Bronx. Jesus, this is terrific. The Indian wants the Bronx.

JOEY [*Sits on a trash can*]. He ain't gonna find no Bronx on this bus.

MURPH. Old Indian, pal. You ain't going to find the Bronx on this bus, unless they changed commissioners again. Now I've got a terrific idea for fun and profit. [*Pauses*]

INDIAN. K-yah kah-ha toom-nay? (*Excuse me?*)

MURPH. Right. Now why don't you come home and meet my mother? Or maybe you'd like to meet Pussyface, huh? [*To* JOEY] Should we bring him over to Pussyface?

JOEY. He don't even know who Pussyface is. You can't just go getting Indians blind dates without giving him a breakdown.

MURPH. Okay, Chief. Here's the breakdown on Pussyface. She's a pig. She lives right over there. See that pretty building? [*Points over the audience to the back row of seats*] That one. The fancy one. That's Pussyface's hide-away. She's our social worker.

JOEY. That's right.

MURPH. Pussyface got assigned to us when we were tykers, right, Joe?

JOEY. Just little fellers.

MURPH. Pussyface was sent to us by the city. To watch over us. And care for us. And love us like a mother. Not because she wanted to. Because we were bad boys. We stole a car.

JOEY. We stole two cars.

MURPH. We stole two cars. And we knifed a kid.

JOEY. You knifed a kid.

MURPH [*To* JOEY]. Tell it to the judge, Fella!

[*He takes a pocketknife from his pocket and shows it to* THE INDIAN. NOTE: *the pocketknife is on a keychain, tiny, not frightening.*]

JOEY. The Chief thinks you're going to cut him up into a totem pole.

MURPH. Easy, Chief. I've never cut an Indian in my life.

JOEY. You've never *seen* an Indian in your life.

MURPH. Anyway, you got a choice. My mother—who happens to have a terrific personality. Or Pussyface, our beloved social lady.

JOEY. Where's the bus?

MURPH. It's coming.

JOEY. So's Christmas.

MURPH. Hey. Show Turkie my Christmas card for Pussyface. [*To* THE INDIAN] Pussyface gives us fun projects. I had to make Christmas cards last year. [*Back to* JOEY] Go on. Show the Chief the card.

[JOEY *fishes through his wallet, finds a dog-eared photostat, hands it to* THE INDIAN, *who accepts curiously*]

INDIAN. Yeh k-yah hai? (*What is this?*)

MURPH. I made that with my own two cheeks. Tell him, Joe.

JOEY. Stupid, he don't speak English.

MURPH. It don't matter. He's interested, ain't he?

JOEY. You're a fink-jerk.

MURPH. Oooo. I'll give you noogies up the kazzooo. [*Takes the card away from* THE INDIAN *and explains*] This is a Christmas card. I made it! I made it! Get me? Pussyface got us Christmas jobs last year. She got me one with the city. With the war on poverty. I ran the Xerox machine.

JOEY. Jesus. You really are stupid. He don't understand one word you're saying.

MURPH [*Mimes the entire scene, slowly*]. He's interested, ain't he? That's more than I can say for most of them. [*To* THE INDIAN] Want to know how you can make your own Christmas cards with your simple Xerox 2400? It's easy. Watch. [*He mimes*] First you lock the door to the stat room, so no one can bust in. Then you turn the machine on. Then you set the dial at the number of people you want to send cards to. Thirty, forty.

JOEY. Three or four.

MURPH. Right, fella. Then you take off your pants. And your underpants that's underneath. You sit on the glass. You push the button. The lights flash. When the picture's developed, you write "Noel" across it! [*Pauses*] That's how you make Christmas cards. [*Waits for a reaction from* THE INDIAN, *then turns back to* JOEY, *dismayed*] He's waiting for the bus.

JOEY. Me too. Jesus. Am I ever late!

MURPH. Tell her to stuff it. You're a big boy now.

JOEY. She gets frightened, that's all. She really don't care how late I come in, as long as I tell her when I'm coming. If I tell her one, and I don't get in until one-thirty, she's purple when I finally get in. [*Pauses*] She's all right. Where's the Goddamned bus, huh? [*Calls across the park*] Pussyface, did you steal the bus, you dirty old whore? Pussyface, I'm calling you! [*Pauses*] She's all right, Murph. Christ, she's my mother. I didn't ask for her. She's all right.

MURPH. Who's all right? That Turkie-humper? [*To* THE INDIAN] His old lady humps Turkies, you know that? [*Smiles, but* THE INDIAN *doesn't respond*] Hey, Turkie's blowin' his cool a little. Least you got somebody waitin'. My old lady wouldn't know if I was gone a year.

JOEY. What? That Turkie-humper?

MURPH [*To* THE INDIAN]. Hey! [THE INDIAN *jumps, startled.* MURPH *laughs*] You got any little Indians runnin' around your tepee? No? Yeah? No? Aw, ya' stupid Indian. Where is the Goddamn bus?

JOEY. Let's walk it.

MURPH. Screw that. A hundred blocks? Besides, we gotta keep this old Turkie company, right? We couldn't let him stand all alone in this big ole city. Some nasty boys might come along and chew him up, right?

JOEY. We can walk it. Let the Indian starve.

MURPH. So walk it, jerk. I'm waiting with the Chief. [MURPH *stands next to* THE INDIAN]

JOEY. Come on, we'll grab the subway.

MURPH. Joe, the trains are running crazy now. Anyway, I'm waitin' with my friend the Chief, here. You wanna go, go. [*Murmurs*] Where is it, Chief? Is that it? Here it comes, huh?

JOEY [*Considers it*]. Yeah, we gotta watch out for Turkie. [JOEY *stands on the other side of* THE INDIAN, *who finally walks slowly back to the bus stop area*]

MURPH. See that, Turkie, little Joe's gonna keep us company. That's nice, huh? [THE INDIAN *looks for the bus*] You know, Joey, this Turk's a pain in my ass. He don't look at me when I talk to him.

JOEY. He oughta look at you when you talk. He oughta be polite.

[*They pass the card in a game.* THE INDIAN *smiles*]

MURPH. I don't think he learned many smarts in Indiana. Any slob knows enough to look when they're being talked to. Huh?

JOEY. This ain't just any slob. This is a definite Turkie-Indian slob.

[*They pass the card behind their backs*]

MURPH. He's one of them commie slobs, probably. Warmongering bastard. [*Flatly*] Pinko here rapes all the little kids.

JOEY. Terrible thing. Too bad we can't give him some smarts. Maybe he could use a couple.

[*The game ends.* JOEY *has the card as in a magic act*]

MURPH. We'll give him plenty of smarts. [*Calling him upstage*] Want some smarts? Chief?

INDIAN. Bna-ee mai toom-maree bah-at nah-hee sah-maj-sak-tah. (*I can't understand you. Please?*)

JOEY. Hey, look. He's talking out of the side of his mouth. Sure, that's right . . . Hey, Murph. Ain't Indian broads s'posed to have sideways breezers? Sure.

MURPH [*Grins*]. You mean chinks, Joey.

JOEY. Naw. Indian broads too. All them foreign broads. Their breezers are sideways. That's why them foreign cars have the back seat facing the side, right?

MURPH. Is that right, Turkie? Your broads have horizontal snatches?

INDIAN [*Stares at him nervously*]. Mai toom-haree bah-at nah-hee sah-maj sak-tah. (*I can't understand you.*)

MURPH [*Repeating him in the same language*]. Nah-hee sah-maj sak-tah.

INDIAN [*Recognizing the language finally. He speaks with incredible speed*]. Toom-haree bah-sha nah-hee sah-maj-tah. Moo-jhay mah-af kar-nah par ah-bhee moo-jhay toom-ha-ray desh aye kuh-chah hee din toh Hu-yay hain. Moo-jhay toom-ha-ree bah-sha see-kh-nay kah ah-bhee sah-mai hee nah-hee milah. (*Yes, that's correct. I can't understand your language. I'm sorry, but I've only been in your country for a few days. I haven't had time to understand your language. Please forgive me.*)

MURPH [*Does a take. Flatly*]. This Turkie's a real pain in the ass.

JOEY. Naw. I think he's pretty interesting. I never saw an Indian before.

MURPH. Oh. It's fascinating. It's marvelous. This city's a regular melting pot. Turkies. Kikes like you. [*Pause*] I even had me a real French lady once. [*Looks at the ground. Pauses*] I thought I saw a dime here. [*Ponders*] I knew it. [*He picks up a dime and pockets it proudly*]

JOEY. A French lady, huh?

MURPH. Yep. A real French broad.

JOEY [*Holds a beat*]. You been at your mother again?

MURPH [*Hits him on the arm*]. Wise-ass. Just what nobody likes. A wise-ass.

JOEY. Where'd you have this French lady, huh?

MURPH. I found her in the park over there. [*Points*] Just

sitting on a bench. She was great. [*Boasts*] A real *talent*.

JOEY. Yeah, sure thing. [*Calls into the park*] Hello, talent. Hello, talent! [*Pauses*] I had a French girl, too. [*Turns to avoid* MURPH's *eyes, caught in a lie*] Where the hell's that bus?

MURPH [*Simply*]. Sure you did. Like the time you had a mermaid?

JOEY. You better believe I did. She wasn't really French. She just lived there a long time. I went to first grade with her. Geraldine. She was my first girl friend. [*Talks very quickly*] Her old man was in the Army or something, 'cause they moved to France. She came back when we were in high school.

MURPH. Then what happened?

JOEY. Nothin'. She just came back, that's all.

MURPH. I thought you said you *had* her . . .

JOEY. No, she was just my girl friend.

MURPH. In high school?

JOEY. No, ya stoop. In the first grade. I just told you.

MURPH. You had her in the first grade?

JOEY. Jesus, you're stupid. She was my girl friend. That's all.

MURPH [*Feigns excitement*]. Hey . . . that's a *sweet little story*. [*Flatly*] What the hell's wrong with you?

JOEY. What do ya' mean?

MURPH. First you say you had a French girl, then you say you had a girl friend in first grade, who went to France. What the hell kind of story's that?

JOEY. It's a true one, that's all. Yours is full of crap.

MURPH. What's full of crap?

JOEY. About the French lady in the park. You never had any French lady, unless you been at your own old lady again. Or maybe you've been at Pussyface?

MURPH. Jesus, you're lookin' for it, aren't you?
   [*They pretend to fistfight*]

JOEY. I mean, if you gotta tell lies to your best buddy, you're in bad shape, that's all.

MURPH [*Gives* JOEY *a "high-sign"*]. Best buddy? You?
   [*The sign to* THE INDIAN. *He returns the obscene gesture, thinking it a berserk American sign of welcome*]

JOEY. Is that how it is in Ceylon, sir?

MURPH. Say-lon? What the hell is say-long?

JOEY. See, ya jerk, Ceylon's part of India. That's where they grow tea.

MURPH. No kiddin'? Boy it's terrific what you can learn just standin' here with a schmuck like you. Tea, huh? [*To* THE INDIAN *he screams*] Hey! [THE INDIAN *turns around, startled*] How's your teabags? [*No response*] No? [*To* JOEY] Guess you're wrong again. He don't know teabags.

JOEY. Look at the bags under his eyes. That ain't chopped liver.

> [MURPH *screams "Hey!"*—THE INDIAN *smiles. They dance a war dance around him, beating a rhythm on the trashcans, hissing and cat-calling for a full minute.* MURPH *ends the dance with a final "Hey!"* THE INDIAN *jumps in fear. Now that they sense his fear, the comedy has ended*]

MURPH. Turkie looks like he's getting bored.

JOEY. Poor old Indian. Maybe he wants to play a game.

MURPH. You know any poor old Indian games?

JOEY. We could burn him at the stake. [*He laughs*] That ain't such a terrible idea, you know. Maybe make an Indian stew.

MURPH. Naw, we couldn't burn a nice fellow like Turkie. That's nasty.

JOEY. We got to play a game. Pussyface always tells us to play games. [*To the apartment, the back of the audience*] Ain't that right, Pussyface? You always want us to play games.

MURPH. I know a game . . .

JOEY. Yeah?

MURPH. Yeah. [*Screams at* THE INDIAN] "Indian, Indian, where's the Indian?"

JOEY. That's a sweet game. I haven't played that for years.

MURPH. Wise-ass. You want to play a game, don't you?

JOEY. Indian-Indian. Where's the Indian?

MURPH. Sure. It's just like ring-a-leave-eo. Only with a spin.

JOEY. That sounds terrific.

MURPH. Look. I spin the hell out of you until you're dizzy. Then you run across the street and get Pussyface. I'll grab the Indian and hide him. Then Pussyface and you come over here and try to find us.

JOEY. We're going to spin, huh?

MURPH. Sure.

JOEY. Who's going to clean up after you? Remember the Ferris wheel, big shot? All those happy faces staring up at you?

MURPH. I ain't the spinner. You're the spinner. I'll hide the Chief. Go on. Spin.

JOEY. How about if we set the rules as we go along? [*To* THE INDIAN] How does that grab you, Chief?

INDIAN. Moo-jhay mah-afkar-nah. Mai toom-nakee bah-sha na-hee sah-maj sak-ta. (*I'm sorry, but I can't understand your language.*)

MURPH. He's talking Indiana again. He don't understand. Go on. Spin. I'll grab the Chief while you're spinning . . . count the ten . . . hide the Chief, while you're after Pussyface. Go on. Spin.

JOEY. I ain't going to spin. I get sick.

MURPH. Ain't you going to play?

JOEY. I'll play. But I can't spin any better than you can. I get sick. You know that. How about if you spin and I hide the Chief? You can get Pussyface. She likes you better than me, anyhow.

MURPH. Pussyface ain't home. You know that. She's in New Jersey.

JOEY. Then what the hell's the point of this game, anyway?

MURPH. It's just a game. We can pretend.

JOEY. You can play marbles for all I care. I just ain't going to spin, that's all. And neither are you. So let's forget the whole game.

MURPH [*Fiercely*]. Spin! Spin!

JOEY. You spin.

MURPH. Hey. I told you to spin.

[MURPH *squares off against* JOEY *and slaps him menacingly.* JOEY *looks* MURPH *straight in the eye for a moment*]

JOEY. Okay. Big deal. So I'll spin. Then I get Pussyface, right? You ready to get the Chief?

MURPH. Will you stop talking and start spinning?

JOEY. All right. All right. Here I go. [JOEY *spins himself meekly, as* MURPH *goes toward* THE INDIAN *and the trash can.* JOEY *giggles as he spins ever so slowly.* MURPH *glances at* JOEY *as* JOEY *pretends.* MURPH *is confused*] There. I spun. Is that okay?

MURPH. That's a spin?

JOEY. Well, it wasn't a fox trot.

MURPH. I told you to spin! Any slob knows that ain't no spin! Now spin, God damn it! Spin!

JOEY. This is stupid. You want to play games. You want a decent spin. You spin.

    [*He walks straight to* MURPH—*a challenge.* JOEY *slaps* MURPH. *He winces*]

MURPH [*Squares off viciously. Raises his arms. Looks at* JOEY *cruelly. Orders*]. Spin me.

    [JOEY *brings* MURPH's *arms behind* MURPH's *back and holds* MURPH's *wrists firmly so that he is helpless.* JOEY *spins him. Slowly at first. Then faster. Faster.* JOEY's *hostility is released; he laughs*]

JOEY. You wanted to spin. Spin. Spin.

    [JOEY *spins* MURPH *frantically.* THE INDIAN *watches in total horror, not knowing what to do; he cuddles next to the bus stop sign, his island of safety*]

MURPH [*Screaming*]. Enough, you little bastard.

JOEY [*Continues to spin him*]. Now *you* get Pussyface. Go on. [*Spins* MURPH *all the faster as in a grotesque dance gone berserk*] I'll hide the Chief. This is your game! This is your game. *You* get Pussyface. I'll hide the Chief. Go on, Murphy. You want some more spin? [JOEY *has stopped the spinning now, as* MURPH *is obviously ill*] You want to spin some more?

MURPH. Stop it, Joey. I'm sick.

JOEY [*Spins* MURPH *once more around*]. You want to spin some more, or are you going to get Pussyface and come find the Chief and me?

MURPH. You little bastard.

JOEY [*Spins* MURPH *once again, still holding* MURPH *helpless with his arms behind his back*]. I'll hide the Chief. YOU get Pussyface and find us. Okay? Okay? Okay?

MURPH. Okay . . . you bastard . . . okay.

JOEY. Here's one more for good luck.

> [JOEY *spins* MURPH *three more times, fiercely, then shoves him offstage.* MURPH *can be heard retching, about to vomit, during the final spins.* JOEY *then grabs* THE INDIAN, *who pulls back in terror*]

INDIAN. Na-hee bha-yee toom ah-b k-yah kah-rogay? (*No, please, what are you going to do?*)

JOEY. Easy, Chief. It's just a game. Murph spun out on us. It's just a game. I've got to hide you now.

> [MURPH's *final puking sounds can be heard well in the distance*]

INDIAN. Na-hee na-hee bha-yee. Mai mah-afee mah-ng-ta. Hoon. (*No. No. Please. I beg you.*)

JOEY. Easy, Chief. Look. I promise you, this ain't for real. This is only a game. A game. Get it? It's all a game! Now I got to count to ten. [*Grabs* THE INDIAN *and forces him down behind a city litter basket. He covers* THE INDIAN's *scream with his hand, as he slaps* THE INDIAN—*a horrifying sound*] One. Two. Three. Murphy? [*He laughs*] Four. Five. Murph? Come get us. Six. Seven. Pussyface is waiting. Eight. Nine. [*Pauses*] Murphy? Murph? Hey, buddy. [*Stands up. Speaks*] Ten. [*Lights are narrowing on* JOEY *and* THE INDIAN. THE INDIAN *tries to escape.* JOEY *subdues him easily.* JOEY *turns slowly back to* THE INDIAN, *who responds with open fear*] Get up. Up. [*No response*] Get up, Turkie. [*Moves to* THE INDIAN, *who recoils sharply.* JOEY *persists and pulls* THE INDIAN *to his feet.* THE INDIAN *shudders, stands and faces his captor.* THE INDIAN *shakes from fear and from a chill. There is a moment's silence as* JOEY *watches. He removes his own sweater and offers it to* THE INDIAN] Here. Here. Put it on. It's okay. [THE INDIAN *is bewildered, but* JOEY *forces the sweater into his hands*] Put it on. [THE INDIAN *stares at the sweater.* JOEY *takes it from his hands and begins to cover* THE INDIAN, *who is amazed*] I hope I didn't hurt you too much. You okay? [*No response*] You ain't sick too bad, huh? [*Pause*] Huh? [*Checks* THE INDIAN *for cuts*] You look okay. You're okay, huh? [*No response*] I didn't mean to rough you up like that, but . . . you know. Huh? [THE INDIAN *raises his eyes to meet* JOEY'S. JOEY *looks down to avoid the stare*] I hope you ain't mad at me or nothin'. [*Pause*] Boy it's gettin' chilly. I mean, it's cold, right? Sure is quiet all of a sudden. Kind of spooky, huh? [*Calls*] Hey, Murphy! [*Laughs aloud*] Murph ain't a bad guy. He's my best buddy, see? I mean, he gets kinda crazy sometimes, but that's all. Everybody gets kind of crazy sometime, right? [*No response*] Jesus, you're a stupid Indian. Can't you speak any English? No? Why the hell did you come here, anyway? Especially if you can't talk any English. You ought to say something. Can't you even say "Thank you"?

　　[THE INDIAN *recognizes those words, finally, and mimics them slowly and painfully*]

INDIAN [*In English, very British and clipped*]. Thank you.

JOEY. I'll be Goddamned! You're welcome. [*Slowly, indicating for* THE INDIAN *to follow*] You're welcome. [*He waits*]

INDIAN [*In English*]. You are welcome.

JOEY. That's terrific. You are welcome. [*Smiles, as though all is forgiven. In relief*] How are you?

INDIAN. You are welcome.

JOEY. No. How are ya? [JOEY *is excited.* THE INDIAN *might be a second friend*]

INDIAN [*In English—very "Joey"*]. How are ya?

JOEY [*Joyously*]. Jesus. You'll be talking like us in no time! You're okay, huh? You ain't bleeding or anything. I didn't wanna hurt you none. But Murph gets all worked up. You know what I mean. He gets all excited. This ain't the first time, you know. No, sir!

INDIAN [*In English*]. No, sir.

JOEY. That's right. He's especially crazy around broads.

INDIAN [*In English*]. Broads.

JOEY [*Forgetting that* THE INDIAN *is only mimicking*]. That's right. Broads. [*Pauses and remembers, deeply*] What am I yakking for? Tell me about India, huh? I'd like to go to India sometime. Maybe I will. You think I'd like India? India? [*No response.* THE INDIAN *recognizes the word, but doesn't understand the question*] That's where you're from, ain't it? Jesus, what a stupid Indian.

India! [*Spells the word*] I-N-D-I-A. Nothin'. Schmuck.
*India!*

INDIAN [*A guess still*]. Hindi?

JOEY. Yeah! Tell me about India! [*Long pause as they
stand staring at each other*] No? You're not talking,
huh? Well, what do you want to do? Murph oughta be
back soon. [*Discovers a coin in his pocket*] You wanna
flip for quarters? Flip? No? Look, a Kennedy half!
[*Goes through three magic tricks with the coin:* (1) *He
palms the coin, offers the obvious choice of hand, then
uncovers the coin in his other hand.* THE INDIAN *raises
his hand to his turban in astonishment*] Like that, huh?
[(2) *Coin is slapped on his breast*] This hand right? Is
it this hand, this hand? No, it's *this* hand! Back to your
dumb act? Here. Here's the one you liked! [*Does* (1).
*This time* THE INDIAN *points to the correct hand instantly*] You're probably some kind of hustler. Okay. Double
or nothing. [*Flips*] Heads, you live. Tails, you die.
Okay? [*Uncovers the coin*] I'll be a son of a bitch. You
got Indian luck. Here. [*He hands the coin to* THE
INDIAN]

INDIAN [*Stares in question*]. Na-hff? (*No?*)

JOEY [*Considers cheating*]. Take it. You won. No, go
ahead. Keep it. I ain't no Indian giver. [*Pause. He laughs
at his own joke. No response*] You ain't got no sense of
humor, that's what. [*Stares upstage*] Murph's my best
buddy, you know? Me and him were buddies when we
were kids. Me and Murph, all the time. You think my
old lady's bad? She's nothing. His old lady's a pro. You
know? She don't even make a living at it, either. That's
the bitch of it. Not even a living. She's a dog. I mean, I
wouldn't even pay her a nickel. Not a nickel. Not that
I'd screw around with Murphy's old lady. Oh! Not that
she doesn't try. She tries plenty. [*His fantasy begins*]
That's why I don't come around to his house much. She
tries it all the time. She wouldn't charge me anything,
probably. But it ain't right screwing your best buddy's
old lady, right? I'd feel terrible if I did. She ain't that
bad, but it just ain't right. I'd bet she'd even take Murph
on. She probably tries it with him, too. That's the bitch

of it. She can't even make a living. His own Goddamned mother. The other one—Pussyface. You think Pussyface is a help? That's the biggest joke yet. [THE INDIAN *is by now thoroughly confused on all counts. He recognizes the name "Pussyface," and reacts slightly. Seeing* JOEY's *anxiety, he cuddles him. For a brief moment they embrace—an insane father-and-son tableau*] Pussyface. There's a brain. You see what she gave us for Christmas [*Fishes his knife out of his pocket*] Knives. Brilliant, huh? Murph's up on a rap for slicing a kid, and she gives us knives for Christmas. To whittle with. She's crazier than Murphy. Hah. [*Flashes his open knife at* THE INDIAN, *who misinterprets the move as spelling disaster.* THE INDIAN *waits, carefully scrutinizing* JOEY, *until* JOEY *begins to look away.* JOEY *now wanders to the spot where he pushed* MURPH *offstage*] Hey, Murph! [THE INDIAN *moves slowly to the other side of the stage.* JOEY *sees his move at once and races after him, thinking* THE INDIAN *was running away*] Hey. Where are you going? [THE INDIAN *knows he'll be hit. He tries to explain with mute gestures and attitude. It's futile. He knows at once and hits* JOEY *as best he can and races across the stage.* JOEY *recovers from the blow and starts after him, as* THE INDIAN *murmurs one continuous frightening scream.* JOEY *dives after* THE INDIAN *and tackles him on the other side of the stage.* THE INDIAN *fights more strongly than ever, but* JOEY's *trance carries him ferociously into this fight. He batters* THE INDIAN *with punches to the body.* THE INDIAN *squeals as* JOEY *sobs*] You were gonna run off. Right? Son of a bitch. You were gonna tell Murphy.

[THE INDIAN *makes one last effort to escape and runs the length of the stage, screaming a bloodcurdling, anguished scream.* MURPH *enters, stops, stares incredulously as* THE INDIAN *runs into his open arms.* JOEY *races to* THE INDIAN *and strikes a karate chop to the back of his neck.* JOEY *is audibly sobbing.* THE INDIAN *drops to the stage as* JOEY *stands frozen above him.* MURPH *stares, first at* JOEY *and then at* THE INDIAN]

MURPH. Pussyface isn't home yet. She's still in New Jersey. Ring-a-leave-eo.

JOEY [*Sobbing, senses his error*]. Indians are dumb.

MURPH [*Stares again at* JOEY. *Then to* THE INDIAN. *Spots* JOEY's *sweater on* THE INDIAN. *Fondles it, then stares at* JOEY *viciously*]. Pussyface isn't home. I rang her bell. She don't answer. I guess she's still on vacation. She ruined our game.

JOEY [*Sobbing*]. Oh, jumping Jesus Christ. Jesus. Jesus. Jesus. Indians are dumb.

MURPH. Pussyface ruins everything. She don't really care about our games. She ruins our games. Just like Indians. They don't know how to play our games either.

JOEY. Indians are dumb. Dumb. [*He sobs.* MURPH *slaps* JOEY *across the face. He straightens up and comes back to reality*]

MURPH. What the hell's going on?

JOEY. He tried to run. I hit him.

MURPH. Yeah. I saw that. You hit him, all right. [*Stares at* THE INDIAN] Is he alive?

[THE INDIAN *groans, pulls himself to his knees*]

JOEY. He was fighting. I hit him.

MURPH. Okay, you hit him.

[THE INDIAN *groans again. Then he speaks in a plea*]

INDIAN [*Praying*]. Moo-jhay or nah sah-tao. Maih-nay toom-hara k-yah bigarah hai. Moo-jhay or nah sah-tao. Moo-jhay in-seh. (*Please. Don't hurt me any more. What have I done? Please don't hurt me. Don't let them hurt me*)

MURPH. He's begging for something. Maybe he's begging for his life. Maybe he is. Sure, maybe he is.

JOEY [*Embarrassed, starts to help* THE INDIAN *to his feet*]. C'mon there, Chief. Get up and face the world. C'mon, Chief. Everything's going to be all right.

MURPH. What's got into you, anyway?

JOEY. C'mon, Chief. Up at the world. Everything's okay.

[THE INDIAN *ad libs words of pleading and pain*]

MURPH. Leave him be. [*But* JOEY *continues to help* THE INDIAN] Leave him be. What's with you? Hey, Joey! I said leave him be! [MURPH *pushes* JOEY *and* THE INDIAN *pulls back with fear*]

JOEY. Okay, Murph. Enough's enough.

MURPH. Just tell me what the hell's wrong with you?

JOEY. He tried to run away, that's all. Change the subject.
Change the subject. It ain't important. I hit him, that's
all.

MURPH. Okay, so you hit him.

JOEY. Okay! Where were you? Sick. Were you a little bit
sick? I mean, you couldn't have been visiting, 'cause
there ain't no one to visit, right?

MURPH. What *do* you mean?

JOEY. Where the hell were you? [*Looks at* MURPH *and
giggles*] You're a little green there, Irish.

MURPH. You're pretty funny. What the hell's so funny?

JOEY. Nothing's funny. The Chief and I were just having a
little pow-wow and we got to wondering where you ran
off to. Just natural for us to wonder, ain't it? [*To* THE
INDIAN] Right, Chief.

MURPH. Hey, look at that. Turkie's got a woolly sweater
just like yours. Ain't that a terrific coincidence. You two
been playing strip poker?

JOEY. Oh, sure. Strip poker. The Chief won my sweater
and I won three of his feathers and a broken arrow. [*To*
THE INDIAN, *he feigns a deep authoritative voice*] You
wonder who I am, don't you? Perhaps this silver bullet
will help to identify me? [*Extends his hand.* THE INDIAN
*peers into* JOEY's *empty palm quizzically. As he does,*
MURPH *quickly taps the underside of* JOEY's *hand, forc-
ing the hand to rise and slap* THE INDIAN's *chin sharply.*
THE INDIAN *pulls back at the slap.* JOEY *turns on*
MURPH, *quickly*] What the hell did you do that for, ya'
jerk. The Chief didn't do nothing.

MURPH. Jesus, you and your Chief are pretty buddy-buddy,
ain't you? [*Mimics* JOEY] "The Chief didn't do nothing." Jesus. You give him your sweater. Maybe you'd
like to have him up for a beer . . .

JOEY. Drop it, Murph. You're giving me a pain in the ass.

MURPH [*Retorts fiercely*]. You little pisser. Who the hell
do you think you're talking to?

[*The telephone rings in the booth. They are all startled,
especially* THE INDIAN, *who senses hope*]

JOEY [*After a long wait, speaking the obvious flatly*]. It's
the phone.

MURPH [*To* THE INDIAN]. The kid's a whiz. He guessed that right away.

[*The phone rings a second time*]

JOEY. Should we answer it?

MURPH. What for? Who'd be calling here? It's a wrong number.

[*The phone rings menacingly a third time. Suddenly* THE INDIAN *darts into the phone booth and grabs the receiver.* JOEY *and* MURPH *are too startled to stop him until he has blurted out his hopeless plea, in his own language*]

INDIAN. Prem k-yah woh may-rah ar-kah hai. Prem (prayem) bay-tah moo-jhay bachah-low. Mai fah ns ga-yah hoon yeh doh goon-day moo-jhay mar ra-hay hain. Mai ba-hoot ghah-bara gaya hoon. Pray-em. (*Prem? Is this my son? Prem? Please help me. I'm frightened. Please help me. Two boys are hurting me . . . I'm frightened. Please. Prem?*)

[THE INDIAN *stops talking sharply and listens. He crumbles as the voice drones the wrong reply. He drops the receiver and stares with horror at the boys.* MURPH *realizes* THE INDIAN's *horror and begins to laugh hysterically.* JOEY *stares silently.* THE INDIAN *begins to mumble and weep. He walks from the phone booth. The voice is heard as a drone from the receiver. The action freezes*]

MURPH [*Laughing*]. What's the matter, Turkie? Don't you have a dime? Give Turkie a dime, Joe. Give him a dime.

JOEY. Jesus Christ. I'd hate to be an Indian.

MURPH. Hey, the paper! C'mon, Joey, get the paper from him. We'll call the Bronx.

JOEY. Cut it out, Murph. Enough's enough.

MURPH. Get the frigging piece of paper. What's the matter with you, anyway?

JOEY. I just don't think it's such a terrific idea, that's all.

MURPH. You're chicken. That's what you are.

JOEY. Suppose his son has called the police. What do you think? You think he hasn't called the police? He knows the old man don't speak any English. He called the police. Right? And they'll trace our call.

MURPH. You're nuts. They can't trace any phone calls. Anyway, we'll be gone from here. You're nuts.

JOEY. I don't want to do it.

MURPH. For Christ's sake. They can't trace nothing to nobody. Who's going to trace? Get the paper.

JOEY. Get it yourself. Go on. Get it yourself. I ain't going to get it.

MURPH. C'mon, Joey. It's not real. This is just a game. It ain't going to hurt anybody. You know that. It's just a game.

JOEY. Why don't we call somebody else? We'll call somebody else and have the Indian talk. That makes sense. Imagine if an Indian called you up and talked to you in Indian. I bet the Chief would go for that all right. Jesus, Murphy.

MURPH. Get the paper and picture.

INDIAN. Ah-b toom k-yah kah-rogay. Mai-nay soh-chah thah sha-yahd woh. Pray-em hoh. (*What are you going to do now? That's who I thought it was. Prem.*)

MURPH. Prem. That's the name. [*Plays the rhyme*]

INDIAN. Pray-aim. (*Prem?*)

MURPH. Yes, Prem. I want to call Prem. Give me the paper with his name.

INDIAN. Toom pray-aim kay ba-ray may k-yah kah ra-hay. (*What are you saying about Prem?*)

MURPH. Shut up already and give me the paper.

JOEY. Jesus, Murph.

MURPH [*Turning* THE INDIAN *around so that they face each other*]. This is ridiculous. [*Searches* THE INDIAN, *who resists a bit at first, and then not at all. Finally,* MURPH *finds the slip of paper*] I got it. I got it. Terrific. "Prem Gupta." In the Bronx. In the frigging Bronx. This is terrific. [*Pushes* THE INDIAN *to* JOEY] Here. Hold him.

INDIAN. Toom k-yah kar ra-hay ho k-yah toom pray-aim k-oh boo-lah ra-hay ho. (*What are you doing? Are you going to call my son?*)

MURPH. Shut him up. [*Fishes for a dime*] Give me a dime, God damn it. This is terrific.

JOEY [*Finds the coins in his pocket*]. Here's two nickels. [*Hands them over*] I think this is a rotten idea, that's what I think. [*Pauses*] And don't forget to pay me back those two nickels either.

MURPH. Just shut up. [*Dials the information operator*] Hello. Yeah, I want some information . . . I want a number up in the Bronx . . . Gupta . . . G-U-P-T-A . . . an Indian kid . . . His first name's Prem . . . P-R-E-M . . . No . . . I can't read the street right . . . Wait a minute. [*Reads the paper to himself*] For Christ's sake. How many Indians are up in the Bronx? There must be only one Indian named Gupta.

JOEY. What's she saying?

MURPH. There are two Indians named Gupta. [*To the operator*] Is the two of them named Prem? [*Pauses*] Well, that's what I told you . . . Jesus . . . wait a minute . . . okay . . . okay. Say that again . . . Okay . . . Okay . . . Right. Okay . . . thanks. [*Hurries quickly to return the coins to the slot.* GUPTA *mumbles. To* JOEY] Don't talk to me. [*Dials*] Six . . . seven-four. Oh. One. Seven, seven. [*Pauses*] It's ringing. It's ringing. [*Pauses*] Hello. [*Covers the phone with his hand*] I got him! Hello? Is this Prem Gupta? Oh swell. How are you? [*To* JOEY] I got the kid!

[THE INDIAN *breaks from* JOEY's *arm and runs to the telephone* . . . MURPH *sticks out his leg and holds* THE INDIAN *off.* THE INDIAN *fights, but seems weaker than ever*]

INDIAN [*Screams*]. Cree-payah moo-jhay ad-nay lar-kay say bah-at kar-nay doh. (*Please let me talk to my son.*) [MURPH *slams* THE INDIAN *aside violently.* JOEY *stands frozen, watching.* THE INDIAN *wails and finally talks calmly, as in a trance*] Cree-payah moo-jhay ahd-nay lar-kay say bah-at kar-nay doh. Mai toom-haray hah-th jor-tah hoom mai toom-hay joh mango-gay doon-gar bus moo-jhay oos-say bah-at kar-nay doh. (*Please let me talk to my son. Oh, Prem. Please, I beg of you. Please. I'll give you anything at all. Just tell me what you want of me. Just let me talk with my son. Won't you, please?*)

[MURPH *glares at* THE INDIAN, *who no longer tries to in-*

*terfere, as it becomes obvious that he must listen to
even the language he cannot understand*]

MURPH. Just listen to me, will you, Gupta? I don't know
where the hell your old man is, that's why I'm calling.
We found an old elephant down here in Miami and we
thought it must be yours. You can't tell for sure
whose elephant is whose. You know what I mean?
[MURPH *is laughing now*] What was that? Say that
again. I can't hear you too well. All the distance between
us, you know what I mean? It's a long way down here,
you follow me? No. I ain't got no Indian. I just got an
elephant. And he's eating all my peanuts. Gupta, you're
talking too fast. Slow down.

INDIAN. Pray-aim bhai-yah moo-jhay ah-kay lay ja-oh
moo-jhay ap-nay lar-kay say bah-at kar-nay doh moo-
jhay oos-say bah-at k-yohn nah-hee kar-nay day-tay.
(*Prem! Prem! Please come and get me. Please let me
talk to my son, mister. Why don't you let me talk to my
son?*)

[JOEY *leaps on* THE INDIAN; *tackles him, lays on top of
him in front of the telephone booth*]

MURPH. That was the waiter. I'm in an Indian restaurant.
[*Pauses*] Whoa. Slow down, man. That was nobody.
That was just a myth. Your imagination. [*Pauses.
Screams into the receiver*] Shut up, damn you! And listen. Okay? Okay. Are you listening? [MURPH *tastes the
moment. He silently clicks the receiver back to the hook.*
[*To* JOEY] He was very upset. [*To* THE INDIAN] He was
very upset. [*Pauses*] Well, what the hell's the matter
with you? I only told him we found an elephant, that's
all. I thought maybe he lost his elephant.

[THE INDIAN *whimpers*]

INDIAN. Toom-nay ai-saw k-yohn ki-yah toom-nay may-ray
lar-kay koh k-yah ka-hah hai. (*Why have you done this?
What have you said to my son?*)

MURPH. You don't have to thank me, Turkie. I only told
him your elephant was okay. He was probably worried
sick about your elephant. [MURPH *laughs*] This is terrific,

Joey. Terrific. You should have heard the guy jabber. He was so excited he started talking in Indian just like the Chief. He said that Turkie here and him got separated today. Turkie's only been in the city one day. You're pretty stupid, Turkie. One day in the city . . . and look at the mess you've made. You're pretty stupid. He's stupid, right?

JOEY. Yeah. He's stupid.

MURPH. Hold him. We'll try again. Sure.

[THE INDIAN *jumps on* MURPH. *He tries to strangle* MURPH]

MURPH [*Screaming*]. Get him off of me! [JOEY *pulls* THE INDIAN *down to the ground as* MURPH *pounds the booth four times, screaming hideous sounds of aggression. With this tension released he begins to call, fierce but controlled, too controlled.* MURPH *takes the dime from his pocket, shows it to* JOEY, *and recalls the number. Talking into receiver. He dials number again and waits for reply.*] Hello? Is this Gupta again? Oh, hello there . . . I'm calling back to complain about your elephant . . . hey, slow down, will you? Let me do the talking. Okay? Your elephant is a terrific pain in the balls to me, get it? Huh? Do you follow me so far? [*Pauses*] I don't know what you're saying, man . . . how about if I do the talking, all right? . . .Your elephant scares hell out of me and my pal here. We don't like to see elephants on the street. Spiders and snakes are okay, but elephants scare us. Elephants . . . yeah, that's right. Don't you get it, pal? . . . Look, we always see spiders and snakes. But we never expect to see an elephant . . . What do you mean "I'm crazy"? I don't know nothing about your old man . . . I'm talking about your elephant. Your elephant offends the hell out of me. So why don't you be a nice Indian kid and come pick him up . . . that's right . . . wait a minute . . . I'll have to check the street sign. [*Covers the receiver*] This is terrific. [*Talks again into the telephone*] Jesus, I'm sorry about that. There don't seem to be no street sign . . . that's a bitch. I guess you lose your elephant . . . well, what do you expect me to do, bring your elephant all the way up to the Bronx? Come off it, pal.

You wouldn't ever bring my elephant home. I ain't no kid, you know! I've lost a couple of elephants in my day. [*Listens*] Jesus, you're boring me now . . . I don't know what the hell you're talking about. Maybe you want to talk to your elephant . . . huh? [*Turns to* THE INDIAN] Here, come talk to your "papoose."

[*He offers the telephone.* THE INDIAN *stares in disbelief, then grabs the telephone from* MURPH's *hands and begins to chatter wildly*]

INDIAN. Pray-aim, bhai-yah Pray-aim moo-jhay ah-kay lay jah-oh k-yah? (*Prem? Oh, Prem. Please come and take me away . . . what? I don't know where I am . . .*)

MURPH. You've had enough, Chief.

[MURPH *takes his knife from his pocket, cuts the line.* THE INDIAN *almost falls flat on his face as the line from the receiver to the phone box is cut, since he has been leaning away from* MURPH *and* JOEY *during his plea*]

INDIAN [*Not at once realizing the line must be connected, continues to talk into the telephone in Hindi*]. Pray-aim, Pray-aim, ya-hahn aa-oh sah-rak kah nah-am hai—yeh toom-nay k-yah key-yah. (*Prem. Prem. Please come here. The street sign reads . . .*) [*He now realizes he has been cut off and stares dumbly at* JOEY. *He scolds*] Toom-nay yeh k-yoh key-yah? (*What have you done?*)

[MURPH *waves the severed cord at* THE INDIAN]

MURPH. There it is, Turkie. Who you talkin' to?

INDIAN [*To* JOEY, *screaming a father's fury and disgust*]. Toom-nay yeh k-yohn key-yah cri-payah may-ree mah-dah-d kah-roho. (*Why have you done this? Please. Please help me.*)

[JOEY *has been standing throughout the entire scene, frozen in terror and disgust. He walks slowly toward* MURPH, *who kicks* THE INDIAN]

MURPH [*Screaming*]. Go ahead, Joey. Love him. Love him like a mother.

[JOEY *bolts from the stage, muttering one continuous droning sob.* MURPH *screams after him*]

MURPH. Hey? Joey? What the hell's the matter? C'mon, buddy? [*Turns to* THE INDIAN, *takes his knife and cuts*

THE INDIAN's *hand, so blood is on the knife*] Sorry,
Chief. This is for my buddy, Joey. And for Pussyface.
[*Calls offstage*] Joey! Buddy! What the hell's the mat-
ter? [*Races from the stage after* JOEY] Joey! Wait up.
Joey! I killed the Indian!

> [*He exits.* THE INDIAN *stares dumbly at his hand, drip-
> ping blood. He then looks to the receiver and talks
> into it*]

INDIAN. Pray-aim, Pray-aim. (*Prem. Prem.*)

> [*He walks to center stage, well away from the telephone
> booth*]

INDIAN. Mai ah-pa-nay lar-kay key ah-wah-az k-yon nah-
hee soon sak-tah Pray-aim! Toom-nay may-ray sah-ahth
aih-saw k-yohn key-yaw bay-tah. (*Why can I not hear
my son, Prem? Why have you done this to me?*)

> [*Suddenly the telephone rings again. Once. Twice.* THE
> INDIAN *is startled. He talks into the receiver, while he
> holds the dead line in his bleeding hand*]

> [*The telephone rings a third time*] Pray-aim, Pray-aim,
> bay-tah k-yah toom ho—(*Prem. Prem? Is that you?*)

> [*A fourth ring.* THE INDIAN *knows the telephone is
> dead*] Pray-aim Pray-aim—moo-jhay bah-chald Pray-
> aim. (*Prem. Prem. Help me. Prem.*)

> [*As the telephone rings a fifth time, in the silence of
> the night, the sounds of two boys' singing is heard*]

FIRST BOY.

> I walk the lonely streets at night,
> A-lookin' for your door . . .

SECOND BOY.

> I look and look and look and look . . .

FIRST BOY *and* SECOND BOY.

> But, baby, you don't care.
> But, baby, no one cares.
> But, baby, no one cares.

> [*Their song continues to build as they repeat the lyrics,
> so the effect is one of many, many voices. The tele-
> phone continues its unanswered ring.* THE INDIAN
> screams a final anguished scream of fury to the boys
> offstage. .*

> *The telephone rings a final ring as* THE INDIAN *screams*]

INDIAN [*Desperately, holding the telephone to the audience as an offer. He speaks in English into the telephone. The only words he remembers are those from his lesson*]. How are you? You're welcome. You're welcome. Thank you. [*To the front*] Thank you!

BLACKOUT

THE PLAY IS OVER

# THE BOYS
# IN THE BAND

*by Mart Crowley*

*For Howard Jeffrey*
*and Douglas Murray*

The Boys in the Band *was first performed in January 1968 at the Playwrights Unit, Vandam Theatre, Charles Gnys, managing director.*

The Boys in the Band *was first produced on the New York stage by Richard Barr and Charles Woodward Jr., at Theatre Four on April 14, 1968. The play was designed by Peter Harvey and directed by Robert Moore.*

*The original cast was:*

MICHAEL, *Kenneth Nelson*
DONALD, *Frederick Combs*
EMORY, *Cliff Gorman*
LARRY, *Keith Prentice*
HANK, *Laurence Luckinbill*
BERNARD, *Reuben Greene*
COWBOY, *Robert La Tourneaux*
HAROLD, *Leonard Frey*
ALAN, *Peter White*

## CHARACTERS

| | |
|---|---|
| MICHAEL | *Thirty, average face, smartly groomed* |
| DONALD | *Twenty-eight, medium blond, wholesome American good looks* |
| EMORY | *Thirty-three, small, frail, very plain* |
| LARRY | *Twenty-nine, extremely handsome* |
| HANK | *Thirty-two, tall, solid, athletic, attractive* |
| BERNARD | *Twenty-eight, Negro, nice looking* |
| COWBOY | *Twenty-two, light blond, muscle-bound, too pretty* |
| HAROLD | *Thirty-two, dark, lean, strong limbs, unusual Semitic face* |
| ALAN | *Thirty, aristocratic Anglo-Saxon features* |

*The play is divided into two acts. The action is continuous and occurs one evening within the time necessary to perform the script.*

## Act one

*A smartly appointed duplex apartment in the East Fifties, New York, consisting of a living room and, on a higher level, a bedroom. Bossa nova music blasts from a phonograph.*

MICHAEL, *wearing a robe, enters from the kitchen, carrying some liquor bottles. He crosses to set them on a bar, looks to see if the room is in order, moves toward the stairs to the bedroom level, doing a few improvised dance steps en route. In the bedroom, he crosses before a mirror, studies his hair—sighs. He picks up comb and a hair drier, goes to work.*

*The downstairs front-door buzzer sounds. A beat.* MICHAEL *stops, listens, turns off the drier. More buzzing.* MICHAEL *quickly goes to the living room, turns off the music, opens the door to reveal* DONALD, *dressed in khakis and a Lacoste shirt, carrying an airline zipper bag.*

MICHAEL. Donald! You're about a day and a half early!

DONALD [*Enters*]. The doctor canceled!

MICHAEL. Canceled! How'd you get inside?

DONALD. The street door was open.

MICHAEL. You wanna drink?

DONALD [*Going to bedroom to deposit his bag*]. Not until I've had my shower. I want something to work out today —I want to try to relax and enjoy *something*.

MICHAEL. You in a blue funk because of the doctor?

DONALD [*Returning*]. Christ, no. I was depressed long before I got *there*.

MICHAEL. Why'd the prick cancel?

DONALD. A virus or something. He looked awful.

MICHAEL [*Holding up a shopping bag*]. Well, this'll pick you up. I went shopping today and bought all kind of goodies. Sandalwood soap . . .

DONALD [*Removing his socks and shoes*]. I feel better already.

MICHAEL [*Producing articles*]. . . . . Your very own toothbrush because I'm sick to death of your using mine.

DONALD. How do you think *I* feel.

MICHAEL. You've had worse things in your mouth. [*Holds up a cylindrical can*] And, also for you . . . something called "Control." Notice nowhere is it called hair spray —just simply "Control." And the words "For Men" are written about thirty-seven times all over the goddamn can!

DONALD. It's called Butch Assurance.

MICHAEL. Well, it's *still* hair spray—no matter if they call it "*Balls*"! [DONALD *laughs*] It's all going on your very own shelf, which is to be labeled: Donald's Saturday Night Douche Kit. By the way, are you spending the night?

DONALD. Nope. I'm driving back. I still get very itchy when I'm in this town too long. I'm not that well yet.

MICHAEL. That's what you say every weekend.

DONALD. Maybe after about ten more years of analysis I'll be able to stay one night.

MICHAEL. Maybe after about ten more years of analysis you'll be able to move back to town permanently.

DONALD. If I live that long.

MICHAEL. You will. If you don't kill yourself on the Long Island Expressway some early Sunday morning. I'll never know how you can tank up on martinis and make it back to the Hamptons in one piece.

DONALD. Believe me, it's easier than getting here. Ever had an anxiety attack at sixty miles an hour? Well, tonight I was beside myself to get to the doctor—and just as I finally make it, rush in, throw myself on the couch, and vomit out how depressed I am, he says, "Donald, I have to cancel tonight—I'm just too sick."

MICHAEL. Why didn't you tell him you're sicker than he is.

DONALD. He already knows *that*. [DONALD *goes to the bed-*

*room, drops his shoes and socks.* MICHAEL *follows*]

MICHAEL. Why didn't the prick call you and cancel. Suppose you'd driven all this way for nothing.

DONALD [*Removing his shirt*]. Why do you keep calling him a prick?

MICHAEL. Whoever heard of an analyst having a session with a patient for two hours on Saturday evening.

DONALD. He simply prefers to take Mondays off.

MICHAEL. Works late on Saturday and takes Monday off— what is he, a psychiatrist or a hairdresser?

DONALD. Actually, he's both. He shrinks my head and combs me out. [*Lies on the bed*] Besides, I had to come in town to a birthday party anyway. Right?

MICHAEL. You had to remind me. If there's one thing I'm not ready for, it's five screaming queens singing Happy Birthday.

DONALD. Who's coming?

MICHAEL. They're really all Harold's friends. It's *his* birthday and I want everything to be just the way he'd want it. I don't want to have to listen to him kvetch about how nobody ever does anything for anybody but themselves.

DONALD. Himself.

MICHAEL. Himself. I think you know everybody anyway— they're the same old tired fairies you've seen around since the day one. Actually, there'll be seven, counting Harold and you and me.

DONALD. Are you calling me a screaming queen or a tired fairy?

MICHAEL. Oh, I beg your pardon—six tired screaming fairy queens and one anxious queer.

DONALD. You don't think Harold'll mind my being here, do you? Technically, I'm *your* friend, not his.

MICHAEL. If she doesn't like it, she can twirl on it. Listen, I'll be out of your way in just a second. I've only got one more thing to do.

DONALD. Surgery, so early in the evening?

MICHAEL. Sunt! That's French, with a cedilla. [*Gives him a crooked third finger, goes to mirror*] I've just got to comb my hair for the thirty-seventh time. Hair—that's singular. My hair, without exaggeration, is clearly falling on the floor. And *fast*, baby!

DONALD. You're totally paranoid. You've got plenty of hair.

MICHAEL. What you see before you is a masterpiece of deception. My hairline starts about here. [*Indicates his crown*] All this is just tortured forward.

DONALD. Well, I hope, for your sake, no strong wind comes up.

MICHAEL. If one does, I'll be in terrible trouble. I will then have a bald head and shoulder-length fringe. [*Runs his fingers through his hair, holds it away from his scalp, dips the top of his head so that* DONALD *can see.* DONALD *is silent*] Not good, huh?

DONALD. Not the best.

MICHAEL. It's called, "getting old." Ah, life is such a grand design—spring, summer, fall, winter, death. Who*ever* could have thought it up?

DONALD. No one *we* know, that's for sure.

MICHAEL [*Turns to study himself in the mirror, sighs*]. Well, one thing you can say for masturbation . . . you certainly don't have to look your best. [*Slips out of the robe, flings it at* DONALD. DONALD *laughs, takes the robe, exits to the bath.* MICHAEL *takes a sweater out of a chest, pulls it on*]

MICHAEL. What are you so depressed about? I mean, other than the usual *everything*. [*A beat*]

DONALD [*Reluctantly*]. I really don't want to get into it.

MICHAEL. Well, if you're not going to tell me, how can we have a conversation *in depth*—a warm, rewarding, meaningful friendship?

DONALD. Up yours!

MICHAEL [*Southern accent*]. Why, Cap'n Butler, how you talk!

[*Pause.* DONALD *appears in the doorway holding a glass of water and a small bottle of pills.* MICHAEL *looks up*]

DONALD. It's just that today I finally realized that I was *raised* to be a failure. I was *groomed* for it. [*A beat*]

MICHAEL. You know, there was a time when you could

have said that to me and I wouldn't have known what the hell you were talking about.

DONALD [*Takes some pills*]. Naturally, it all goes back to Evelyn and Walt.

MICHAEL. Naturally. When doesn't it go back to Mom and Pop. Unfortunately, we all had an Evelyn and a Walt. The crumbs! Don't you love that word—crumb? Oh, I love it! It's a real Barbara Stanwyck word. [*A la Stanwyck's frozen-lipped Brooklyn accent*] "Cau'll me a keab, you kr-rumm."

DONALD. Well, I see all vestiges of sanity for this evening are now officially shot to hell.

MICHAEL. Oh, Donald, you're so serious tonight! You're fun-starved, baby, and I'm eating for two! [*Sings*] "Forget your troubles, c'mon get happy! You better chase all your blues away. Shout, 'Hallelujah!' c'mon get happy . . ." [*Sees* DONALD *isn't buying it*]—what's more boring than a queen doing a Judy Garland imitation?

DONALD. A queen doing a Bette Davis imitation.

MICHAEL. Meanwhile—back at the Evelyn and Walt Syndrome.

DONALD. America's Square Peg and America's Round Hole.

MICHAEL. Christ, how sick analysts must get of hearing how mommy and daddy made their darlin' into a fairy.

DONALD. It's beyond just that now. Today I finally began to see how some of the other pieces of the puzzle relate to them.—Like why I never finished anything I started in my life . . . my neurotic compulsion to not succeed. I've realized it was always when I failed that Evelyn loved me the most—because it displeased Walt, who wanted perfection. And when I fell short of the mark she was only too happy to make up for it with her love. So I began to identify failing with winning my mother's love. And I began to fail on purpose to get it. I didn't finish Cornell—I couldn't keep a job in this town. I simply retreated to a room over a garage and scrubbing floors in order to keep alive. Failure is the only thing with which I feel at home. Because it is what I was taught at home.

MICHAEL. Killer whales is what they are. Killer whales.

How many whales could a killer whale kill . . .

DONALD. A lot, especially if they get them when they were babies.

> [*Pause.* MICHAEL *suddenly tears off his sweater, throws it in the air, letting it land where it may, whips out another, pulls it on as he starts down the stairs for the living room.* DONALD *follows*]

Hey! Where're you going?

MICHAEL. To make drinks! I think we need about thirty-seven!

DONALD. Where'd you get *that* sweater?

MICHAEL. This clever little shop on the right bank called Hermes.

DONALD. I work my ass off for forty-five lousy dollars a week *scrubbing* floors and you waltz around throwing cashmere sweaters on them.

MICHAEL. The one on the floor in the bedroom is vicuña.

DONALD. I *beg* your pardon.

MICHAEL. You could get a job doing something else. Nobody holds a gun to your head to be a charwoman. That is, how you say, your neurosis.

DONALD. Gee, and I thought it's why I was born.

MICHAEL. Besides, just because I *wear* expensive clothes doesn't necessarily mean they're paid for.

DONALD. That is, how you say, *your* neurosis.

MICHAEL. I'm a spoiled brat, so what do I know about being mature. The only thing mature means to me is *Victor* Mature, who was in all those pictures with Betty Grable. [*Sings à la Grable*] "I can't begin to tell you, how much you mean to me . . ." Betty sang that in 1945. '45?—'43. No, '43 was "Coney Island," which was re-made in '50 as "Wabash Avenue." Yes, "Dolly Sisters" was in '45.

DONALD. How did I manage to miss these momentous events in the American cinema. I can understand people having an affinity for the stage—but movies are such garbage, who can take them seriously.

MICHAEL. Well, I'm sorry if your sense of art is offended. Odd as it may seem, there wasn't any Shubert Theatre in Hot Coffee, Mississippi!

DONALD. However—thanks to the silver screen, your neurosis has got style. It takes a certain flair to squander one's unemployment check at Pavillion.

MICHAEL. What's so snappy about being head over heels in debt. The only thing smart about it is the ingenious ways I dodge the bill collectors.

DONALD. Yeah. Come to think of it, you're the type that gives faggots a bad name.

MICHAEL. And you, Donald, *you* are a credit to the homosexual. A reliable, hard-working, floor-scrubbing, bill-paying fag who don't owe nothin' to nobody.

DONALD. *I* am a model fairy.

[MICHAEL *has taken some ribbon and paper and begun to wrap* HAROLD's *birthday gift*]

MICHAEL. You think it's just nifty how I've always flitted from Beverly Hills to Rome to Acapulco to Amsterdam, picking up a lot of one-night stands and a lot of custom-made duds along the trail, but I'm here to tell you that the only place in all those miles—the only place I've ever been *happy*—was on the goddamn plane. [*Puffs up the bow on the package, continues*] Bored with Scandinavia, try Greece. Fed up with dark meat, try light. Hate tequila, what about slivovitz. Tired of boys, what about girls—or how about boys and girls mixed and in what combination? And if you're sick of people, what about poppers? Or pot or pills or the hard stuff. And can you think of anything else the bad baby would like to indulge his spoiled-rotten, stupid, empty, boring, selfish, self-centered self in? Is that what you think has style, Donald? Huh? Is that what you think you've missed out on—my hysterical escapes from country to country, party to party, bar to bar, bed to bed, hangover to hangover, and all of it, hand to mouth! [*A beat*] Run, charge, run, buy, borrow, make, spend, run, squander, beg, run, run, run, waste, waste, *waste!* [*A beat*] And why? And why?

DONALD. Why, Michael? Why?

MICHAEL. I really don't want to get into it.

DONALD. Then how can we have a conversation in depth?

MICHAEL. Oh, you know it all by heart anyway. Same song, second verse. Because my Evelyn refused to let me grow up. She was determined to keep me a child forever and she did one helluva job of it. And my Walt stood by and let her do it. [*A beat*] What you see before you is a thirty-year-old infant. And it was all done in the name of love—what *she* labeled love and probably sincerely believed to be love, when what she was really doing was feeding her own need—satisfying her own loneliness. [*A beat*] She made me into a girl-friend dash lover. [*A beat*] We went to all those goddamn cornball movies together. I picked out her clothes for her and told her what to wear and she'd take me to the beauty parlor with her and we'd both get our hair bleached and a permanent and a manicure. [*A beat*] *And Walt let this happen.* [*A beat*] And she convinced me that I was a sickly child who couldn't run and play and sweat and get knocked around—oh, no! I was frail and pale and, to hear her tell it, practically female. I can't tell you the thousands of times she said to me, "I declare, Michael, you should have been a girl." And I guess I should have—I was frail and pale and bleached and curled and bedded down with hot-water bottles and my dolls and my paper dolls, and my doll clothes and my doll houses! [*Quick beat*] *And Walt bought them for me!* [*Beat. With increasing speed*] And she nursed me and put Vicks salve on my chest and cold cream on my face and told me what beautiful eyes I had and what pretty lips I had. She bathed me in the same tub with her until I grew too big for the two of us to fit. She made me sleep in the same bed with her until I was fourteen years old—until I finally flatly refused to spend one more night there. She didn't want to prepare me for life or how to be out in the world on my own or I might have left her. But I left anyway. This goddamn cripple finally wrenched free and limped away. And here I am—unequipped, undisciplined, untrained, unprepared and unable to live! [*A beat*] And do you know until this day she still says, "I don't care if you're seventy years old, you'll always be my baby." And can I tell you how that drives me mad! Will that bitch never understand that what I'll always *be* is her son—but that I haven't been her baby for twenty-five years! [*A beat*]

And don't get me wrong. I know it's easy to cop out and blame Evelyn and Walt and say it was *their* fault. That we were simply the helpless put-upon victims. But in the end, we are responsible for ourselves. And I guess—I'm not sure—but I want to believe it—that in their own pathetic, *dangerous* way, they just loved us too much. [*A beat*] Finis. Applause.

[DONALD *hesitates, walks over to* MICHAEL, *puts his arms around him and holds him. It is a totally warm and caring gesture*]

There's nothing quite as good as feeling sorry for yourself, is there?

DONALD. Nothing.

MICHAEL [*A la Bette Davis*]. I adore cheap sentiment. [*Breaks away*] Okay, I'm taking orders for drinks. What'll it be?

DONALD. An extra-dry-Beefeater-martini-on-the-rocks-with-a-twist.

MICHAEL. Coming up.

[DONALD *exits up the stairs into the bath;* MICHAEL *into the kitchen.*

*Momentarily,* MICHAEL *returns, carrying an ice bucket in one hand and a silver tray of cracked crab in the other, singing "Acapulco" or "Down Argentine Way" or some other forgotten Grable tune.*

*The telephone rings*]

MICHAEL [*Answering it*]. Backstage, "New Moon." [*A beat*] Alan? My God, I don't believe it. How *are* you? *Where* are you? In town! Great! When'd you get in? Is Fran with you? Oh, What? No. No, I'm tied up tonight. No, tonight's no good for me. —You mean, *now?* Well, Alan, ole boy, it's a friend's birthday and I'm having a few people. —No, you wouldn't exactly call it a birthday party—well, yes, actually I guess you would. I mean, what else would you call it. A *wake,* maybe. I'm sorry I can't ask you to join us—but—well, kiddo, it just wouldn't work out. —No, it's not place cards or anything. It's just that—well, I'd hate to just see you for ten minutes and . . . Alan? Alan? What's the matter? —Are you—are you crying? —Oh, Alan, what's wrong?

—Alan, listen, come on over. No, no, it's perfectly all right. Well, just hurry up. I mean, come on by and have a drink, okay? Alan . . . are you all right? Okay. Yeah. Same old address. Yeah. Bye. [*Slowly hangs up, stares blankly into space.* DONALD *appears, bathed and changed. He strikes a pose*]

DONALD. Well. Am I stunning?

   [MICHAEL *looks up*]

MICHAEL [*Tonelessly*]. You're absolutely stunning. —You *look* like shit, but I'm absolutely stunned.

DONALD [*Crestfallen*]. Your grapes are, how you say, sour.

MICHAEL. Listen, you won't believe what just happened.

DONALD. Where's my drink?

MICHAEL. I didn't make it—I've been on the phone.

   [DONALD *goes to the bar, makes himself a martini*]

MICHAEL. My old roommate from Georgetown just called.

DONALD. Alan what's-his-name?

MICHAEL. McCarthy. He's up here from Washington on business or something and he's on his way over here.

DONALD. Well, I hope he knows the lyrics to Happy Birthday.

MICHAEL. Listen, asshole, what am I going to do? He's *straight*. And *Square City!* ["*Top Drawer*" *accent through clenched teeth*] I mean, he's rally vury proper. Auffully good family.

DONALD [*Same accent*]. That's *so* important.

MICHAEL [*Regular speech*]. I mean, they look down on people in the *theatre*—so whatta you think he'll feel about this *freak show* I've got booked for dinner?

DONALD [*Sipping his drink*]. Christ, is that good.

MICHAEL. Want some cracked crab?

DONALD. Not just yet. Why'd you invite him over?

MICHAEL. He invited himself. He said he had to see me to-night. *Immediately.* He absolutely lost his spring on the phone—started crying.

DONALD. Maybe he's feeling sorry for himself too.

MICHAEL. Great heaves and sobs. Really boo-hoo-hoo-time —and that's not his style at all. I mean, he's so pulled-together he wouldn't show any emotion if he were in a plane crash. What am I going to do?

DONALD. What the hell do you care what he thinks.

MICHAEL. Well, I don't really but . . .

DONALD. Or are you suddenly ashamed of your friends?

MICHAEL. Donald, *you* are the only person I know of whom I am truly ashamed. Some people *do* have different standards from yours and mine, you know. And if we don't acknowledge them, we're just as narrow-minded and backward as we think they are.

DONALD. You know what you are, Michael? You're a *real* person.

MICHAEL. Thank you and fuck you. [MICHAEL *crosses to take a piece of crab and nibble on it*] Want some?

DONALD. No, thanks. How could you ever have been friends with a bore like that?

MICHAEL. Believe it or not, there was a time in my life when I didn't go around *announcing* that I was a faggot.

DONALD. That must have been before speech replaced sign language.

MICHAEL. Don't give me any static on that score. I didn't come out until I left college.

DONALD. It seems to me that the first time we tricked we met in a gay bar on Third Avenue during your *junior* year.

MICHAEL. Cunt.

DONALD. I thought you'd never say it.

MICHAEL. Sure you don't want any cracked crab?

DONALD. *Not yet! If you don't mind!*

MICHAEL. Well, it can only be getting colder. What time is it?

DONALD. I don't know. Early.

MICHAEL. Where the hell is Alan?

DONALD. Do you want some more club soda?

MICHAEL. What?

DONALD. There's nothing but club soda in that glass. It's not gin—like mine. You want some more?

MICHAEL. No.

DONALD. I've been watching you for several Saturdays now. You've actually stopped drinking, haven't you?

MICHAEL. And smoking too.

DONALD. And smoking too. How long's it been?

MICHAEL. Five weeks.

DONALD. That's amazing.

MICHAEL. I've found God.

DONALD. It *is* amazing—for you.

MICHAEL. Or is God dead?

DONALD. Yes, thank God. And don't get panicky just because I'm paying you a compliment. I can tell the difference.

MICHAEL. You always said that I held my liquor better than
anybody you ever saw.

DONALD. I could always tell when you were getting high—
one way.

MICHAEL. I'd get hostile.

DONALD. You seem happier or something now—and that
shows.

MICHAEL [*Quietly*]. Thanks.

DONALD. What made you stop—the analyst?

MICHAEL. He certainly had a lot to do with it. Mainly, I
just didn't think I could survive another hangover, that's
all. I don't think I could get through that morning-after
ick attack.

DONALD. Morning-after what?

MICHAEL. Icks! Anxiety! Guilt! Unfathomable guilt—either
real or imagined—from that split second your eyes pop
open and you say, "Oh, my God, what did I do last
night!" and ZAP, Total recall!

DONALD. *Tell* me about it!

MICHAEL. Then, the coffee, aspirin, Alka-Seltzer, Darvon,
Daprisal, and a quick call to I.A.—Icks Anonymous.

DONALD. "Good morning, I.A."

MICHAEL. "Hi! Was I too bad last night? Did I do anything
wrong? I didn't do anything terrible, did I?"

DONALD [*Laughing*]. How many times! How many times!

MICHAEL. And from then on, that struggle to live till lunch,
when you have a double Bloody Mary—that is, if you've
*waited* until lunch—and then you're half pissed again
and useless for the rest of the afternoon. And the only
sure cure is to go to bed for about thirty-seven hours, but

who ever does that. Instead, you hang on till cocktail
time, and by then you're ready for what the night holds
—which hopefully is another party, where the whole
goddamn cycle starts over! [*A beat*] Well, I've been on
that merry-go-round long enough and I either had to get
off or die of centrifugal force.

DONALD. And just how does a clear head stack up with the
dull fog of alcohol?

MICHAEL. Well, all those things you've always heard are
true. Nothing can compare with the experience of one's
faculties functioning at their maximum natural capacity.
The only thing is . . . I'd *kill* for a drink.

   [*The wall-panel buzzer sounds*]

DONALD. Joe College has finally arrived.

MICHAEL. Suddenly, I have such an ick! [*Presses the wall-
panel button*] Now listen, Donald . . .

DONALD [*Quick*]. Michael, don't insult me by giving me
any lecture on acceptable social behavior. I promise tō
sit with my legs spread apart and keep my voice in a
deep register.

MICHAEL. Donald, you are a real *card-carrying cunt.*

   [*The apartment door buzzes several times.* MICHAEL
   *goes to it, pauses briefly before it, tears it open to re-
   veal* EMORY, LARRY *and* HANK. EMORY *is in Bermuda
   shorts and a sweater.* LARRY *has on a turtleneck and
   sandals.* HANK *is in a dark Ivy League suit with a vest
   and has on cordovan shoes.* LARRY *and* HANK *carry
   birthday gifts.* EMORY *carries a large covered dish*]

EMORY [*Bursting in*]. ALL RIGHT THIS IS A RAID!
EVERYBODY'S UNDER ARREST!

   [*This entrance is followed by loud raucous laugh as*
   EMORY *throws his arms around* MICHAEL *and gives
   him a big kiss on the cheek. Referring to dish*]

Hello, darlin'! Connie Casserole. Oh, Mary, don't ask.

MICHAEL [*Weary already*]. Hello, Emory. Put it in the
kitchen.

   [EMORY *spots* DONALD]

EMORY. Who is this exotic woman over here?

MICHAEL. Hi, Hank. Larry.

   [*They say, "Hi," shake hands, enter.* MICHAEL *looks*

*out in the hall, comes back into the room, closes the door]*

DONALD. Hi, Emory.

EMORY. My dear, I thought you had perished! Where have you been hiding your classically chiseled features?

DONALD [*To* EMORY]. I don't live in the city any more.

MICHAEL [*To* LARRY *and* HANK, *referring to the gifts]*. Here, I'll take those. Where's yours, Emory?

EMORY. It's arriving later.

[EMORY *exits to the kitchen.* LARRY *and* DONALD's *eyes have met.* HANK *has handed* MICHAEL *his gift—*LARRY *is too preoccupied]*

HANK. Larry!—Larry!

LARRY. What!

HANK. Give Michael the gift!

LARRY. Oh. Here. [*To* HANK] Louder. So my mother in Philadelphia can hear you.

HANK. Well, you were just standing there in a trance.

MICHAEL [*To* LARRY *and* HANK *as* EMORY *reenters]*. You both know Donald, don't you?

DONALD. Sure. Nice to see you. [*To* HANK] Hi.

HANK [*Shaking hands]*. Nice to meet you.

MICHAEL. Oh, I thought you'd met.

DONALD. Well . . .

LARRY. We haven't exactly met but we've . . . Hi.

DONALD. Hi.

HANK. But you've what?

LARRY. . . . . *Seen* . . . each other before.

MICHAEL. Well, *that* sounds murky.

HANK. You've never met but you've seen each other.

LARRY. What was wrong with the way *I* said it.

HANK. Where?

EMORY [*Loud aside to* MICHAEL]. I think they're going to have their first fight.

LARRY. The first one since we got out of the taxi.

MICHAEL [*Referring to* EMORY]. Where'd you find this trash.

LARRY. Downstairs leaning against a lamppost.

EMORY. With an orchid behind my ear and big wet lips painted over the lipline.

MICHAEL. Just like Maria Montez.

DONALD. Oh, *please!*

EMORY [*To* DONALD]. What have you got against Maria—she was a good woman.

MICHAEL. Listen, everybody, this old college friend of mine is in town and he's stopping by for a fast drink on his way to dinner somewhere. But, listen, he's *straight*, so . . .

LARRY. *Straight!* If it's the one I met, he's about as straight as the Yellow Brick Road.

MICHAEL. No, you met Justin Stuart.

HANK. I don't remember anybody named Justin Stuart.

LARRY. Of course you don't, dope. *I* met him.

MICHAEL. Well, this is someone else.

DONALD. Alan McCarthy. A very close total stranger.

MICHAEL. It's not that I care what he would think of me, really—it's just that *he's* not ready for it. And he never will be. You understand that, don't you, Hank?

HANK. Oh, sure.

LARRY. You honestly think he doesn't know about you?

MICHAEL. If there's the slightest suspicion, he's never let on one bit.

EMORY. What's he had, a lobotomy? [*He exits up the stairs into the bath*]

MICHAEL. I was super-careful when I was in college and I still am whenever I see him. I don't know why, but I am.

DONALD. Tilt.

MICHAEL. You may think it was a crock of shit, Donald, but to him I'm sure we were close friends. The closest. To pop that balloon now just wouldn't be fair to him. Isn't that right?

LARRY. Whatever's fair.

MICHAEL. Well, of course. And if that's phony of me, Donald, then that's phony of me and make something of it.

DONALD. I pass.

MICHAEL. Well, even you have to admit it's much simpler to deal with the world according to its rules and then go right ahead and do what you damn well please. You do understand *that*, don't you?

DONALD. Now that you've put it in layman's terms.

MICHAEL. I was just like Alan when I was in college. Very large in the dating department. Wore nothing but those

constipated Ivy League clothes and those ten-pound cordovan shoes. [*To* HANK] No offense.

HANK. Quite all right.

MICHAEL. I butched it up quite a bit. And I didn't think I
was lying to myself. I really thought I was straight.

EMORY [*Coming downstairs tucking a Kleenex into his
sleeve*]. Who do you have to fuck to get a drink around
here?

MICHAEL. Will you *light* somewhere? [EMORY *sits on
steps*] Or I thought I thought I was straight. I know I
didn't come out till after I'd graduated.

DONALD. What about all those weekends up from school?

MICHAEL. I still wasn't out. I was still in the "Christ-was-I-
drunk-last-night syndrome."

LARRY. The *what?*

MICHAEL. The Christ-was-I-drunk-last-night syndrome.
You know, when you made it with some guy in school
and the next day when you had to face each other there
was always a lot of shit-kicking crap about, "Man, was I
drunk last night! Christ, I don't remember a thing!"
   [*Everyone laughs*]

DONALD. You were just guilty because you were Catholic,
that's all.

MICHAEL. That's not true. The Christ-was-I-drunk-last-
night syndrome knows no religion. It has to do with im-
maturity. Although I will admit there's a high percentage
of it among Mormons.

EMORY. Trollop.

MICHAEL. We all somehow managed to justify our actions
in those days. I later found out that even Justin Stuart,
my closest friend . . .

DONALD. Other than Alan McCarthy.

MICHAEL [*A look to* DONALD]. . . . was doing the same
thing. Only Justin was going to Boston on weekends.
   [EMORY *and* LARRY *laugh*]

LARRY [*To* HANK]. Sound familiar?

MICHAEL. Yes, long before Justin or I or God only knows
how many others *came out,* we used to get drunk and
"horse around" a bit. You see, in the Christ-was-I-
drunk-last-night syndrome, you really *are* drunk. That

part of it is true. It's just that you also *do remember everything.* [*General laughter*] Oh God, I used to have to get loaded to go in a gay bar!

DONALD. Well, times certainly have changed.

MICHAEL. They *have.* Lately I've gotten to despise the bars. Everybody just standing around and standing around— it's like one eternal intermission.

HANK [*To* LARRY]. Sound familiar?

EMORY. I can't stand the bars either. All that cat-and-mouse business—you hang around *staring* at each other all night and wind up going home alone.

MICHAEL. And pissed.

LARRY. A lot of guys have to get loaded to have sex. [*Quick look to* HANK, *who is unamused*] So I've been told.

MICHAEL. If you remember, Donald, the first time we made it I was so drunk I could hardly stand up.

DONALD. You were so drunk you could hardly *get* it up.

MICHAEL [*Mock innocence*]. Christ, I was so drunk I don't remember.

DONALD. Bullshit, you remember.

MICHAEL [*Sings to* DONALD]. "Just friends, lovers no more . . ."

EMORY. You may as well be. Everybody thinks you are anyway.

DONALD. We never *were—really.*

MICHAEL. We didn't have time to be—we got to know each other too fast. [*Door buzzer sounds*] Oh, Jesus, it's Alan! Now, please everybody, do me a favor and cool it for the few minutes he's here.

EMORY. Anything for a sis, Mary.

MICHAEL. That's *exactly* what I'm talking about, Emory. *No camping!*

EMORY. Sorry. [*Deep, deep voice to* DONALD] Think the Giants are gonna win the pennant this year?

DONALD [*Deep, deep voice*]. Fuckin' A, Mac.

[MICHAEL *goes to the door, opens it to reveal* BERNARD, *dressed in a shirt and tie and sport jacket. He carries a birthday gift and two bottles of red wine*]

EMORY [*Big scream*]. Oh, it's only another queen!

BERNARD. And it ain't the Red one, either.

EMORY. It's the queen of spades!

[BERNARD *enters.* MICHAEL *looks out in the hall*]

MICHAEL. Bernard, is the downstairs door open?

BERNARD. It was, but I closed it.

MICHAEL. Good.

[BERNARD *starts to put wine on bar*]

MICHAEL [*Referring to the two bottles of red wine*]. I'll take those. You can put your present with the others.

[MICHAEL *closes the door.* BERNARD *hands him the gift. The phone rings*]

BERNARD. Hi, Larry. Hi, Hank.

MICHAEL. *Christ of the Andes!* Donald, will you bartend please.

[MICHAEL *gives* DONALD *the wine bottles, goes to the phone*]

BERNARD [*Extending his hand to* DONALD]. Hello, Donald. Good to see you.

DONALD. Bernard.

MICHAEL [*Answers phone*]. Hello? Alan?

EMORY. Hi, Bernadette. Anybody ever tell you you'd look divine in a hammock, surrounded by louvres and ceiling fans and lots and lots of lush tropical ferns?

BERNARD [*To* EMORY]. You're *such* a fag. You take the cake.

EMORY. Oh, what *about* the cake—whose job was that?

LARRY. Mine. I ordered one to be delivered.

EMORY. How many candles did you say put on it—eighty?

MICHAEL. . . . What? Wait a minute. There's too much noise. Let me go to another phone. [*Presses the hold button, hangs up, dashes toward stairs*]

LARRY. Michael, did the cake come?

MICHAEL. No.

DONALD [*To* MICHAEL *as he passes*]. What's up?

MICHAEL. Do *I* know?

LARRY. Jesus, I'd better call. Okay if I use the private line?

MICHAEL [*Going upstairs*]. Sure. [*Stops dead on stairs, turns*] Listen, everybody, there's some cracked crab there. Help yourselves.

[DONALD *shakes his head.* MICHAEL *continues up the stairs to the bedroom.* LARRY *crosses to the phone, presses the free-line button, picks up receiver, dials Information*]

DONALD. Is everybody ready for a drink?

[HANK *and* BERNARD *say, "Yeah"*]

EMORY [*Flipping up his sweater*]. *Ready!* I'll be your topless cocktail waitress.

BERNARD. Please spare us the sight of your sagging tits.

EMORY [*To* HANK, LARRY]. What're you having, kids?

MICHAEL [*Having picked up the bedside phone*]. . . . Yes, Alan . . .

LARRY. Vodka and tonic. [*Into phone*] Could I have the number for the Marseilles Bakery in Manhattan.

EMORY. A vod and ton and a . . .

HANK. Is there any beer?

EMORY. Beer! Who drinks beer before dinner?

BERNARD. Beer drinkers.

DONALD. That's telling him.

MICHAEL. . . . No, Alan, don't be silly. What's there to apologize for?

EMORY. Truck drivers do. Or . . . or wallpaperers. Not school teachers. They have sherry.

HANK. This one has beer.

EMORY. Well, maybe school teachers in *public* schools. [*To* LARRY] How can a sensitive artist like you live with an insensitive bull like that?

LARRY [*Hanging up the phone and redialing*]. I can't.

BERNARD. Emory, you'd live with Hank in a minute, if he'd ask you. In fifty-eight seconds. Lord knows, you're *sss*sensitive.

EMORY. Why don't you have a piece of watermelon and hush up!

MICHAEL. . . . Alan, don't be ridiculous.

DONALD. Here you go, Hank.

HANK. Thanks.

LARRY. Shit, they don't answer.

DONALD. What're you having, Emory?

BERNARD. A Pink Lady.

EMORY. A vodka martini on the rocks, please.

LARRY [*Hangs up*]. Well, let's just hope.

> [DONALD *hands* LARRY *his drink—their eyes meet again. A faint smile crosses* LARRY's *lips.* DONALD *returns to the bar to make* EMORY's *drink*]

MICHAEL. Lunch tomorrow will be great. One o'clock—the Oak Room at the Plaza okay? Fine.

BERNARD [*To* DONALD]. Donald, read any new libraries lately?

DONALD. One or three. I did the complete works of Doris Lessing this week. I've been depressed.

MICHAEL. Alan, forget it, will you? Right. Bye. [*Hangs up, starts to leave the room—stops. Quickly pulls off the sweater he is wearing, takes out another, crosses to the stairs*]

DONALD. You must not work in Circulation any more.

BERNARD. Oh, I'm still there—every day.

DONALD. Well, since I moved, I only come in on Saturday evenings. [*Moves his stack of books off the bar*]

HANK. Looks like you stock up for the week.

> [MICHAEL *rises and crosses to steps landing*]

BERNARD. Are you kidding—that'll last him two days.

EMORY. It would last *me* two years. I still haven't finished *Atlas Shrugged,* which I started in 1912.

MICHAEL [*To* DONALD]. Well, he's not coming.

DONALD. It's just as well now.

BERNARD. Some people eat, some people drink, some take dope . . .

DONALD. I read.

MICHAEL. And read and read and read. It's a wonder your eyes don't turn back in your head at the sight of a dust jacket.

HANK. Well, at least he's a constructive escapist.

MICHAEL. Yeah, what do I do—take planes. No, I don't do that any more. Because I don't have the *money* to do that any more. I go to the baths. That's about it.

EMORY. I'm about to do both. I'm flying to the West Coast—

BERNARD. You still have that act with a donkey in Tijuana?

EMORY. I'm going to *San Francisco* on a well-earned vacation.

LARRY. No shopping?

EMORY. Oh, I'll look for a few things for a couple of clients, but I've been so busy lately I really couldn't care less if I never saw another piece of fabric or another stick of furniture as long as I live. I'm going to the Club Baths and I'm not out till they announce the departure of TWA one week later.

BERNARD [*To* EMORY]. You'll never learn to stay out of the baths, will you. The last time Emily was taking the vapors, this big hairy number strolled in. Emory said, "I'm just resting," and the big hairy number said, "I'm just *arr*esting!" It was the vice!

  [*Everybody laughs*]

EMORY. You have to tell everything, don't you.

  [DONALD *crosses to give* EMORY *his drink*]

  Thanks, sonny. You live with your parents?

DONALD. Yeah, but it's all right—they're gay.

  [EMORY *roars, slaps* HANK *on the knee,* HANK *gets up, moves away.* DONALD *turns to* MICHAEL]

  What happened to Alan?

MICHAEL. He suddenly got terrible icks about having broken down on the phone. Kept apologizing over and over. Did a big about-face and reverted to the old Alan right before my very eyes.

DONALD. Ears.

MICHAEL. Ears. Well, the cracked crab obviously did not work out. [*Starts to take away the tray*]

EMORY. Just put that down if you don't want your hand slapped. I'm about to have some.

MICHAEL. It's really very good. [*Gives* DONALD *a look*] I don't know why everyone has such an aversion to it.

DONALD. Sometimes you remind me of the Chinese water torture. I take that back. Sometimes you remind me of the *relentless* Chinese water torture.

MICHAEL. Bitch.

  [HANK *has put on some music*]

BERNARD. Yeah, baby, let's hear that sound.

EMORY. A drumbeat and their eyes sparkle like Cartier's.

[BERNARD *starts to snap his fingers and move in time with the music.* MICHAEL *joins in*]

I wonder where Harold is.

EMORY. Yeah, where *is* the frozen fruit?

MICHAEL [*To* DONALD]. Emory refers to Harold as the frozen fruit because of his former profession as an ice skater.

EMORY. She used to be the Vera Hruba Ralston of the Borscht Circuit.

[MICHAEL *and* BERNARD *are now dancing freely*]

BERNARD [*To* MICHAEL]. If your mother could see you now, she'd have a stroke.

MICHAEL. Got a camera on you?

[*The door panel buzzes.* EMORY *lets out a yelp*]

EMORY. Oh my God, it's Lily Law! Everybody three feet apart!

[MICHAEL *goes to the panel, presses the button.* HANK *turns down the music.* MICHAEL *opens the door a short way, pokes his head out*]

BERNARD. It's probably Harold now.

[MICHAEL *leans back in the room*]

MICHAEL. No, it's the delivery boy from the bakery.

LARRY. Thank God.

[MICHAEL *goes out into the hall, pulling the door almost closed behind him*]

EMORY [*Loudly*]. Ask him if he's got any hot-cross buns!

HANK. Come on, Emory, knock it off.

BERNARD. You can take her anywhere but out.

EMORY [*To* HANK]. You remind me of an old-maid school teacher.

HANK. You remind me of a chicken wing.

EMORY. I'm sure you meant that as a compliment.

[HANK *turns the music back up*]

MICHAEL [*In hall*]. Thank you. Good night.

[MICHAEL *returns with a cake box, closes the door, and takes it into the kitchen*]

LARRY. Hey, Bernard, you remember that thing we used to do on Fire Island? [LARRY *starts to do a kind of Madison*]

BERNARD. That was "in" so far back I think I've forgotten.

EMORY. *I* remember. [*Pops up—starts doing the steps.* LARRY *and* BERNARD *start to follow*]

LARRY. Yeah. That's it.

[MICHAEL *enters from the kitchen, falls in line with them*]

MICHAEL. Well, if it isn't the Geriatrics Rockettes.

[*Now they all are doing practically a precision routine.* DONALD *comes to sit on the arm of a chair, sip his drink, and watch in fascination.* HANK *goes to the bar to get another beer.*

*The door buzzer sounds. No one seems to hear it. It buzzes again.* HANK *turns toward the door, hesitates. Looks toward* MICHAEL, *who is now deeply involved in the intricacies of the dance. No one, it seems, has heard the buzzer but* HANK, *who goes to the door, opens it wide to reveal* ALAN. *He is dressed in black tie.*

*The dancers continue, turning and slapping their knees and heels and laughing with abandon. Suddenly* MICHAEL *looks up, stops dead.* DONALD *sees this and turns to see what* MICHAEL *has seen. Slowly he stands up.*

MICHAEL *goes to the record player, turns it off abruptly.* EMORY, LARRY, *and* BERNARD *come to out-of-step halts, look to see what's happened*]

MICHAEL. I thought you said you weren't coming.

ALAN. I . . . well, I'm sorry . . .

MICHAEL [*Forced lightly*]. We were just—acting silly . . .

ALAN. . . . Actually, when I called I was in a phone booth around the corner. My dinner party is not far from here. And . . .

MICHAEL. . . . Emory was just showing us this . . . silly dance.

ALAN. . . . Well, then I walked past and your downstairs door was open and . . .

MICHAEL. This is Emory. [EMORY *curtsies.* MICHAEL *glares at him*] Everybody, this is Alan McCarthy. Counterclockwise, Alan: Larry, Emory, Bernard, Donald, and Hank. [*They all mumble "Hello," "Hi"*] Would you like a drink?

ALAN. Thanks, no. I . . . I can't stay . . . long . . . really.

MICHAEL. Well, you're here now, so stay. What would you like?

ALAN. Do you have any rye?

MICHAEL. I'm afraid I don't drink it any more. You'll have to settle for gin or Scotch or vodka.

DONALD. Or beer.

ALAN. Scotch, please.

    [MICHAEL *starts for bar*]

DONALD. I'll get it. [*Goes to bar*]

HANK [*Forced laugh*]. Guess I'm the only beer drinker.

ALAN [*Looking around group*]. Whose . . . birthday . . . is it?

LARRY. Harold's.

ALAN [*Looking from face to face*]. Harold?

BERNARD. He's not here yet.

EMORY. She's never been on time . . . [MICHAEL *shoots* EMORY *a withering glance*] He's never been on time in his . . .

MICHAEL. Alan's from Washington. We went to college together. Georgetown. [*A beat. Silence*]

EMORY. Well, isn't that fascinating.

    [DONALD *hands* ALAN *his drink*]

DONALD. If that's too strong, I'll put some water in it.

ALAN [*Takes a quick gulp*]. It's fine. Thanks. Fine.

HANK. Are you in the government?

ALAN. No. I'm a lawyer. What . . . what do you do?

HANK. I teach school.

ALAN. Oh. I would have taken you for an athlete of some sort. You look like you might play sports . . . of some sort.

HANK. Well, I'm no professional but I was on the basketball team in college and I play quite a bit of tennis.

ALAN. I play tennis too.

HANK. Great game.

ALAN. Yes. Great. [*A beat. Silence*] What . . . do you teach?

HANK. Math.

ALAN. Math?

HANK. Yes.

ALAN. Math. Well.

EMORY. Kinda makes you want to rush out and buy a slide rule, doesn't it?

MICHAEL. Emory. I'm going to need some help with dinner and you're elected. Come on!

EMORY. I'm *always* elected.

BERNARD. You're a natural-born domestic.

EMORY. Said the African queen! You come on, too—you can fan me while I make the salad dressing.

MICHAEL [*Glaring. Phony smile*]. RIGHT THIS WAY, EMORY!

> [MICHAEL *pushes the swinging door aside for* EMORY *and* BERNARD *to enter. They do and he follows. The door swings closed, and the muffled sound of* MICHAEL's *voice can be heard*]

[*Offstage*] You son-of-a-bitch!

EMORY [*Offstage*]. What the hell do you want from me?

HANK. Why don't we all sit down.

ALAN. . . . Sure.

> [HANK *and* ALAN *sit on the couch.* LARRY *crosses to the bar, refills his drink.* DONALD *comes over to refill his*]

LARRY. Hi.

DONALD. . . . Hi.

ALAN. I really feel terrible—barging in on you fellows this way.

LARRY [*To* DONALD]. How've you been?

DONALD. Fine, thanks.

HANK [*To* ALAN]. . . . Oh, that's okay.

DONALD [*To* LARRY]. . . . And you?

LARRY. Oh . . . just fine.

ALAN [*To* HANK]. You're married?

> [LARRY *hears this, turns to look in the direction of the couch.* MICHAEL *enters from the kitchen*]

HANK [*Watching* LARRY *and* DONALD]. What?

ALAN. I see you're married. [*Points to* HANK's *wedding band*]

HANK. Oh.

MICHAEL [*Glaring at* DONALD]. Yes. Hank's married.

ALAN. You have any kids?

HANK. Yes. Two. A boy nine, and a girl seven. You should see my boy play tennis—really puts his dad to shame.

DONALD [*Avoiding* MICHAEL's *eyes*]. I better get some ice. [*Exits to the kitchen*]

ALAN [*To* HANK]. I have two kids too. Both girls.

HANK. Great.

MICHAEL. How *are* the girls, Alan?

ALAN. Oh, just sensational. [*Shakes his head*] They're something, those kids. God, I'm nuts about them.

HANK. How long have you been married?

ALAN. Nine years. Can you believe it, Mickey?

MICHAEL. No.

ALAN. Mickey used to go with my wife when we were all in school.

MICHAEL. Can you believe that?

ALAN [*To* HANK]. You live in the city?

LARRY. Yes, we do. [LARRY *comes over to couch next to* HANK]

ALAN. Oh.

HANK. I'm in the process of getting a divorce. Larry and I are—roommates.

MICHAEL. Yes.

ALAN. Oh. I'm so sorry. Oh, I mean . . .

HANK. I understand.

ALAN [*Gets up*]. I . . . I . . . I think I'd like another drink . . . If I may.

MICHAEL. Of course. What was it?

ALAN. I'll do it . . . if I may. [*Gets up, starts for the bar. Suddenly there is a loud crash offstage.* ALAN *jumps, looks toward swinging door*]
What was that?
[DONALD *enters with the ice bucket*]

MICHAEL. Excuse me. Testy temperament out in the kitch!
[MICHAEL *exits through the swinging door.* ALAN *continues to the bar—starts nervously picking up and putting down bottles, searching for the Scotch*]

HANK [*To* LARRY]. Larry, where do you know that guy from?

LARRY. What guy?

HANK. *That* guy.

LARRY. I don't know. Around. The bars.

DONALD. Can I help you, Alan?

ALAN. I . . . I can't seem to find the Scotch.

DONALD. You've got it in your hand.

ALAN. Oh. Of course. How . . . stupid of me.

　　[DONALD *watches* ALAN *fumble with the Scotch bottle and glass*]

DONALD. Why don't you let me do that.

ALAN [*Gratefully hands him both*]. Thanks.

DONALD. Was it water or soda?

ALAN. Just make it straight—over ice.

　　[MICHAEL *enters*]

MICHAEL. You see, Alan, I told you it wasn't a good time to talk. But we . . .

ALAN. It doesn't matter. I'll just finish this and go . . . [*Takes a long swallow*]

LARRY. Where can Harold be?

MICHAEL. Oh, he's always late. You know how neurotic he is about going out in public. It takes him hours to get ready.

LARRY. Why *is* that?

　　[EMORY *breezes in with an apron tied around his waist, carrying a stack of plates which he places on a drop-leaf table.* MICHAEL *does an eye roll*]

EMORY. Why is what?

LARRY. Why does Harold spend hours getting ready before he can go out?

EMORY. Because she's a sick lady, that's why. [*Exits to the kitchen.* ALAN *finishes his drink*]

MICHAEL. Alan, as I was about to say, we can go in the bedroom and talk.

ALAN. It really doesn't matter.

MICHAEL. Come on. Bring your drink.

ALAN. I . . . I've finished it.

MICHAEL. Well, make another and bring it upstairs.

　　[DONALD *picks up the Scotch bottle and pours into the glass* ALAN *has in his hand.* MICHAEL *has started for the stairs*]

ALAN [*To* DONALD]. Thanks.

DONALD. Don't mention it.

ALAN [*To* HANK]. Excuse us. We'll be down in a minute.

LARRY. He'll still be here. [*A beat*]

MICHAEL [*On the stairs*]. Go ahead, Alan. I'll be right there.

> [ALAN *turns awkwardly, exits to the bedroom.* MICHAEL *goes into the kitchen. A beat*]

HANK [*To* LARRY]. What was *that* supposed to mean?

LARRY. What was what supposed to mean?

HANK. You know.

LARRY. You want another beer?

HANK. No. You're jealous, aren't you? [HANK *starts to laugh.* LARRY *doesn't like it*]

LARRY. I'm Larry. *You're* jealous. [*Crosses to* DONALD] Hey, Donald, where've you been hanging out these days? I haven't seen you in a long time . . .

> [MICHAEL *enters to witness this disapprovingly. He turns, goes up the stairs.*
>
> *In the bedroom* ALAN *is sitting on the edge of the bed.* MICHAEL *enters, pauses at the mirror to adjust his hair.*
>
> *Downstairs* HANK *gets up, exits into the kitchen.* DONALD *and* LARRY *move to a corner of the room, sit facing upstage and talk quietly*]

ALAN [*To* MICHAEL]. This is a marvelous apartment.

MICHAEL. It's too expensive. I work to pay rent.

ALAN. What are you doing these days?

MICHAEL. Nothing.

ALAN. Aren't you writing any more?

MICHAEL. I haven't looked at a typewriter since I sold the very very wonderful, very very marvelous *screenplay* which never got produced.

ALAN. That's right. The last time I saw you, you were on your way to California. Or was it Europe?

MICHAEL. Hollywood. Which is not in Europe, nor does it have anything whatsoever to do with California.

ALAN. I've never been there but I would imagine it's awful. Everyone must be terribly cheap.

MICHAEL. No, not everyone. [ALAN *laughs. A beat.*

MICHAEL *sits on the bed*] Alan, I want to try to explain this evening . . .

ALAN. What's there to explain? Sometimes you just can't invite everybody to every party and some people take it personally. But I'm not one of them. I should apologize for inviting myself.

MICHAEL. That's not exactly what I meant.

ALAN. Your friends all seem like very nice guys. That Hank is really a very attractive fellow.

MICHAEL. . . . Yes. He is.

ALAN. We have a lot in common. What's his roommate's name?

MICHAEL. Larry.

ALAN. What does *he* do?

MICHAEL. He's a commercial artist.

ALAN. I liked Donald too. The only one I didn't care too much for was—what's his name—Emory?

MICHAEL. Yes. Emory.

ALAN. I just can't stand that kind of talk. It just grates on me.

MICHAEL. What kind of talk, Alan?

ALAN. Oh, you know. His brand of humor, I guess.

MICHAEL. He can be really quite funny sometimes.

ALAN. I suppose so. If you find that sort of thing amusing. He just seems like such a goddamn little pansy. [*Silence. A pause*] I'm sorry I said that. I didn't mean to say that. That's such an awful thing to say about *anyone*. But you know what I mean, Michael—you have to admit he *is* effeminate.

MICHAEL. He is a bit.

ALAN. A bit! He's like a . . . a butterfly in heat! I mean, there's no wonder he was trying to teach you all a dance. He *probably* wanted to dance *with* you! [*Pause*] Oh, come on, man, you know me—you know how I feel—your priv te life is your own affair.

MICHAEL [*Icy*]. No. I *don't* know that about you.

ALAN. I cou dn't care less what people do—as long as they don't do it in public—or—or try to force their ways on the whole damned world.

MICHAEL. Alan, what was it you were crying about on the telephone?

ALAN. Oh, I feel like such a fool about that. I could shoot myself for letting myself act that way. I'm so embarrassed I could die.

MICHAEL. But, Alan, if you were genuinely upset—that's nothing to be embarrassed about.

ALAN. All I can say is—please accept my apology for making such an ass of myself.

MICHAEL. You must have been upset or you wouldn't have said you were and that you wanted to see me—*had* to see me and had to talk to me.

ALAN. Can you forget it? Just pretend it never happened. I know *I* have. Okay?

MICHAEL. Is something wrong between you and Fran?

ALAN. Listen, I've really got to go.

MICHAEL. Why are you in New York?

ALAN. I'm dreadfully late for dinner.

MICHAEL. *Whose* dinner? Where are you going?

ALAN. Is this the loo?

MICHAEL. Yes.

ALAN. Excuse me.

> [*Quickly goes into the bathroom, closes the door.* MICHAEL *remains silent—sits on the bed, stares into space.*
>
> *Downstairs,* EMORY *pops in from the kitchen to discover* DONALD *and* LARRY *in quiet, intimate conversation*]

EMORY. What's-going-on-in-here-oh-Mary-don't-ask!

> [*Puts a salt cellar and pepper mill on the table.* HANK *enters, carrying a bottle of red wine and a corkscrew. Looks toward* LARRY *and* DONALD. DONALD *sees him, stands up*]

DONALD. Hank, why don't you come and join us?

HANK. That's an interesting suggestion. Whose idea is that?

DONALD. Mine.

LARRY [*To* HANK]. He means in a conversation.

> [BERNARD *enters from the kitchen, carrying four wine glasses*]

EMORY [*To* BERNARD]. Where're the rest of the wine glasses?

BERNARD. Ahz workin' as fas' as ah can!

EMORY. They have to be told everything. Can't let 'em out of your sight.

>[*Breezes out to the kitchen.*
>
>DONALD *leaves* LARRY'*s side and goes to the coffee table, helps himself to the cracked crab.* HANK *opens the wine, puts it on the table.*
>
>MICHAEL *gets up from the bed and goes down the stairs.*
>
>*Downstairs,* HANK *crosses to* LARRY]

HANK. I thought maybe you were abiding by the agreement.

LARRY. We have no agreement.

HANK. We *did*.

LARRY. *You* did. I never agreed to anything!

>[DONALD *looks up to see* MICHAEL, *raises a crab claw toward him*]

DONALD. To your health.

MICHAEL. Up yours.

DONALD. Up my health?

BERNARD. Where's the gent?

MICHAEL. In the gent's room. If you can all hang on for five more minutes, he's about to leave [*The door buzzes.* MICHAEL *crosses to it*]

LARRY. Well, at last!

>[MICHAEL *opens the door to reveal a muscle-bound young* MAN *wearing boots, tight Levi's, a calico neckerchief, and a cowboy hat. Around his wrist there is a large card tied with a ribbon*]

COWBOY. [*Singing fast*].

"Happy birthday to you,
Happy birthday to you,
Happy birthday, dear Harold.
Happy birthday to you."

>[*And with that, he throws his arms around* MICHAEL *and gives him a big kiss on the lips. Everyone stands in stunned silence*]

MICHAEL. Who the hell are you?

[EMORY *swings in from the kitchen*]

EMORY. She's Harold's present from me and she's *early!* [*Quick, to* COWBOY] And that's not even Harold, you *idiot!*

COWBOY. You said whoever answered the door.

EMORY. But *not until midnight!* [*Quickly, to group*] He's supposed to be a *midnight cowboy!*

DONALD. He *is* a midnight cowboy.

MICHAEL. He looks right out of a William Inge play to me.

EMORY [*To* COWBOY]. . . . Not until midnight and you're supposed to sing to the right person, for Chrissake! I *told* you Harold has very, very tight, tight, black curly hair. [*Referring to* MICHAEL] This number's practically bald!

MICHAEL. Thank you and fuck you.

BERNARD. It's a good thing *I* didn't open the door.

EMORY. Not that tight and not that black.

COWBOY. I forgot. Besides, I wanted to get to the bars by midnight.

MICHAEL. He's a class act all the way around.

EMORY. What do you mean—get to the bars! Sweetie, I paid you for the whole night, remember?

COWBOY. I hurt my back doing my exercises and I wanted to get to bed early tonight.

BERNARD. Are you ready for this one?

LARRY [*To* COWBOY]. That's too bad, what happened?

COWBOY. I lost my grip doing my chin-ups and fell on my heels and twisted my back.

EMORY. You shouldn't *wear* heels when you do chin-ups.

COWBOY [*Oblivious*]. I shouldn't do chin-ups—I got a weak grip to begin with.

EMORY. A weak grip. In my day it used to be called a limp wrist.

BERNARD. Who can remember that far back?

MICHAEL. Who was it that always used to say, "You show me Oscar Wilde in a cowboy suit, and I'll show you a gay caballero."

DONALD. I don't know. Who *was* it who always used to say that?

MICHAEL [*Katharine Hepburn voice*]. I don't know. Somebody.

LARRY [*To* COWBOY]. What does your card say?

COWBOY [*Holds up his wrist*]. Here. Read it.

LARRY [*Reading card*]. "Dear Harold, bang, bang, you're alive. But roll over and play dead. Happy birthday, Emory."

BERNARD. Ah, sheer poetry, Emmy.

LARRY. And in your usual good taste.

MICHAEL. Yes, so conservative of you to resist a sign in Times Square.

EMORY [*Glancing toward stairs*]. Cheese it! Here comes the socialite nun.

MICHAEL. Goddammit, Emory!

[ALAN *comes down the stairs into the room. Everybody quiets*]

ALAN. Well, I'm off. . . . Thanks, Michael, for the drink.

MICHAEL. You're entirely welcome, Alan. See you tomorrow?

ALAN. . . . No. No, I think I'm going to be awfully busy. I may even go back to Washington.

EMORY. Got a heavy date in Lafayette Square?

ALAN. What?

HANK. Emory.

EMORY. Forget it.

ALAN [*Sees* COWBOY]. Are you . . . Harold?

EMORY. No, he's not Harold. He's *for* Harold.

[*Silence.* ALAN *lets it pass. Turns to* HANK]

ALAN. Goodbye, Hank. It was nice to meet you.

HANK. Same here. [*They shake hands*]

ALAN. If . . . if you're ever in Washington—I'd like for you to meet my wife.

LARRY. That'd be fun, wouldn't it, Hank.

EMORY. Yeah, they'd love to meet him—*her*. I have such a problem with pronouns.

ALAN [*Quick, to* EMORY]. How many esses are there in the word pronoun?

EMORY. How'd you like to kiss my ass—that's got two or more *essess* in it!

ALAN. How'd you like to blow me!

EMORY. What's the matter with your *wife*, she got lockjaw?

ALAN [*Lashes out*]. Faggot, fairy, pansy . . . [*Lunges at* EMORY] . . . queer, cocksucker! I'll kill you, you goddamn little mincing swish! You goddamn freak! FREAK! FREAK!

[*Pandemonium.*

ALAN *beats* EMORY *to the floor before anyone recovers from surprise and reacts*]

EMORY. Oh, my God, somebody help me! Bernard! He's killing me!

[BERNARD *and* HANK *rush forward.* EMORY *is screaming. Blood gushes from his nose*]

HANK. Alan! ALAN! ALAN!

EMORY. Get him off me! Get him off me! Oh, my God, he's broken my nose! I'm BLEEDING TO DEATH!

[LARRY *has gone to shut the door.*

*With one great athletic move,* HANK *forcefully tears* ALAN *off* EMORY, *and drags him backward across the room.* BERNARD *bends over* EMORY, *puts his arm around him and lifts him*]

BERNARD. Somebody get some ice! And a cloth!

[LARRY *runs to the bar, grabs the bar towel and the ice bucket, rushes to put it on the floor beside* BERNARD *and* EMORY. BERNARD *quickly wraps some ice in the towel, holds it to* EMORY'S *mouth*]

EMORY. Oh, my face!

BERNARD. He busted your lip, that's all. It'll be all right.

[HANK *has gotten* ALAN *down on the floor on the opposite side of the room.* ALAN *relinquishes the struggle, collapses against* HANK, *moaning and beating his fists rhythmically against* HANK'S *chest.* MICHAEL *is still standing in the same spot in the center of the room, immobile.* DONALD *crosses past the* COWBOY]

DONALD [*To* COWBOY]. Would you mind waiting over there with the gifts.

[COWBOY *moves over to where the gift-wrapped packages have been put.* DONALD *continues past to observe the mayhem, turns up his glass, takes a long swallow. The door buzzes.* DONALD *turns toward* MICHAEL,

waits. MICHAEL *doesn't move.* DONALD *goes to the
door, opens it to reveal* HAROLD]

Well, Harold! Happy birthday. You're just in time for the
floor show, which, as you see, is on the floor. [*To*
COWBOY] Hey, you, *this* is Harold!

[HAROLD *looks blankly toward* MICHAEL. MICHAEL
*looks back blankly*]

COWBOY [*Crossing to* HAROLD].
"Happy birthday to you,
Happy birthday to you,
Happy birthday, dear Harold.
Happy birthday to you."

[*Throws his arms around* HAROLD *and gives him a big
kiss.* DONALD *looks toward* MICHAEL, *who observes
this stoically.* HAROLD *breaks away from* COWBOY, *reads
the card, begins to laugh.*

MICHAEL *turns to survey the room.* DONALD *watches
him. Slowly* MICHAEL *begins to move. Walks over to
the bar, pours a glass of gin, raises it to his lips, downs
it all.* DONALD *watches silently as* HAROLD *laughs and
laughs and laughs*]

**CURTAIN**

## Act two

*A moment later.* HAROLD *is still laughing.* MICHAEL, *still at the bar, lowers his glass, turns to* HAROLD

MICHAEL. What's so fucking funny?

HAROLD [*Unintimidated. Quick hand to hip*]. Life. Life is a goddamn laff-riot. You remember life.

MICHAEL. *You're stoned.* It shows in your arm.

LARRY. Happy birthday, Harold.

MICHAEL [*To* HAROLD]. You're stoned and you're late! You were supposed to arrive at this location at approximately eight-thirty dash nine o'clock!

HAROLD. What I *am*, Michael, is a thirty-two-year-old, ugly, pockmarked Jew fairy—and if it takes me a while to pull myself together and if I smoke a little grass before I can get up the nerve to show this face to the world, it's nobody's goddamn business but my own. [*Instant switch to chatty tone*] And how are *you* this evening?

[HANK *lifts* ALAN *to the couch.* MICHAEL *turns away from* HAROLD, *pours himself another drink.* DONALD *watches.*

HAROLD *sweeps past* MICHAEL *over to where* BERNARD *is helping* EMORY *off the floor.* LARRY *returns the bucket to the bar.* MICHAEL *puts some ice in his drink*]

EMORY. Happy birthday, Hallie.

HAROLD. What happened to *you*?

EMORY [*Groans*]. Don't ask!

HAROLD. Your lips are turning blue; you look like you been rimming a snowman.

EMORY. That piss-elegant kooze hit me!

[*Indicates* ALAN. HAROLD *looks toward the couch.*
ALAN *has slumped his head forward into his own lap*]

MICHAEL. Careful, Emory, that kind of talk just makes him
s'nervous.

[ALAN *covers his ears with his hands*]

HAROLD. Who is she? Who was she? Who does she hope to
be?

EMORY. Who knows, who cares!

HANK. His name is Alan McCarthy.

MICHAEL. Do forgive me for not formally introducing you.

HAROLD [*Sarcastically, to* MICHAEL]. Not the famous college *chum.*

MICHAEL [*Takes an ice cube out of his glass, throws it at*
HAROLD]. Do a figure eight on that.

HAROLD. Well, well, well. I finally get to meet dear ole Alan
after all these years. And in black tie too. Is this my surprise from you, Michael?

LARRY. I think Alan is the one who got the surprise.

DONALD. And, if you'll notice, he's absolutely speechless.

EMORY. I *hope* she's in *shock!* She's a beast!

COWBOY [*Indicating* ALAN]. Is it his birthday too?

EMORY [*Indicates* COWBOY *to* HAROLD]. *That's* your surprise.

LARRY. Speaking of beasts.

EMORY. From me to you, darlin'. How do you like it?

HAROLD. Oh, I suppose he has an interesting face and body
—but it turns me right off because he can't talk intelligently about art.

EMORY. Yeah, ain't it a shame.

HAROLD. I could never *love* anyone like that.

EMORY. Never. *Who could?*

HAROLD. *I* could and *you* could, that's who could! Oh,
Mary, she's *gorgeous!*

EMORY. She may be dumb, but she's all yours!

HAROLD. In affairs of the heart, there are no rules! Where'd
you ever find him?

EMORY. Rae knew where.

MICHAEL [*To* DONALD]. Rae is Rae Clark. That's R-A-E.
She's Emory's dike friend who sings at a place in the Village. She wears pin-striped suits and bills herself "Miss

Rae Clark—Songs Tailored To Your Taste."

EMORY. Miss Rae Clark. Songs tailored to your taste!

MICHAEL. Have you ever heard of anything so crummy in your life?

EMORY. Rae's a fabulous chanteuse. I adore the way she does: "Down in the Depths on the Ninetieth Floor."

MICHAEL. The faggot national anthem. [*Exits to the kitchen singing "Down in the Depths" in a butch baritone*]

HAROLD [*To* EMORY]. All I can say is thank God for Miss Rae Clark. I think my present is a super-surprise. I'm so thrilled to get it I'd kiss you but I don't want to get blood all over me.

EMORY. Ohhh, look at my sweater!

HAROLD. Wait'll you see your face.

BERNARD. Come on, Emory, let's clean you up. Happy birthday, Harold.

HAROLD [*Smiles*]. Thanks, love.

EMORY. My sweater is ruined!

MICHAEL [*From the kitchen*]. Take one of mine in the bedroom.

DONALD. The one on the floor is vicuña.

BERNARD [*To* EMORY]. You'll feel better after I bathe your face.

EMORY. Cheer-up-things-could-get-worse-I-did-and-they-did. [BERNARD *leads* EMORY *up the stairs*]

HAROLD. Just another birthday party with the folks. [MICHAEL *returns with a wine bottle and a green crystal white-wine glass, pouring en route*]

MICHAEL. Here's a cold bottle of Pouilly-Fuissé I bought especially for you, kiddo.

HAROLD. Pussycat, all is forgiven. You can stay. No. You can stay, but not all is forgiven. Cheers.

MICHAEL. I didn't want it this way, Hallie.

HAROLD [*Indicating* ALAN]. Who asked Mr. Right to celebrate my birthday?

DONALD. There are no accidents.

HAROLD [*Referring to* DONALD]. And who asked *him?*

MICHAEL. *Guilty again.* When I make problems for myself, I go the whole route.

HAROLD. Always got to have your crutch, haven't you.

DONALD. I'm *not* leaving. [*Goes to the bar, makes himself another martini*]

HAROLD. Nobody ever thinks completely of somebody else. They always please themselves; they always cheat, if only a little bit.

LARRY [*Referring to* ALAN]. Why is he sitting there with his hands over his ears?

DONALD. I think he has an ick. [DONALD *looks at* MICHAEL. MICHAEL *returns the look, steely*]

HANK [*To* ALAN]. Can I get you a drink?

LARRY. How can he hear you, dummy, with his hands over his ears?

HAROLD. He can hear every word. In fact, he wouldn't miss a word if it killed him.

[ALAN *removes his hands from his ears*]
What'd I tell you?

ALAN. I . . . I . . . feel sick. I think . . . I'm going to . . . throw up.

HAROLD. Say that again and I won't have to take my appetite depressant.

[ALAN *looks desperately toward* HANK]

HANK. Hang on. [HANK *pulls* ALAN's *arm around his neck, lifts him up, takes him up the stairs*]

HAROLD. Easy does it. One step at a time.

[BERNARD *and* EMORY *come out of the bath*]

BERNARD. There. Feel better?

EMORY. Oh, Mary, what would I do without you?

[EMORY *looks at himself in the mirror*] I am not ready for my close-up, Mr. De Mille. Nor will I be for the next two weeks.

[BERNARD *picks up* MICHAEL's *sweater off the floor.* HANK *and* ALAN *are midway up the stairs*]

ALAN. I'm going to throw up! Let me go! Let me go! [*Tears loose of* HANK, *bolts up the remainder of the stairs. He and* EMORY *meet head-on.* EMORY *screams*]

EMORY. Oh, my God, he's after me again! [EMORY *recoils as* ALAN *whizzes past him into the bathroom, slamming the door behind him.* HANK *has reached the bedroom*]

HANK. He's sick.

BERNARD. Yeah, sick in the head. Here, Emory, put this on.

EMORY. Oh, Mary, take me home. My nerves can't stand any more of this tonight.

> [EMORY *takes the vicuña sweater from* BERNARD, *starts to put it on.*
> *Downstairs,* HAROLD *flamboyantly takes out a ciga-rette, takes a kitchen match from a striker, steps up on the seat of the couch and sits on the back of it*]

HAROLD. TURNING ON! [*With that, he strikes the match on the sole of his shoe and lights up. Through a strained throat*] Anybody care to join me? [*Waves the cigarette in a slow pass*]

MICHAEL. Many thanks, No. [HAROLD *passes it to* LARRY, *who nods negatively*]

DONALD. No, thank you.

HAROLD [*To* COWBOY]. How about you, Tex?

COWBOY. Yeah. [COWBOY *takes the cigarette, makes some audible inhalations through his teeth*]

MICHAEL. I find the sound of the ritual alone utterly hu-miliating. [*Turns away, goes to the bar, makes another drink*]

LARRY. I hate the smell poppers leave on your fingers.

HAROLD. Why don't you get up and wash your hands?

> [EMORY *and* BERNARD *come down the stairs*]

EMORY. Michael, I left the casserole in the oven. You can take it out any time.

MICHAEL. You're not going.

EMORY. I couldn't eat now anyway.

HAROLD. Well, *I'm* absolutely ravenous. I'm going to eat until I have a fat attack.

MICHAEL [*To* EMORY]. I said, you're *not going.*

HAROLD [*To* MICHAEL]. Having a cocktail this evening, are we? In my honor?

EMORY. It's your favorite dinner, Hallie. I made it myself.

BERNARD. *Who* fixed the casserole?

EMORY. Well, *I* made the sauce!

BERNARD. Well, *I* made the salad!

LARRY. Girls, please.

MICHAEL. Please *what!*

HAROLD. Beware the hostile fag. When he's sober, he's dan-gerous. When he drinks, he's lethal.

MICHAEL [*Referring to* HAROLD]. Attention must *not* be paid.

HAROLD. I'm starved, Em, I'm ready for some of your Alice B. Toklas' opium-baked lasagna.

EMORY. Are you really? Oh, that makes me so pleased maybe I'll just serve it before I leave.

MICHAEL. *You're not leaving.*

BERNARD. I'll help.

LARRY. I better help too. We don't need a nose-bleed in the lasagna.

BERNARD. When the sauce is on it, you wouldn't be able to tell the difference anyway.

   [EMORY, BERNARD, *and* LARRY *exit to the kitchen*]

MICHAEL [*Proclamation*]. Nobody's going anywhere!

HAROLD. You are going to have schmertz tomorrow you wouldn't believe.

MICHAEL. May I kiss the hem of your schmata, Doctor Freud?

COWBOY. What are you two talking about? I don't understand.

DONALD. He's working through his Oedipus complex, sugar. With a machete.

COWBOY. Huh?

   [HANK *comes down the stairs*]

HANK. Michael, is there any air spray?

HAROLD. Hair spray! You're supposed to be holding his head, not doing his hair.

HANK. *Air* spray, not *hair* spray.

MICHAEL. There's a can of floral spray right on top of the john.

HANK. Thanks. [HANK *goes back upstairs*]

HAROLD [*To* MICHAEL]. Aren't you going to say "If it was a snake, it would have bitten you."

MICHAEL [*Indicating* COWBOY]. That is something only your friend would say.

HAROLD [*To* MICHAEL]. I am turning on and you are just turning. [*To* DONALD] I keep my grass in the medicine cabinet. In a Band-Aid box. Somebody told me it's the safest place. If the cops arrive, you can always lock yourself in the bathroom and flush it down the john.

DONALD. *Very cagey.*

HAROLD. It makes more sense than where I *was* keeping it—in an oregano jar in the spice rack. I kept forgetting and accidentally turning my hateful mother on with the salad. [*A beat*] But I think she liked it. No matter what meal she comes over for—even if it's breakfast—she says, "Let's have a salad!"

COWBOY [*To* MICHAEL]. Why do you say I would say "If it was a snake, it would have bitten you." I think that's what I *would* have said.

MICHAEL. Of course you would have, baby. That's the kind of remark your pint-size brain thinks of. You are definitely the type who still moves his lips when he reads and who sits in a steam room and says things like "Hot enough for you?"

COWBOY. I never use the steam room when I go to the gym. It's bad after a workout. It flattens you down.

MICHAEL. Just after you've broken your back to blow yourself up like a poisoned dog.

COWBOY. Yeah.

MICHAEL. You're right, Harold. Not only can he not talk intelligently about art, he can't even follow from one sentence to the next.

HAROLD. *But he's beautiful.* He has *unnatural* natural beauty. [*Quick palm upheld*] Not that that means anything.

MICHAEL. It doesn't mean *everything.*

HAROLD. Keep telling yourself that as your hair drops out in handfuls. [*Quick palm upheld*] Not that it's not *natural* for one's hair to recede as one reaches seniority. Not that those wonderful lines that have begun creasing our countenances don't make all the difference in the world because they add so much *character.*

MICHAEL. Faggots are worse than women about their age. They think their lives are over at thirty. Physical beauty is not that goddamned important!

HAROLD. Of course not. How could it be—it's only in the eye of the beholder.

MICHAEL. And it's only skin deep—don't forget that one.

HAROLD. Oh, no, I haven't forgotten that one at all. It's only skin deep and it's *transitory* too. It's *terribly* transitory. I mean, how long does it last—thirty or forty or fifty years at the most—depending on how well you take care of yourself. And not counting, of course, that you might die before it runs out anyway. Yes, it's too bad about this poor boy's face. It's tragic. He's absolutely cursed! [*Takes* COWBOY's *face in his hands*] How can *his* beauty ever compare with *my* soul? And although I have never seen my soul, I understand from my mother's rabbi that it's a knockout. I, however, cannot seem to locate it for a gander. And if I could, I'd sell it in a flash for some skin-deep, transitory, meaningless beauty!

[ALAN *walks weakly into the bedroom and sits on the bed. Downstairs,* LARRY *enters from the kitchen with salad plates.* HANK *comes into the bedroom and turns out the lamps.* ALAN *lies down. Now only the light from the bathroom and the stairwell illuminate the room*]

MICHAEL [*Makes sign of the cross with his drink in hand*]. Forgive him, Father, for he know not what he do.

[HANK *stands still in the half darkness*]

HAROLD. Michael, you kill me. You don't know what side of the fence you're on. If somebody says something pro-religion, you're against them. If somebody denies God, you're against *them*. One might say that you have some problem in that area. You can't live with it and you can't live without it.

[EMORY *barges through the swinging door, carrying the casserole*]

EMORY. Hot stuff! Coming through!

MICHAEL. [*To* EMORY]. One could murder you with very little effort.

HAROLD [*To* MICHAEL]. You hang on to that great insurance policy called The Church.

MICHAEL. That's right. I believe in God, and if it turns out that there really isn't one, okay. Nothing lost. But if it turns out that there *is*—I'm covered.

[BERNARD *enters, carrying a huge salad bowl. He puts it down, lights table candles*]

EMORY [*To* MICHAEL]. Harriet Hypocrite, that's who you are.

MICHAEL. Right. I'm one of those truly rotten Catholics

who gets drunk, sins all night and goes to Mass the next morning.

EMORY. Gilda Guilt. It depends on what you think sin is.

MICHAEL. Would you just shut up your goddamn minty mouth and get back to the goddamn kitchen!

EMORY. Say anything you want—*just don't hit me!* [*Exits. A beat*]

MICHAEL. Actually, I suppose Emory has a point—I only go to confession before I get on a plane.

BERNARD. Do you think God's power only exists at thirty thousand feet?

MICHAEL. It must. On the ground, I *am* God. In the air, I'm just one more scared son of a bitch. [*A beat*]

BERNARD. I'm scared on the ground.

COWBOY. Me, too. [*A beat*] That is, when I'm not high on pot or up on acid.

   [HANK *comes down the stairs*]

LARRY [*To* HANK]. Well, is it bigger than a breadstick?

HANK [*Ignores last remark. To* MICHAEL]. He's lying down for a minute.

HAROLD. How does the bathroom smell?

HANK. Better.

MICHAEL. Before it smelled like somebody puked. Now it smells like somebody puked in a gardenia patch.

LARRY. And how does the big hero feel?

HANK. Lay off, will you.

   [EMORY *enters with a basket of napkin-covered rolls, deposits them on the table*]

EMORY. *Dinner is served!*

   [HAROLD *comes to the buffet table*]

HAROLD. Emory, it looks absolutely fabulous.

EMORY. I'd make somebody a good wife. [EMORY *serves pasta.* BERNARD *serves the salad, pours wine.* MICHAEL *goes to the bar, makes another drink*] I could cook and do an apartment and entertain . . . [*Grabs a long-stem rose from an arrangement on the table, clenches it between his teeth, snaps his fingers and strikes a pose*] Kiss me quick, I'm Carmen! [HAROLD *just looks at him blankly, passes on.* EMORY *takes the flower out of his mouth*] One really needs castanets for that sort of thing.

MICHAEL. And a getaway car.

[HANK *comes up to the table*]

EMORY. What would you like. big boy?

LARRY. Alan McCarthy, and don't ho'd the mayo.

EMORY. I can't keep up with you two—[*Indicating* HANK, *then* LARRY]—I thought you were mad at him—now he's bitchin' you. What gives?

LARRY. Never mind.

[COWBOY *comes over to the table.* EMORY *gives him a plate of food.* BERNARD *gives him salad and a glass of wine.*

HANK *moves to the couch, sits and puts his plate and glass on the coffee table.*

HAROLD *moves to sit on the stairs and eat*]

COWBOY. What is it?

LARRY. Lasagna.

COWBOY. It looks like spaghetti and meatballs sorta flattened out.

DONALD. It's been in the steam room.

COWBOY. It has?

MICHAEL [*Contemptuously*]. It looks like spaghetti and meatballs sorta flattened out. Ah, yes, Harold, truly enviable.

HAROLD. As opposed to you who knows so much about *haute cuisine.* [*A beat*] Raconteur, gourmet, troll.

[LARRY *takes a plate of food, goes to sit on the back of the couch from behind it*]

COWBOY. It's good.

HAROLD [*Quick*]. You like it, eat it.

MICHAEL. Stuff your mouth so that you can't say anything.

[DONALD *takes a plate*]

HAROLD. Turning.

BERNARD [*To* DONALD]. Wine?

DONALD. No, thanks.

MICHAEL. Aw, go on, kiddo, force yourself. Have a little *vin ordinaire* to wash down all that depressed pasta.

HAROLD. Sommelier, connoisseur, pig.

[DONALD *takes the glass of wine, moves up by the bar, puts the glass of wine on it, leans against the wall, eats his food.* EMORY *hands* BERNARD *a plate*]

BERNARD [*To* EMORY]. Aren't you going to have any?

EMORY. No. My lip hurts too much to eat.

MICHAEL [*Crosses to table, picks up knife*]. I hear if you puts a knife under de bed it cuts de pain.

HAROLD [*To* MICHAEL]. I hear if you put a knife under your chin it cuts your throat.

EMORY. Anybody going to take a plate up to Alan?

MICHAEL. The punching bag has now dissolved into Flo Nightingale.

LARRY. Hank?

HANK. I don't think he'd have any appetite.

> [ALAN, *as if he's heard his name, gets up from the bed, moves slowly to the top of the stairwell.* BERNARD *takes his plate, moves near the stairs, sits on the floor.* MICHAEL *raps the knife on an empty wine glass*]

MICHAEL. Ladies and gentlemen. Correction: Ladies and ladies, I would like to announce that you have just eaten Sebastian Venable.

COWBOY. Just eaten *what*?

MICHAEL. Not *what*, stupid. *Who.* A character in a play. A fairy who was eaten alive. I mean the chop-chop variety.

COWBOY. Jesus.

HANK. Did Edward Albee write that play?

MICHAEL. No. Tennessee Williams.

HANK. Oh, yeah.

MICHAEL. Albee wrote *Who's Afraid of Virginia Woolf?*

LARRY. Dummy.

HANK. I know that. I just thought maybe he wrote that other one too.

LARRY. Well, you made a mistake.

HANK. So I made a mistake.

LARRY. That's right, you made a mistake.

HANK. What's the difference! You can't add.

COWBOY. Edward who.

MICHAEL [*To* EMORY]. How much did you pay for him?

EMORY. He was a steal.

MICHAEL. He's a ham sandwich—fifty cents any time of the day or night.

HAROLD. King of the Pig People.

[MICHAEL *gives him a look.* DONALD *returns his plate to the table*]

EMORY [*To* DONALD]. Would you like some more?

DONALD. No, thank you, Emory. It was very good.

EMORY. Did you like it?

COWBOY. I'm not a steal. I cost twenty dollars.

[BERNARD *returns his plate*]

EMORY. More?

BERNARD [*Nods negatively*]. It was delicious—even if I did make it myself.

EMORY. Isn't anybody having seconds?

HAROLD. I'm having seconds and thirds and maybe even fifths. [*Gets up off the stairs, comes toward the table*] I'm absolutely desperate to keep the weight up.

[BERNARD *bends to whisper something in* EMORY's *ear.* EMORY *nods affirmatively and* BERNARD *crosses to* COWBOY *and whispers in his ear. A beat.* COWBOY *returns his plate to the buffet and follows* EMORY *and* BERNARD *into the kitchen*]

MICHAEL [*Parodying* HAROLD]. You're *absolutely* paranoid about *absolutely* everything.

HAROLD. Oh, yeah, well, why don't you *not* tell me about it.

MICHAEL. You starve yourself all day, living on coffee and cottage cheese so that you can gorge yourself at one meal. Then you feel guilty and moan and groan about how fat you are and how ugly you are when the truth is you're no fatter or thinner than you ever are.

EMORY. Polly Paranoia. [EMORY *moves to the coffee table to take* HANK's *empty plate*]

HANK. Just great, Emory.

EMORY. Connie Casserole, no-trouble-at-all-oh-Mary, D.A.

MICHAEL. [*To* HAROLD]. . . . And this pathological lateness. It's downright *crazy*.

HAROLD. Turning.

MICHAEL. Standing before a bathroom mirror for hours and hours before you can walk out on the street. And looking no different after Christ knows how many applications of Christ knows how many ointments and salves and creams and masks.

HAROLD. I've got bad skin, what can I tell you.

MICHAEL. Who wouldn't after they deliberately take a pair of tweezers and *deliberately* mutilate their pores—no wonder you've got holes in your face after the hack job you've done on yourself year in and year out!

HAROLD. [*Coolly but definitely*]. You hateful sow.

MICHAEL. Yes, you've got scars on your face—but they're not that bad and if you'd leave yourself alone you wouldn't have any more than you've already awarded yourself.

HAROLD. You'd really like me to compliment you now for being so honest, wouldn't you. For being my best friend who will tell me what even my best friends won't tell me. Swine.

MICHAEL. And the pills! [*Announcement to group*] Harold has been gathering, saving, and storing up barbiturates for the last year like a goddamn squirrel. Hundreds of Nembutals, hundreds of Seconals. All in preparation for and anticipation of the long winter of his death. [*Silence*] But I tell you right now, Hallie. When the time comes, you'll never have the guts. It's not always like it happens in plays, not all faggots bump themselves off at the end of the story.

HAROLD. What you say may be true. Time will undoubtedly tell. But, in the meantime, you've left out one detail—the cosmetics and astringents are *paid* for, the bathroom is *paid* for, the tweezers are *paid* for, and the pills *are paid for!*

[EMORY *darts in and over to the light switch, plunges the room into darkness except for the light from the tapers on the buffet table, and begins to sing "Happy Birthday." Immediately* BERNARD *pushes the swinging door open and* COWBOY *enters carrying a cake ablaze with candles. Everybody has now joined in with "Happy birthday, dear Harold, happy birthday to you." This is followed by a round of applause.* MICHAEL *turns, goes to the bar, makes another drink*]

EMORY. Blow out your candles, Mary, and make a wish!

MICHAEL [*To himself*]. Blow out your candles, *Laura.*

[COWBOY *has brought cake over in front of* HAROLD.

*He thinks a minute, blows out the candles. More applause]*

EMORY. Awwww, she's thirty-two years young!

HAROLD [*Groans, holds his head*]. Ohh, my God!

[BERNARD *has brought in cake plates and forks. The room remains lit only by candlelight from the buffet table.* COWBOY *returns the cake to the table and* BERNARD *begins to cut it and put the pieces on the plates*]

HANK. Now you have to open your gifts.

HAROLD. Do I have to open them here?

EMORY. Of course you've got to open them here. [*Hands* HAROLD *a gift.* HAROLD *begins to rip the paper off*]

HAROLD. Where's the card?

EMORY. Here.

HAROLD. Oh. From Larry. [*Finishes tearing off the paper*] It's *heaven!* Oh, I just love it, Larry. [HAROLD *holds up a graphic design—a large-scale deed to Boardwalk, like those used in a Monopoly game*]

COWBOY. What is it?

HAROLD. It's the deed to Boardwalk.

EMORY. Oh, gay pop art!

DONALD [*To* LARRY]. It's sensational. Did you do it?

LARRY. Yes.

HAROLD. Oh, it's super, Larry. It goes up the minute I get home. [HAROLD *gives* LARRY *a peck on the cheek*]

COWBOY [*To* HAROLD]. I don't get it—you cruise Atlantic City or something?

MICHAEL. Will somebody get him out of here!

[HAROLD *has torn open another gift, takes the card from inside*]

HAROLD. Oh, what a nifty sweater! Thank you, Hank.

HANK. You can take it back and pick out another one if you want to.

HAROLD. I think this one is just nifty.

[DONALD *goes to the bar, makes himself a brandy and soda*]

BERNARD. Who wants cake?

EMORY. Everybody?

DONALD. None for me.

MICHAEL. I'd just like to sleep on mine, thank you.

[HANK *comes over to the table.* BERNARD *gives him a plate of cake, passes another one to* COWBOY *and a third to* LARRY. HAROLD *has torn the paper off another gift. Suddenly laughs aloud*]

HAROLD. Oh, Bernard! How divine! Look, everybody! Bejeweled knee pads! [*Holds up a pair of basketball knee pads with sequin initials*]

BERNARD. Monogrammed!

EMORY. Bernard, you're a camp!

MICHAEL. Y'all heard of Gloria DeHaven and Billy de Wolfe, well, dis here is Rosemary De Camp!

BERNARD. Who?

EMORY. I never miss a Rosemary De Camp picture.

HANK. I've never heard of her.

COWBOY. Me neither.

HANK. Not all of us spent their childhood in a movie house, Michael. Some of us played baseball.

DONALD. And mowed the lawn.

EMORY. Well, *I* know who Rosemary De Camp is.

MICHAEL. You would. It's a cinch you wouldn't recognize a baseball or a lawnmower.

[HAROLD *has unwrapped his last gift. He is silent. Pause*]

HAROLD. Thank you, Michael.

MICHAEL. What? [*Turns to see the gift*] Oh. [*A beat*] You're welcome. [MICHAEL *finishes off his drink, returns to the bar*]

LARRY. What is it, Harold? [*A beat*]

HAROLD. It's a photograph of him in a silver frame. And there's an inscription engraved and the date.

BERNARD. What's it say?

HAROLD. Just . . . something personal.

[MICHAEL *spins round from the bar*]

MICHAEL. Hey, Bernard, what do you say we have a little music to liven things up!

BERNARD. Okay.

EMORY. Yeah, I feel like dancing.

MICHAEL. How about something good and ethnic; Emory —one of your specialties, like a military toe tap with sparklers.

EMORY. I don't do that at birthdays—only on the Fourth of July.

> [BERNARD *puts on a romantic record*. EMORY *goes to* BERNARD. *They start to dance slowly*]

LARRY. Come on, Michael.

MICHAEL. I only lead.

LARRY. I can follow.

> [*They start to dance*]

HAROLD. Come on, Tex, you're on.

> [COWBOY *gets to his feet, but is a washout as a dancing partner*. HAROLD *gives up, takes out another cigarette, strikes a match. As he does, he catches sight of someone over by the stairs, walks over to* ALAN. *Blows out match*]

Wanna dance?

EMORY [*Sees* ALAN]. Uh-oh. Yvonne the Terrible is back.

MICHAEL. Oh, hello, Alan. Feel better? This is where you came in, isn't it?

> [ALAN *starts to cross directly to the door.* MICHAEL *breaks away*]

Excuse me, Larry . . .

> [ALAN *has reached the door and has started to open it as* MICHAEL *intercepts, slams the door with one hand, and leans against it, crossing his legs*]

As they say in the Deep South, don't rush off in the heat of the day.

HAROLD. Revolution complete.

> [MICHAEL *slowly takes* ALAN *by the arm, walks him slowly back into the room*]

MICHAEL. . . . You missed the cake—and you missed the opening of the gifts—but you're still in luck. You're just in time for a party game.

> [*They have reached the phonograph.* MICHAEL *rejects the record. The music stops, the dancing stops.* MICHAEL *releases* ALAN, *claps his hands*]

. . . Hey, everybody! Game time!

> [ALAN *starts to move.* MICHAEL *catches him gently by the sleeve*]

HAROLD. Why don't you just let him go, Michael?

MICHAEL. He can go if he wants to—but not before we play a little game.

EMORY. What's it going to be—movie-star gin?

MICHAEL. That's too faggy for Alan to play—he wouldn't be any good at it.

BERNARD. What about Likes and Dislikes?

[MICHAEL *lets go of* ALAN, *takes a pencil and pad from the desk*]

MICHAEL. It's too much trouble to find enough pencils, and besides, Emory always puts down the same thing. He dislikes artificial fruit and flowers and coffee grinders made into lamps—and he likes Mabel Mercer, poodles, and *All About Eve*—the screenplay of which he will then recite *verbatim*.

EMORY. I put down other things sometimes.

MICHAEL. Like a tan out of season?

EMORY. I just always put down little "Chi-Chi" because I adore her so much.

MICHAEL. If one is of the masculine gender, a poodle is the *insignia* of one's deviation.

BERNARD. You know why old ladies like poodles—because they go down on them.

EMORY. *They do not!*

LARRY. We could play B for Botticelli.

MICHAEL. We *could* play *Spin* the Botticelli, but we're not going to. [*A beat*]

HAROLD. What would you like to play, Michael—the Truth Game?

[MICHAEL *chuckles to himself*]

MICHAEL. Cute, Hallie.

HAROLD. Or do you want to play Murder? You all remember that one, don't you?

MICHAEL [*To* HAROLD]. Very, very cute.

DONALD. As I recall, they're quite similar. The rules are the same in both—you kill somebody.

MICHAEL. In affairs of the heart, there are no rules. Isn't that right, Harold?

HAROLD. That's what I always say.

MICHAEL. Well, that's the name of the game. The Affairs of the Heart.

COWBOY. I've never heard of that one.

MICHAEL. Of course you've never heard of it—I just made it up, baby doll. Affairs of the Heart is a combination of both the Truth Game and Murder—with a new twist.

HAROLD. I can hardly wait to find out what that is.

ALAN. Mickey, I'm leaving. [*Starts to move*]

MICHAEL [*Firmly, flatly*]. Stay where you are.

HAROLD. Michael, let him go.

MICHAEL. He really doesn't *want* to. If he did, he'd have left a long time ago—or he wouldn't have come here in the first place.

ALAN. [*Holding his forehead*]. . . . Mickey, I don't *feel* well!

MICHAEL [*Low tone, but distinctly articulate*] My name is Michael. I am called Michael. You must never call anyone called Michael Mickey. Those of us who are named Michael are very nervous about it. If you don't believe it—try it.

ALAN. I'm sorry. I can't think.

MICHAEL. You can think. What you can't do—is leave. It's like watching an accident on the highway—you can't look at it and you can't look away.

ALAN. I . . . feel . . . weak . . .

MICHAEL. You are weak. Much weaker than I think you realize. [*Takes ALAN by the arm, leads him to a chair. Slowly, deliberately, pushes him down into it*] Now! Who's going to play with Alan and me? Everyone?

HAROLD. I have no intention of playing.

DONALD. Nor do I.

MICHAEL. Well, not everyone is a participant in *life*. There are always those who stand on the sidelines and watch.

LARRY. What's the game?

MICHAEL. Simply this: we all have to call on the telephone the *one person* we truly believe we have loved.

HANK. I'm not playing.

LARRY. Oh, yes, you are.

HANK. You'd like for me to play, wouldn't you?

LARRY. You bet I would. I like to know who you'd call after all the fancy speeches I've heard lately. Who would you call? Would you call me?

MICHAEL [*To* BERNARD]. Sounds like there's, how you say, trouble in paradise.

HAROLD. If there isn't, I think you'll be able to stir up some.

HANK. And who would *you* call? Don't think I think for one minute it would be me. Or that one call would do it. You'd have to make several, wouldn't you? About three long-distance and God only knows how many locals.

COWBOY. I'm glad I don't have to pay the bill.

MICHAEL. Quiet!

HAROLD [*Loud whisper to* COWBOY]. Oh, don't worry, Michael won't pay it either.

MICHAEL. Now, here's how it works.

LARRY. I thought you said there were no rules.

MICHAEL. That's right. In Affairs of the Heart, there are no rules! This is the goddamn point system! [*No response from anyone. A beat*] If you make the call, you get one point. If the person you are calling answers, you get two more points. If somebody else answers, you get only one. If there's no answer at all, you're screwed.

DONALD. You're screwed if you make the call.

HAROLD. You're a *fool*—if you screw yourself.

MICHAEL. . . . When you get the person whom you are calling on the line—if you tell them who you are, you get two points. And then—if you tell them that you *love* them—you get a bonus of five more points!

HAROLD. Hateful.

MICHAEL. Therefore you can get as many as ten points and as few as one.

HAROLD. You can get as few as none—if you know how to work it.

MICHAEL. The one with the highest score wins.

ALAN. Hank. Let's get out of here.

EMORY. Well, now. Did you hear that!

MICHAEL. Just the two of you together. The pals . . . the guys . . . the buddy-buddies . . . the he-men.

EMORY. I think Larry might have something to say about that.

BERNARD. Emory.

MICHAEL. The duenna speaks. [*Crosses to take the telephone from the desk, brings it to the group*] So who's playing? Not including Cowboy, who, as a gift, is neuter. And, of course, le voyeur. [*A beat*] Emory? Bernard?

BERNARD. I don't think I want to play.

MICHAEL. Why, Bernard! Where's your fun-loving spirit?

BERNARD. I don't think this game is fun.

HAROLD. It's absolutely hateful.

ALAN. Hank, leave with me.

HANK. You don't understand, Alan. I can't. You can . . . but I can't.

ALAN. Why, Hank? Why can't you?

LARRY [*To* HANK]. If he doesn't understand, why don't you explain it to him?

MICHAEL. *I'll* explain it.

HAROLD. I had a feeling you might.

MICHAEL. Although I doubt that it'll make any difference. That type refuses to understand that which they do not wish to accept. They reject certain facts. And Alan is decidedly from The Ostrich School of Reality. [*A beat*] Alan . . . Larry and Hank are lovers. Not just roommates, *bed*mates. *Lovers*.

ALAN. Michael!

MICHAEL. No man's still got a *roommate* when he's over thirty years old. If they're not lovers, they're sisters.

LARRY. Hank is the one who's over thirty.

MICHAEL. Well, you're pushing it!

ALAN. . . . Hank? [*A beat*]

HANK. Yes, Alan. Larry is my lover.

ALAN. But . . . but . . . you're married.

[MICHAEL, LARRY, EMORY, *and* COWBOY *are sent into instant gales of laughter*]

HAROLD. I think you said the wrong thing.

MICHAEL. Don't you love that quaint little idea—if a man is married, then he is automatically heterosexual. [*A beat*] Alan—Hank swings both ways—with a definite preference. [*A beat*] Now. Who makes the first call? Emory?

EMORY. You go, Bernard.

BERNARD. I don't want to.

EMORY. I don't want to either. I don't want to at all.

DONALD [*To himself*]. There are no accidents.

MICHAEL. Then, may I say, on your way home I hope you *will* yourself over an embankment.

EMORY [*To* BERNARD]. Go on. Call up Peter Dahlbeck. That's who you'd like to call, isn't it?

MICHAEL. Who is Peter Dahlbeck?

EMORY. The boy in Detroit whose family Bernard's mother has been a laundress for since he was a pickaninny.

BERNARD. I worked for them too—after school and every summer.

EMORY. It's always been a large order of Hero Worship.

BERNARD. I think I've loved him all my life. But he never knew I was alive. Besides, he's straight.

COWBOY. So nothing ever happened between you?

EMORY. Oh, they finally made it—in the pool house one night after a drunken swimming party.

LARRY. With the right wine and the right music there're damn few that aren't curious.

MICHAEL. Sounds like there's a lot of Lady Chatterley in Mr. Dahlbeck, wouldn't you say, Donald?

DONALD. I've never been an O'Hara fan myself.

BERNARD. . . . And afterwards we went swimming in the nude in the dark with only the moon reflecting on the water.

DONALD. Nor Thomas Merton.

BERNARD. It was beautiful.

MICHAEL. How romantic. And then the next morning you took him his coffee and Alka-Seltzer on a tray.

BERNARD. It was in the afternoon. I remember I was worried sick all morning about having to face him. But he pretended like nothing at all had happened.

MICHAEL. Christ, he must have been so drunk he didn't remember a thing.

BERNARD. Yeah. I was sure relieved.

MICHAEL. Odd how that works. And now, for ten points, get that liar on the phone.

[*A beat.* BERNARD *picks up the phone, dials*]

LARRY. You *know* the number?

BERNARD. Sure. He's back in Grosse Pointe, living at home. He just got separated from his third wife.

[*All watch* BERNARD *as he puts the receiver to his ear, waits. A beat. He hangs up quickly*]

EMORY. D.A. or B.Y.?

MICHAEL. He didn't even give it time to find out. [*Coaxing*] Go ahead, Bernard. Pick up the phone and dial. You'll think of something. You know you want to call him. You know that, don't you? Well, go ahead. Your curiosity has got the best of you now. So . . . go on, call him.

HAROLD. Hateful.

COWBOY. What's D.A. or B.Y.?

EMORY. That's operator lingo. It means—"Doesn't Answer" or "Busy."

BERNARD. . . . Hello?

MICHAEL. One point. [*Efficiently takes note on the pad*]

BERNARD. Who's speaking? Oh . . . Mrs. Dahlbeck.

MICHAEL [*Taking note*]. One point.

BERNARD. . . . It's Bernard—Francine's boy.

EMORY. *Son,* not *boy.*

BERNARD. . . . How are you? Good. Good. Oh, just fine, thank you. Mrs. Dahlbeck . . . is . . . Peter . . . at home? Oh. Oh, I see.

MICHAEL [*Shakes his head*]. Shhhhiiii . . .

BERNARD. . . . Oh, no. No, it's nothing important. I just wanted to . . . to tell him . . . that . . . to tell him I . . . I . . .

MICHAEL [*Prompting flatly*]. I love him. That I've always loved him.

BERNARD. . . . that I was sorry to hear about him and his wife.

MICHAEL. No points!

BERNARD. . . . My mother wrote me. Yes. It is. It really is. Well. Would you just tell him I called and said . . . that I was . . . just . . . very, very sorry to hear and I . . . hope . . . they can get everything straightened out. Yes. Yes. Well, good night. Goodbye.

[*Hangs up slowly.* MICHAEL *draws a definite line across his pad, makes a definite period*]

MICHAEL. Two points total. Terrible. Next!

[MICHAEL *whisks the phone out of* BERNARD'S *hands, gives it to* EMORY]

EMORY. Are you all right, Bernard?

BERNARD [*Almost to himself*]. Why did I call? Why did I do that?

LARRY [*To* BERNARD]. Where was he?

BERNARD. Out on a date.

MICHAEL. Come on, Emory. Punch in.

[EMORY *picks up the phone, dials information. A beat*]

EMORY. Could I have the number, please—in the Bronx— for a Delbert Botts.

LARRY. A Delbert Botts! How many can there be!

BERNARD. Oh, I wish I hadn't called now.

EMORY. . . . No, the residence number, please. [*Waves his hand at* MICHAEL, *signaling for the pencil.* MICHAEL *hands it to him. He writes on the white, plastic phone case*] . . . Thank you. [*A beat. And he indignantly slams down the receiver*] I do wish information would stop calling me "Ma'am"!

MICHAEL. By all means, scribble all over the telephone. [*Snatches the pencil from* EMORY'S *hands*]

EMORY. It comes off with a little spit.

MICHAEL. Like a lot of things.

LARRY. Who the hell is Delbert Botts?

EMORY. The one person I have always loved. [*To* MICHAEL] That's who you said call, isn't it?

MICHAEL. That's right, Emory board.

LARRY. How could you love anybody with a name like that?

MICHAEL. Yes, Emory, you couldn't love anybody with a name like that. It wouldn't look good on a place card. Isn't that right. Alan? [MICHAEL *slaps* ALAN *on the shoulder.* ALAN *is silent.* MICHAEL *snickers*]

EMORY. I admit his name is not so good—but he is absolutely beautiful. At least, he was when I was in high school. Of course, I haven't seen him since and he was about seven years older than I even then.

MICHAEL. Christ, you better call him quick before he dies.

EMORY. I've loved him ever since the first day I laid eyes on him, which was when I was in the fifth grade and he was a senior. Then, he went away to college and by the time he got out *I* was in high school, and he had become a dentist.

MICHAEL [*With incredulous disgust*]. A dentist!

EMORY. Yes. Delbert Botts, D.D.S. And he opened his office in a bank building.

HAROLD. And you went and had every tooth in your head pulled out, right?

EMORY. No. I just had my teeth cleaned, that's all.

[DONALD *turns from the bar with two drinks in his hands*]

BERNARD [*To himself*]. Oh, I shouldn't have called.

MICHAEL. Will you shut up, Bernard! And take your boring, sleep-making icks somewhere else. *Go!* [MICHAEL *extends a pointed finger toward the steps.* BERNARD *takes the wine bottle and his glass and moves toward the stairs, pouring himself another drink on the way*]

EMORY. I remember I looked right into his eyes the whole time and I kept wanting to bite his fingers.

HAROLD. Well, it's absolutely mind boggling.

MICHAEL. Phyllis Phallic.

HAROLD. It absolutely boggles the mind.

[DONALD *brings one of the drinks to* ALAN. ALAN *takes it, drinks it down*]

MICHAEL [*Referring to* DONALD]. Sara Samaritan.

EMORY. . . . I told him I was having my teeth cleaned for the Junior-Senior Prom, for which I was in charge of decorations. I told him it was a celestial theme and I was cutting stars out of tin foil and making clouds out of chicken wire and angel's-hair. [*A beat*] He couldn't have been less impressed.

COWBOY. I got angel's-hair down my shirt once at Christmas time. Gosh, did it itch!

EMORY. . . . I told him I was going to burn incense in pots so that white fog would hover over the dance floor and it would look like heaven—just like I'd seen it in a Rita Hayworth movie. I can't remember the title.

MICHAEL. The picture was called *Down to Earth*. Any *kid* knows that.

COWBOY. . . . And it made little tiny cuts in the creases of

my fingers. Man, did they sting! It would be terrible if
you got that stuff in your . . . [MICHAEL *circles slowly
toward him*] I'll be quiet.

EMORY. He was engaged to this stupid-ass girl named
Loraine whose mother was truly Supercunt.

MICHAEL. Don't digress.

EMORY. Well, anyway, I was a wreck. I mean a total mess.
I couldn't eat, sleep, stand up, sit down, *nothing*. I could
hardly cut out silver stars or finish the clouds for the
prom. So I called him on the telephone and asked if I
could see him alone.

HAROLD. Clearly not the coolest of moves.

    [DONALD *looks at* ALAN. ALAN *looks away*]

EMORY. He said okay and told me to come by his house. I
was so nervous my hands were shaking and my voice
was unsteady. I couldn't look at him this time—I just
stared straight in space and blurted out why I'd come. I
told him . . . I wanted him to be my friend. I said that I
had never had a friend who I could talk to and tell everything and trust. I asked him if he would be my friend.

COWBOY. You poor bastard.

MICHAEL. Shhhhhh!

BERNARD. What'd he say?

EMORY. He said he would be glad to be my friend. And any
time I ever wanted to see him or call him—to just call
him and he'd see me. And he shook my trembling wet
hand and I left on a cloud.

MICHAEL. One of the ones you made yourself.

EMORY. And the next day I went and bought him a gold-
plated cigarette lighter and had his initials monogrammed on it and wrote a card that said "From your
friend, Emory."

HAROLD. Seventeen years old and already big with the gifts.

COWBOY. Yeah. And cards too.

EMORY. . . . And then the night of the prom I found out.

BERNARD. Found out what?

EMORY. I heard two girls I knew giggling together. They
were standing behind some goddamn corrugated cardboard Greek columns I had borrowed from a department store and had draped with yards and yards of god-

damn cheesecloth. Oh, Mary, it takes a fairy to make
something pretty.

MICHAEL. *Don't digress.*

EMORY. This girl who was telling the story said she had
heard it from her mother—and her mother had heard it
from Loraine's mother. [*To* MICHAEL] You see, Loraine
and her mother were not beside the point. [*Back to the
group*] Obviously, Del had told Loraine about my calling and about the gift. [*A beat*] Pretty soon everybody
at the dance had heard about it and they were laughing
and making jokes. Everybody knew I had a crush on
Doctor Delbert Botts and that I had asked him to be my
friend. [*A beat*] What they didn't know was that I *loved*
him. And that I would go on loving him years after they
had all forgotten my funny secret. [*Pause*]

HAROLD. Well, I for one need an insulin injection.

MICHAEL. *Call him.*

BERNARD. Don't, Emory.

MICHAEL. Since when are you telling him what to do!

EMORY [*To* BERNARD]. What do I care—I'm pissed! I'll do
anything. Three times.

BERNARD. Don't. *Please!*

MICHAEL. I said call him.

BERNARD. Don't! You'll be sorry. Take my word for it.

EMORY. What have I got to lose?

BERNARD. Your dignity. That's what you've got to lose.

MICHAEL. Well, *that's* a knee-slapper! I love *your* telling
*him* about dignity when you allow him to degrade you
constantly by Uncle Tom-ing you to death.

BERNARD. *He* can do it, Michael. *I* can do it. But *you can't*
do it.

MICHAEL. Isn't that discrimination?

BERNARD. I don't like it from him and I don't like it from
me—but I do it to myself and I let him do it. I let him
do it because it's the only thing that, to him, makes him
my equal. We both got the short end of the stick—but
I got a hell of a lot more than he did and he knows it.
I let him Uncle Tom me just so he can tell himself he's
not a complete loser.

MICHAEL. How very considerate.

BERNARD. It's his defense. You have your defense, Michael. But it's indescribable.

[EMORY *quietly licks his finger and begins to rub the number off the telephone case*]

MICHAEL [*To* BERNARD]. Y'all want to hear a little polite parlor jest from the liberal Deep South? Do you know why *Nigras* have such big lips? Because they're always going P-p-p-p-a-a-a-h!"

[*The labial noise is exasperating with lazy disgust as he shuffles about the room*]

DONALD. Christ, Michael!

MICHAEL [*Unsuccessfully tries to tear the phone away from* EMORY]. I can do without your goddamn spit all over my telephone, you nellie coward.

EMORY. I may be nellie, but I'm no coward. [*Starts to dial*] Bernard, forgive me. I'm sorry. I won't ever say those things to you again.

[MICHAEL *watches triumphant.* BERNARD *pours another glass of wine. A beat*]

B.Y.

MICHAEL. It's busy?

EMORY [*Nods*]. Loraine is probably talking to her mother. Oh, yes, Delbert married Loraine.

MICHAEL. I'm sorry, you'll have to forfeit your turn. We can't wait. [*Takes the phone, hands it to* LARRY, *who starts to dial*]

HAROLD [*To* LARRY]. Well, you're not wasting any time.

HANK. Who are you calling?

LARRY. Charlie.

[EMORY *gets up, jerks the phone out of* LARRY's *hands*]

EMORY. I refuse to forfeit my turn! It's *my turn* and I'm taking it!

MICHAEL. That's the spirit, Emory! *Hit that iceberg—don't miss it! Hit it! Goddamnit!* I want a smash of a finale!

EMORY. Oh, God, I'm drunk.

MICHAEL. A falling-down-drunk-nellie-queen.

HAROLD. Well, that's the pot calling the kettle beige!

MICHAEL [*Snapping. To* HAROLD]. *I am not drunk!* You cannot tell that I am drunk! Donald! I'm not drunk! Am I!

DONALD. *I'm* drunk.

EMORY. So am I. I am a *major drunk.*

MICHAEL [*To* EMORY]. Shut up and dial!

EMORY [*Dialing*]. I am a major drunk of this or any other season.

DONALD [*To* MICHAEL]. Don't you mean shut up and *deal.*

EMORY. . . . It's ringing. It is no longer B.Y. Hello?

MICHAEL [*Taking note*]

EMORY. . . . Who's speaking? Who? . . . Doctor Delbert Botts?

MICHAEL. Two points.

EMORY. Oh, Del, is this really you? Oh, nobody. You don't know me. You wouldn't remember me. I'm . . . just a friend. A falling-down drunken friend. Hello? Hello? Hello? [*Lowers the receiver*] He hung up. [EMORY *hangs up the telephone*]

MICHAEL. Three points total. You're winning.

EMORY. He said I must have the wrong party.

[BERNARD *gets up, goes into the kitchen*]

HAROLD. He's right. We have the wrong party. We should be somewhere else.

EMORY. It's your party, Hallie. Aren't you having a good time?

HAROLD. Simply fabulous. And what about you? Are you having a good time, Emory? Are you having as good a time as you thought you would?

[LARRY *takes the phone*]

MICHAEL. If you're bored, Harold, we could sing Happy Birthday again—to the tune of Havah Nageelah.

[HAROLD *takes out another cigarette*]

HAROLD. Not for all the tea in Mexico. [*Lights up*]

HANK. My turn now.

LARRY. It's my turn to call Charlie.

HANK. No. Let me.

LARRY. Are *you* going to call Charlie?

MICHAEL. The score is three to two. Emory's favor.

ALAN. Don't, Hank. Don't you see—Bernard was right.

HANK [*Firmly to* ALAN]. I want to. [*A beat. Holds out his hand for the phone*] Larry? [*A beat*]

LARRY [*Gives him the phone*]. Be my eager guest.

COWBOY [*To* LARRY]. Is he going to call Charlie for you?
    [LARRY *breaks into laughter*. HANK *starts to dial*]

LARRY. Charlie is all the people I cheat on Hank with.

DONALD. With whom I cheat on Hank.

MICHAEL. The butcher, the baker, the candlestick maker.

LARRY. Right! I love 'em all. And what he refuses to under-
    stand—is that I've got to *have* 'em all. I am *not* the mar-
    rying kind, and I never will be.

HAROLD. Gypsy feet.

LARRY. Who are you calling?

MICHAEL. Jealous?

LARRY. Curious as hell!

MICHAEL. And a little jealous too.

LARRY. Who are you calling?

MICHAEL. Did it ever occur to you that Hank might be
    doing the same thing behind your back that you do be-
    hind his?

LARRY. I wish to Christ he would. It'd make life a hell of a
    lot easier. Who are you calling?

HAROLD. Whoever it is, they're not sitting on top of the
    telephone.

HANK. Hello?

COWBOY. They must have been in the tub.

MICHAEL [*Snaps at* COWBOY]. Eighty-six!
    [COWBOY *goes over to a far corner, sits down*. BERNARD
    *enters, uncorking another bottle of wine. Taking
    note*]
    One point.

HANK. . . . I'd like to leave a message.

MICHAEL. Not in. One point.

HANK. Would you say that Hank called. Yes, it is. Oh,
    good evening, how are you?

LARRY. Who the hell *is* that?

HANK. . . . Yes, that's right—the message is for my room-
    mate, Larry. Just say that I called and . . .

LARRY. It's our answering service!

HANK. . . . and said . . . I love you.

MICHAEL. *Five points!* You said it! You get five goddamn
    points for saying it!

ALAN. Hank! Hank! . . . Are you crazy?

HANK. . . . No. You didn't hear me incorrectly. That's what I said. The message is for Larry and it's from me, Hank, and it is just as I said: *I . . . love . . . you.* Thanks. [*Hangs up*]

MICHAEL. Seven points total! Hank, you're ahead, baby. You're way, way ahead of everybody!

ALAN. Why? . . . Oh, Hank, why? Why did you do that?

HANK. Because I do love him. And I don't care who knows it.

ALAN. Don't say that.

HANK. Why not? It's the truth.

ALAN. I can't believe you.

HANK [*Directly to* ALAN]. I left my wife and family for Larry.

ALAN. I'm really not interested in hearing about it.

MICHAEL. Sure you are. Go ahead, Hankola, tell him all about it.

ALAN. No! I don't want to hear it. It's disgusting! [*A beat*]

HANK. Some men do it for another woman.

ALAN. Well, I could understand *that*. That's *normal*.

HANK. It just doesn't always work out that way, Alan. No matter how you might want it to. And God knows, nobody ever wanted it more than I did. I really and truly felt that I was in love with my wife when I married her. It wasn't altogether my trying to prove something to myself. I did love her and she loved me. But . . . there was always that something there . . .

DONALD. You mean your attraction to your own sex.

HANK. Yes.

ALAN. Always?

HANK. I don't know. I suppose so.

EMORY. I've known what I was since I was four years old.

MICHAEL. Everybody's always known it about *you*, Emory.

DONALD. I've always known it about myself too.

HANK. I don't know when it was that I started admitting it to myself. For so long I either labeled it something else or denied it completely.

MICHAEL. Christ-was-I-drunk-last-night.

HANK. And then there came a time when I just couldn't lie to myself any more . . . I thought about it but I never did anything about it. I think the first time was during my wife's last pregnancy. We lived near New Haven—in the country. She and the kids still live there. Well, anyway, there was a teachers' meeting here in New York. She didn't feel up to the trip and I came alone. And that day on the train I began to think about it and think about it and think about it. I thought of nothing else the whole trip. And within fifteen minutes after I had arrived I had picked up a guy in the men's room of Grand Central Station.

ALAN. [*Quietly*]. Jesus.

HANK. I'd never done anything like that in my life before and I was scared to death. But he turned out to be a nice fellow. I've never seen him again and it's funny I can't even remember his name any more. [*A beat*] Anyway. After that, it got easier.

HAROLD. Practice makes perfect.

HANK. And then . . . sometime later . . . not very long after, Larry was in New Haven and we met at a party my wife and I had gone in town for.

EMORY. And your real troubles began.

HANK. That was two years ago.

LARRY. Why am I always the goddamn villain in the piece! If I'm not thought of as a happy-home wrecker, I'm an impossible son of a bitch to live with!

HAROLD. Guilt turns to hostility. Isn't that right, Michael?

MICHAEL. Go stick your tweezers in your cheek.

LARRY. I'm fed up to the teeth with everybody feeling so goddamn sorry for poor shat-upon Hank.

EMORY. Aw, Larry, everybody knows you're Frieda Fickle.

LARRY. I've never made any promises and I never intend to. It's my right to lead my sex life without answering to *anybody*—Hank included! And if those terms are not acceptable, then we must not live together. Numerous relations is a part of the way I am!

EMORY. You don't have to be gay to be a wanton.

LARRY. By the way I am, I don't mean being gay—I mean my sexual appetite. And I don't think of myself as a wanton. Emory, you are the most promiscuous person I know.

EMORY. I am not promiscuous at all!

MICHAEL. Not by choice. By design. Why would anybody want to go to bed with a flaming little sissy like you?

BERNARD. Michael!

MICHAEL [*To* EMORY]. Who'd make a pass at you—I'll tell you who—nobody. Except maybe some fugitive from the Braille Institute.

BERNARD [*To* EMORY]. Why do you let him talk to you that way?

HAROLD. Physical beauty is not everything.

MICHAEL. Thank you, Quasimodo.

LARRY. What do you think it's like living with the goddamn gestapo! I can't breathe without getting the third degree!

MICHAEL. Larry, it's your turn to call.

LARRY. I can't take all that let's-be-faithful-and-never-look-at-another-person routine. It just doesn't work. If you want to promise that, fine. Then do it and stick to it. But if you *have* to promise it—as far as I'm concerned—nothing finishes a relationship faster.

HAROLD. Give me Librium or give me Meth.

BERNARD [*Intoxicated now*]. Yeah, freedom, baby! Freedom!

LARRY. You gotta have it! It can't work any other way. And the ones who swear their undying fidelity are lying. Most of them, anyway—ninety percent of them. They cheat on each other constantly and lie through their teeth. I'm sorry, I can't be like that and it drives Hank up the wall.

HANK. There is that ten percent.

LARRY. The only way it stands a chance is with some sort of an understanding.

HANK. I've tried to go along with that.

LARRY. Aw, *come on!*

HANK. I agreed to an agreement.

LARRY. Your agreement.

MICHAEL. What agreement?

LARRY. A ménage.

HAROLD. The lover's agreement.

LARRY. Look, I know a lot of people think it's the answer. They don't consider it cheating. But it's not my style.

HANK. Well, *I* certainly didn't want it.

LARRY. Then who suggested it?

HANK. It was a compromise.

LARRY. Exactly.

HANK. And you agreed.

LARRY. I didn't agree to anything. You agreed to your own proposal and *informed me* that I agreed.

COWBOY. I don't understand. What's a me . . . menaa . . .

MICHAEL. A ménage à trois, baby. Two's company—three's a ménage.

COWBOY. Oh.

HANK. It works for some.

LARRY. Well, I'm not one for group therapy. I'm sorry, I can't relate to anyone or anything that way. I'm old-fashioned—I like 'em all, but I like 'em one at a time!

MICHAEL [*To* LARRY]. Did you like Donald as a single side attraction? [*Pause*]

LARRY. Yes. I did.

DONALD. So did I, Larry.

LARRY [*To* DONALD, *referring to* MICHAEL]. Did you tell him?

DONALD. No.

MICHAEL. It was perfectly obvious from the moment you walked in. What was that song and dance about having seen each other but never having met?

DONALD. It was true. We saw each other in the baths and went to bed together but we never spoke a word and never knew each other's name.

EMORY. You had better luck than I do. If I don't get arrested, my trick announces upon departure that he's been exposed to hepatitis!

MICHAEL. In spring a young man's fancy turns to a fancy young man.

LARRY [*To* HANK]. Don't look at me like that. You've been playing footsie with the Blue Book all night.

DONALD. I think he only wanted to show you what's good for the gander is good for the gander.

HANK. That's right.

LARRY [*To* HANK]. I suppose you'd like the three of us to have a go at it.

HANK. At least it'd be together.

LARRY. That point eludes me.

HANK. What kind of an understanding do you *want!*

LARRY. Respect—for each other's freedom. With no need to lie or pretend. In my own way, Hank, I love you, but you have to understand that even though I do want to go on living with you, sometimes there may be others. I don't want to flaunt it in your face. If it happens, I know I'll never mention it. But if you ask me, I'll tell you. I don't want to hurt you but I won't lie to you if you want to know anything about me.

BERNARD. He gets points.

MICHAEL. What?

BERNARD. He said it. He said "I love you" to Hank. He gets the bonus.

MICHAEL. He didn't call him.

DONALD. He called him. He just didn't use the telephone.

MICHAEL. Then he doesn't get any points.

BERNARD. He gets five points!

MICHAEL. He didn't use the telephone. He doesn't get a goddamn thing!

[LARRY *goes to the phone, picks up the receiver, looks at the number of the second line, dials. A beat. The phone rings*]

LARRY. It's for you, Hank. Why don't you take it upstairs?

[*The phone continues to ring.* HANK *gets up, goes up the stairs to the bedroom. Pause. He presses the second-line button, picks up the receiver. Everyone downstairs is silent*]

HANK. Hello?

BERNARD. One point.

LARRY. Hello, Hank.

BERNARD. Two points.

LARRY. . . .This is Larry.

BERNARD. Two more points!

LARRY. . . . For what it's worth, I love you.

BERNARD. Five points bonus!

HANK. I'll . . . I'll try.

LARRY. I will too. [*Hangs up.* HANK *hangs up*]

BERNARD. That's ten points total!

EMORY. Larry's the winner!

HAROLD. Well, that wasn't as much fun as I thought it would be.

MICHAEL. THE GAME ISN'T OVER YET! [HANK *moves toward the bed into darkness*] Your turn, Alan. [MICHAEL *gets the phone, slams it down in front of* ALAN] PICK UP THE PHONE, BUSTER!

EMORY. Michael, don't!

MICHAEL. STAY OUT OF THIS!

EMORY. You don't have to, Alan. You don't have to.

ALAN. Emory . . . I'm sorry for what I did before. [*A beat*]

EMORY. . . . Oh, forget it.

MICHAEL. Forgive us our trespasses. Christ, now you're both joined at the goddamn hip! You can decorate his home, Emory—and he can get you out of jail the next time you're arrested on a morals charge. [*A beat*] Who are you going to call, Alan? [*No response*] Can't remember anyone? Well, maybe you need a minute to think. Is that it? [*No response*]

HAROLD. I believe this will be the final round.

COWBOY. Michael, aren't you going to call anyone?

HAROLD. How could he? He's never loved anyone.

MICHAEL [*Sings the classic vaudeville walk-off to* HAROLD].
"No matter how you figger,
　It's tough to be a nigger [*Indicates* BERNARD],
　But it's tougher
　To be a Jeeeew-ooouuu-oo!"

DONALD. My God, Michael, you're a charming host.

HAROLD. Michael doesn't have charm, Donald. Michael has countercharm.
　　[LARRY *crosses to the stairs*]

MICHAEL. Going somewhere?
　　[LARRY *stops, turns to* MICHAEL]

LARRY. Yes. Excuse me. [*Turns, goes up the stairs*]

MICHAEL. You're going to miss the end of the game.

LARRY [*Pauses on stairs*]. You can tell me how it comes out.

MICHAEL. I never reveal an ending. And no one will be re-seated during the climactic revelation.

LARRY. With any luck, I won't be back until it's all over. [*Turns, continues up the stairs into the dark*]

MICHAEL [*Into* ALAN's *ear*]. What do you suppose is going on up there? Hmmm, Alan? What do you imagine Larry and Hank are doing? Hmmmmm? Shooting marbles?

EMORY. Whatever they're doing, they're not hurting anyone.

HAROLD. And they're minding their own business.

MICHAEL. And you mind yours, Harold. I'm warning you! [*A beat*]

HAROLD [*Coolly*]. Are you now? Are you warning *me*? *Me*? I'm Harold. I'm the one person you don't warn, Michael. Because you and I are a match. And we tread very softly with each other because we both play each other's game too well. Oh, I know this game you're playing. I know it very well. And I *play* it very well. You play it very well too. But you know what, I'm the only one that's better at it than you are. I can beat you at it. So don't push me. I'm warning *you*. [*A beat*. MICHAEL *starts to laugh*]

MICHAEL. You're funny, Hallie. A laff riot. Isn't he funny, Alan? Or, as you might say, isn't he amusing. He's an amusing faggot, isn't he? Or, as you might say, freak. That's what you called Emory, wasn't it? A freak? A pansy? My, what an antiquated vocabulary you have. I'm surprised you didn't say sodomite or pederast. [*A beat*] You'd better let me bring you up to date. Now it's not so new, but it might be new to you— [*A beat*] Have you heard the term "closet queen"? Do you know what that means? Do you know what it means to be "in the closet"?

EMORY. Don't, Michael. It won't help anything to explain what it means.

MICHAEL. He already knows. He knows very, very well what a closet queen is. Don't you, Alan? [*Pause*]

ALAN. Michael, if you are insinuating that I am homosexual, I can only say that you are mistaken.

MICHAEL. Am I? [*A beat*] What about Justin Stuart?

ALAN. . . . What about . . . Justin Stuart?

MICHAEL. You were in love with him, that's what about

him. [*A beat*] And *that* is who you are going to call.

ALAN. Justin and I were very good friends. That is all. Unfortunately, we had a parting of the ways and that was the end of the friendship. We have not spoken for years. I most certainly will not call him now.

MICHAEL. According to Justin, the friendship was quite passionate.

ALAN. What do you mean?

MICHAEL. I mean that you slept with him in college. Several times.

ALAN. That is not true!

MICHAEL. Several times. One time, it's youth. Twice, a phase maybe. Several times, *you like it!*

ALAN. IT'S NOT TRUE!

MICHAEL. Yes, it is. Because Justin Stuart *is* homosexual. He comes to New York on occasion. He calls me. I've taken him to parties. Larry "had" him once. *I* have slept with Justin Stuart. And he has told me all about *you.*

ALAN. Then he told you a lie. [*A beat*]

MICHAEL. You were obsessed with Justin. That's all you talked about, morning, noon, and night. You started doing it about Hank upstairs tonight. What an attractive fellow he is and all that transparent crap.

ALAN. He *is* an attractive fellow. What's wrong with saying so?

MICHAEL. Would you like to join him and Larry right now?

ALAN. I said he was attractive. That's all.

MICHAEL. How many times do you have to say it? How many times did you have to say it about Justin: what a good tennis player he was; what a good dancer he was; what a good body he had; what good taste he had; how bright he was—how *amusing* he was—how the girls were all mad for him—what close friends you were.

ALAN. We . . . we . . . were . . . very close . . . very good . . . friends. *That's all!*

MICHAEL. It was *obvious*—and when you did it around Fran it was downright embarrassing. Even she must have had her doubts about you.

ALAN. *Justin . . . lied.* If he told you that, he lied. It is a lie. A vicious lie. He'd say anything about me now to get even. He could never get over the fact that *I* dropped *him*. But I had to. I had to because . . . he told me . . . he told me about himself . . . he told me that he wanted to be my lover. And I . . . I . . . told him . . . he made me sick . . . I told him I pitied him. [*A beat*]

MICHAEL. You ended the friendship, Alan, because you couldn't face the truth about yourself. You could go along, sleeping with Justin, as long as he lied to himself and you lied to yourself and you both dated girls and labeled yourselves men and called yourselves just fond friends. But Justin finally had to be honest about the truth, and you couldn't take it. You couldn't take it and so you destroyed the friendship and your friend along with it. [MICHAEL *goes to the desk and gets address book*]

ALAN. No!

MICHAEL. Justin could never understand what he'd done wrong to make you cut him off. He blamed himself.

ALAN. No!

MICHAEL. He did until he eventually found out who he was and what he was.

ALAN. No!

MICHAEL. But to this day he still remembers the treatment —the scars he got from you. [*Puts address book in front of* ALAN *on coffee table*]

ALAN. NO!

MICHAEL. Pick up this phone and call Justin. Call him and apologize and tell him what you should have told him twelve years ago. [*Picks up the phone, shoves it at* ALAN]

ALAN. NO! HE LIED! NOT A WORD IS TRUE!

MICHAEL. CALL HIM!
[ALAN *won't take the phone*]
All right then, *I'll dial!*

HAROLD. You're so helpful.
[MICHAEL *starts to dial*]

ALAN. Give it to me. [MICHAEL *hands* ALAN *the receiver.* ALAN *takes it, hangs up for a moment, lifts it again, starts to dial. Everyone watches silently.* ALAN *finishes dialing, lifts the receiver to his ear*] . . . Hello?

MICHAEL. One point.

ALAN. . . . It's . . . it's Alan.

MICHAEL. Two points.

ALAN. . . . Yes, yes, it's *me*.

MICHAEL. Is it Justin?

ALAN. . . . You sound surprised.

MICHAEL. I should hope to think so—after twelve years! Two more points.

ALAN. I . . . I'm in New York. Yes. I . . . won't explain now . . . I . . . I just called to tell you . . .

MICHAEL. THAT I LOVE YOU, GODDAMNIT! I LOVE YOU!

ALAN. I love you.

MICHAEL. You get the goddamn bonus. TEN POINTS TOTAL! JACKPOT!

ALAN. I love you and I beg you to forgive me.

MICHAEL. Give me that! [*Snatches the phone from* ALAN] Justin! Did you hear what the son of a bitch said! [*A beat.* MICHAEL *is speechless for a moment*] . . . Fran? [*A beat*] Well, of course I expected it to be you!. . . [*A beat*] How are you? Me, too. Yes, yes . . . he told me everything. Oh, don't thank *me*. Please . . . Please . . . [*A beat*] I'll . . . I'll put him back on. [*A beat*] My love to the kids . . .

ALAN . . . Darling? I'll take the first plane I can get. Yes. I'm sorry too. I love you very much. [*Hangs up, stands, crosses to the door, stops. Turns around, surveys the group*] Thank you, Michael.

　　　[*Opens the door and exits. Silence.* MICHAEL *slowly sinks down on the couch, covering his face. Pause*]

COWBOY. Who won?

DONALD. It was a tie.

　　　[HAROLD *crosses to* MICHAEL]

HAROLD [*Calmly, coldly, clinically*]. Now it is my turn. And ready or not, Michael, here goes. [*A beat*] You are a sad and pathetic man. You're a homosexual and you don't want to be. But there is nothing you can do to change it. Not all your prayers to your God, not all the analysis you can buy in all the years you've got left to live. You may very well one day be able to know a hetero-

sexual life if you want it desperately enough—if you
pursue it with the fervor with which you annihilate—but
you will always be homosexual as well. Always, Michael.
Always. Until the day you die. [*Turns, gathers his gifts,
goes to* EMORY. EMORY *stands up unsteadily*] Oh,
friends, thanks for the nifty party and the super gift.
[*Looks toward* COWBOY] It's just what I needed.
[EMORY *smiles.* HAROLD *gives him a hug, spots* BERNARD
*sitting on the floor, head bowed*] . . . Bernard, thank
you. [*No response. To* EMORY] Will you get him home?

EMORY. Don't worry about her. I'll take care of everything.

[HAROLD *turns to* DONALD, *who is at the bar making
himself another drink*]

HAROLD. Donald, good to see you.

DONALD. Good night, Harold. See you again sometime.

HAROLD. Yeah. How about a year from Shavuoth? [HAROLD
*goes to* COWBOY] Come on, Tex. Let's go to my place.
[COWBOY *gets up, comes to him*] Are you good in bed?

COWBOY. Well . . . I'm not like the average hustler you'd
meet. I try to show a little affection—it keeps me from
feeling like such a whore. [*A beat.* HAROLD *turns.*
COWBOY *opens the door for them. They start out.*
HAROLD *pauses*]

HAROLD. Oh, Michael . . . thanks for the laughs. Call you
tomorrow. [*No response. A beat.* HAROLD *and* COWBOY
*exit*]

EMORY. Come on, Bernard. Time to go home. [EMORY,
*frail as he is, manages to pull* BERNARD's *arm around his
neck, gets him on his feet*] Oh, Mary, you're a heavy
mother.

BERNARD [*Practically inaudible mumble*]. Why did I call?
Why?

EMORY. Thank you, Michael. Good night, Donald.

DONALD. Goodbye, Emory.

BERNARD. Why . . .

EMORY. It's all right, Bernard. Everything's all right. I'm
going to make you some coffee and everything's going to
be all right.

[EMORY *virtually carries* BERNARD *out.* DONALD *closes
the door. Silence.*

MICHAEL *slowly slips from the couch onto the floor. A beat. Then slowly he begins a low moan that increases in volume—almost like a siren. Suddenly he slams his open hands to his ears*]

MICHAEL [*In desperate panic*]. Donald! Donald! DONALD! DONALD!

[DONALD *puts down his drink, rushes to* MICHAEL. MICHAEL *is now white with fear and tears are bursting from his eyes. He begins to gasp his words*]

Oh, no! No! What have I done! Oh, my God, what have I done! [MICHAEL *writhing.* DONALD *holds him, cradles him in his arms*]

DONALD. Michael! Michael!

MICHAEL. [*Weeping*]. Oh, no! NO! It's beginning! The liquor is starting to wear off and the anxiety is beginning! Oh, NO! No! I feel it! I know it's going to happen. Donald!! Donald! Don't leave me! Please! Please! Oh, my God, what have I done! Oh Jesus, the guilt! I can't handle it any more. I won't make it!

DONALD [*Physically subduing him*]. Michael! Michael! Stop it! Stop it! I'll give you a Valium—I've got some in my pocket!

MICHAEL [*Hysterical*]. No! No! Pills and alcohol—I'll die!

DONALD. I'm not going to give you the whole bottle! Come on, let go of me!

MICHAEL [*Clutching him*]. NO!

DONALD. Let go of me long enough for me to get my hand in my pocket!

MICHAEL. Don't leave!

[MICHAEL *quiets down a bit, lets go of* DONALD *enough for him to take a small plastic bottle from his pocket and open it to give* MICHAEL *a tranquilizer*]

DONALD. Here.

MICHAEL [*Sobbing*]. I don't have any water to swallow it with!

DONALD. Well, if you'll wait one goddamn minute, I'll get you some! [MICHAEL *lets go of him. He goes to the bar, gets a glass of water and returns*] Your water, your Majesty. [*A beat*] Michael, stop that goddamn crying and take this pill!

[MICHAEL *straightens up, puts the pill into his mouth amid choking sobs, takes the water, drinks, returns the glass to* DONALD]

MICHAEL. I'm like Ole Man River—tired of livin' and scared o' dyin'.

[DONALD *puts the glass on the bar, comes back to the couch, sits down.* MICHAEL *collapses into his arms, sobbing. Pause*]

DONALD. Shhhhh. Shhhhhh. Michael. Shhhhh. Michael. Michael. [DONALD *rocks him back and forth. He quiets. Pause*]

MICHAEL. . . . If we . . . if we could just . . . not hate ourselves so much. That's it, you know. If we could just *learn* not to hate ourselves quite so very much.

DONALD. Yes, I know. I know. [*A beat*] Inconceivable as it may be, you used to be worse than you are now. [*A beat*] Maybe with a lot more work you can help yourself some more—if you try.

[MICHAEL *straightens up, dries his eyes on his sleeve*]

MICHAEL. Who was it that used to always say, "You show me a happy homosexual, and I'll show you a gay corpse."

DONALD. I don't know. Who was it who always used to say that?

MICHAEL. And how dare you come on with that holier-than-thou attitude with me! "A lot more work," "if I try," indeed! You've got a long row to hoe before you're perfect, you know.

DONALD. I never said I didn't.

MICHAEL. And while we're on the subject—I think your analyst is a quack. [MICHAEL *is sniffling.* DONALD *hands him a handkerchief. He takes it and blows his nose*]

DONALD. Earlier you said he was a prick.

MICHAEL. That's right. He's a prick quack. Or a quack prick, whichever you prefer.

[DONALD *gets up from the couch, goes for his drink*]

DONALD [*Heaving a sigh*]. Harold was right. You'll never change.

MICHAEL. Come back, Donald. Come back, Shane.

DONALD. I'll come back when you have another anxiety attack.

MICHAEL. I need you. Just like Mickey Mouse needs Minnie Mouse—just like Donald Duck needs Minnie Duck. Mickey needs Donnie.

DONALD. My name is Donald. I am called Donald. You must never call anyone called Donald Donnie . . .

MICHAEL [*Grabs his head, moans*]. Ohhhhh . . . icks! Icks! Terrible icks! Tomorrow is going to be an ick-packed day. It's going to be a Bad Day at Black Rock. A day of nerves, nerves, and more nerves! [MICHAEL *gets up from the couch, surveys the wreckage of the dishes and gift wrappings*] Do you suppose there's any possibility of just burning this room? [*A beat*]

DONALD. Why do you think he stayed, Michael? Why do you think he took all of that from you?

MICHAEL. There are no accidents. He was begging to get killed. He was dying for somebody to let him have it and he got what he wanted.

DONALD. He could have been telling the truth—Justin could have lied.

MICHAEL. Who knows? What time is it?

DONALD. It seems like it's day after tomorrow.

[MICHAEL *goes to the kitchen door, pokes his head in. Comes back into the room carrying a raincoat*]

MICHAEL. It's early. [*Goes to a closet door, takes out a blazer, puts it on*]

DONALD. What does life *hold*? Where're you going?

MICHAEL. The bedroom is ocupado and I don't want to go to sleep anyway until I try to walk off the booze. If I went to sleep like this, when I wake up they'd have to put me in a padded cell—not that that's where I don't belong. [*A beat*] And . . . and . . . there's a midnight mass at St. Malachy's that all the show people go to. I think I'll walk over there and catch it.

DONALD [*Raises his glass*]. Well, pray for me.

MICHAEL [*Indicates bedroom*]. Maybe they'll be gone by the time I get back.

DONALD. Well, *I* will be—just as soon as I knock off that bottle of brandy.

MICHAEL. Will I see you next Saturday?

DONALD. Unless you have other plans.

MICHAEL. No. [*Turns to go*]

DONALD. Michael?

MICHAEL [*Stops, turns back*]. What?

DONALD. Did he ever tell you why he was crying on the phone—what it was he *had* to tell you?

MICHAEL. No. It must have been that he'd left Fran. Or maybe it was something else and he changed his mind.

DONALD. Maybe so. [*A beat*] I wonder why he left her. [*A pause*]

MICHAEL. . . . As my father said to me when he died in my arms, "I don't understand any of it. I never did."

[*A beat.* DONALD *goes to his stack of books, selects one, and sits in a chair*]

Turn out the lights when you leave, will you?

[DONALD *nods.* MICHAEL *looks at him for a long silent moment.* DONALD *turns his attention to his book, starts to read.* MICHAEL *opens the door and exits*]

**CURTAIN**

# The Psychology of Women

☐ **NOTES OF A FEMINIST THERAPIST**
*Elizabeth Friar Williams*

Drawing on actual case studies, the author writes of her professional experience in helping women gain a sense of their own power, self-esteem, and autonomy. She discusses issues like sex, love, loneliness, work, and the sex-role revolution, offering intelligent advice to women who want to lead fuller, freer, and more satisfying lives. "The author is a sane and sensible therapist, and an excellent writer."—*West Coast Review of Books*
$1.50   (36427-2)

☐ **WOMEN & ANALYSIS: Dialogues on Psychoanalytic Views of Femininity**
*Jean Strouse, editor*

An exploration of questions about the nature and status of women, this book brings together key writings on women by leading analytic figures including Sigmund Freud, Margaret Mead, Karen Horney, Erik H. Erikson, Elizabeth Janeway, Juliet Mitchell, and Robert Stoller. "*Women and Analysis* should be required reading for every feminist and every therapist—and anyone who cares about either."—*Erica Jong*   $1.95   (38890-2)

**Laurel Editions** 🌿

# No More Dying:

## THE CONQUEST OF AGING AND THE EXTENSION OF HUMAN LIFE

### Joel Kurtzman and Phillip Gordon

Specialists predict that 75 will soon be just middle age; 150-year-olds will be active and vigorous, with time for multiple careers, interests, and achievements. The decline and deterioration of the aging process will be arrested, even reversed. And ultimately, humans will live without the prospect of death. NO MORE DYING addresses itself to these predictions, surveying exciting new breakthroughs in the battle against aging, its history, terms, techniques, and theories. "An important and revolutionary book. Hard-edged, well-researched."—*L.A. Free Press.* "Tantalizing in its detail of scientific and medical advances."—*Publishers Weekly*

**A Laurel Edition** $1.95